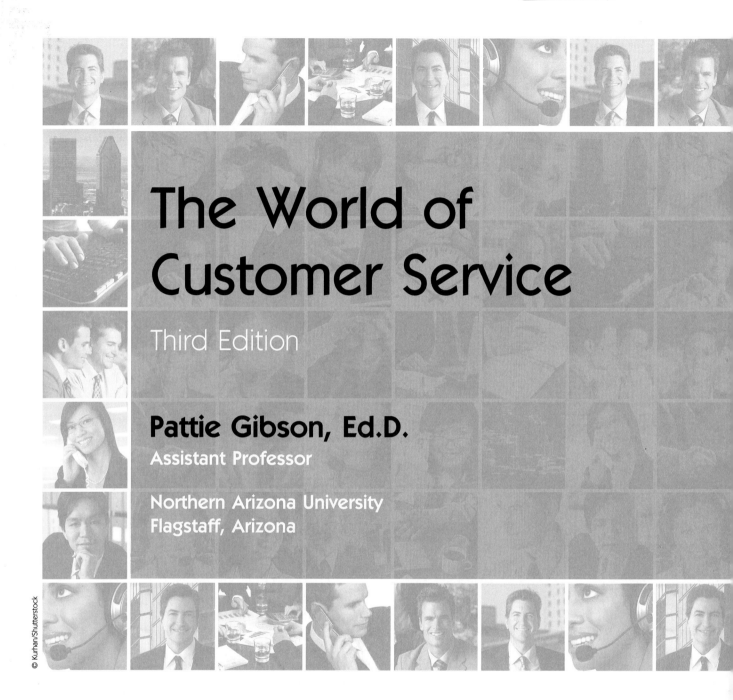

The World of Customer Service

Third Edition

Pattie Gibson, Ed.D.

Assistant Professor

Northern Arizona University
Flagstaff, Arizona

© Kurhan/Shutterstock

SOUTH-WESTERN
CENGAGE Learning™

Australia • Brazil • Japan • Korea • Mexico • Singapore • Spain • United Kingdom • United States

**The World of Customer Service,
Third Edition**

Pattie Gibson, Ed.D.

VP, Editorial Director: Jack W. Calhoun

VP, Editor-in-Chief: Karen Schmohe

Senior Acquisitions Editor: Jane Phelan

Senior Developmental Editor: Karen Caldwell

Associate Marketing Manager: Shanna Shelton

Marketing Communications Manager:
Tom Guenette

Production Manager: Jennifer Ziegler

Rights Acquisitions Specialist—Text:
Sam Marshall

Rights Acquisitions Specialist—Image:
Deanna Ettinger

Photo Researcher: Darren Wright

Senior Media Editor: Mike Jackson

Manufacturing Planner: Kevin Kluck

Senior Art Director: Tippy McIntosh

Content Project Management: PreMediaGlobal

Production House/Compositor: PreMediaGlobal

Internal Designer: PreMediaGlobal

Cover Design: Joe Devine, Red Hangar
Design LLC

Cover Images: © Marcel Mooij, Shutterstock;
© Steve Cole, Getty Images

Library of Congress Control Number: 2011926550

ISBN-13: 978-0-8400-6424-0

ISBN-10: 0-8400-6424-1

South-Western
5191 Natorp Boulevard
Mason, OH 45040
USA

Cengage Learning products are represented in Canada by Nelson Education, Ltd.

For your course and learning solutions, visit **www.cengage.com**

Purchase any of our products at your local college store or at our preferred online store **www.cengagebrain.com**

Printed in the United States of America
1 2 3 4 5 6 7 15 14 13 12 11

© Kurhan/Shutterstock

TABLE OF CONTENTS

PREFACE

The third edition of *The World of Customer Service* is written in a practical, commonsense manner and reflects current customer service accepted wisdom, concepts, and hints. This multidisciplinary textbook is designed to teach exemplary, yet "down-to earth," applied customer service thinking in business organizations—public or private, domestic or international.

The customer service function continues to be a critical element in the success and future of all businesses competing in today's economy. With global markets more common than ever, it is a major challenge for organizations to attract and retain customers because more companies are competing for the same customer. The secret in getting and keeping loyal customers today comes in creating new business and using a customer-centric approach with technology tools to communicate on a global scale.

Successful organizations are emerging with a common focus—*customers*. Further, these thriving organizations live the mantra that each member in an organization is involved in delivering exceptional customer service.

AUDIENCE FOR TEXTBOOK

The World of Customer Service is designed to be used at any level of higher education or for corporate training programs in business and industry. For example, students may be enrolled in a customer service course offered in community colleges or career schools. This text is also ideal for a concentrated study of customer service in career readiness curriculums at the community and career college levels.

AT A GLANCE

Part 1: The Customer Service Environment

In the opening part, Chapters 1–4, the reader is introduced to the basic concepts of customer service. Coverage begins with describing what customer-centric service is and how a customer is defined. Discussion proceeds to identifying the global customers served today and what exceptional customer service is. Finally, customer service strategy and its importance in developing a strong service culture are introduced.

Part 2: Essential Customer Service Skills

Chapters 5–8 focus on the essential personal skills that a customer service representative must demonstrate on the job. This part first addresses time, stress, and anger management, as well as the benefits of teamwork and organizational skills. Next, problem solving, identifying dissatisfied customers, handling their complaints, and then winning them back is covered. Finally, the importance of managing, training, and rewarding service professionals is examined.

Part 3: Communication Skills

Communication skills needed for effective customer service are covered in Chapters 9–12. These skills begin with understanding the essentials of communicating and continue with the importance of customer-focused listening skills, nonverbal communication, dress, and manners. With the emergence of many Web-driven technologies, effective digital communication is also discussed.

NEW TO THIS EDITION

To update and further strengthen coverage of the current research and practice in the customer service field, topics throughout the text are covered in more depth, with an emphasis on the global customer, the impact social media has on customer decision making, and the importance of new digital technologies as a means of gathering and supporting a customer base.

New Chapters

Customer Service Strategy, Chapter 4, focuses on gathering customer intelligence and analyzing marketing and sales information in order to maximize revenue and customer satisfaction.

Critical Workplace Skills, Chapter 5, is a fresh look at time, stress, and anger management, teamwork, and organizational skills.

Problem Solving, Chapter 6, addresses the skills and strategies needed for recognizing, negotiating, and resolving customer complaints.

New Features

Business in Action launches each chapter with a close look at a real-world company and how it handles customer service issues.

Make it a Habit provides information about the qualities and skills that will help students polish their customer service behaviors and attitudes.

Focus on Best Practices offers short case studies of how various businesses address the topic in each chapter.

What Do You Think? asks students to reflect on the concepts they have learned and how they relate to their own experiences and philosophies in a short journal entry.

New Online Supplement

CourseMate—Cengage Learning's CourseMate brings course concepts to life with interactive learning, study, and exam preparation tools that support the printed textbook. Students will have access to an interactive eBook, videos, flashcards, quizzing, and other tools to guide and encourage learning. Watch student comprehension soar as they work with the textbook and the textbook-specific website. Experience it today.

ADDITIONAL FEATURES

Many features remain from the prior edition because they have proven to be well received and hold the reader's attention:

- *Quotations* introduce each chapter with thoughts from famous people or historians that prompt and focus interest.

- *Customer Service Tips* provide practical suggestions from customer service providers.

- *Ethics/Choices* demonstrates ethical dilemmas and gets students thinking about how they would handle difficult situations.

- *Remember This* guides students in reviewing key points in each chapter while serving as a reference tool for addressing on-the-job problems.

- *Industry Profiles* introduce each of the three parts and profile a real person in the customer service profession. These profiles share personal information about attitude, education, and work experience as applied to essential elements of customer service today.

END OF CHAPTER ACTIVITIES

- *Critical Thinking* questions offer challenging ways for students to apply their learning skills.

- *What Do You Think NOW?* requires students to revisit their journal entries and further relate concepts to their philosophy and work experiences.

- *Online Research Activities* are designed to expand on customer service topics. Guided instructions are given to assist students in gathering pertinent data for completing these projects.

- *Communication Skills at Work* presents opportunities for students to apply their communication skills to resolve customer service problems effectively.

- *Decision Making at Work* provides students with the opportunity to apply their decision-making skills as they think through and effectively address customer service concerns.

- *A Case Study* reinforces chapter content using real life scenarios to address important issues in the workplace that include human relations and worker attitude problems.

AVAILABLE SUPPLEMENTS

- **Instructor's Resource CD** includes the Instructor's Manual with chapter outlines, teaching suggestions, and solutions to book activities and projects. The IRCD also includes two variations of the course syllabus, PowerPoint® presentations for each chapter, and **Exam***View*® test banks with solutions for each chapter.

- **Product Website** provides flashcards, crossword puzzles, links to additional Internet resources, and more.

www.cengage.com/marketing/gibson

ACKNOWLEDGMENTS

During the development of this textbook, it underwent several practical and constructive revisions. I would like to recognize and thank all those who helped make this a stronger and more cohesive book. Special thanks to the outstanding reviewers for this edition:

Russell Brown
Navarro College
Corsicana, TX

Amanda McClellan
Antonelli College
Hattiesburg, MS

Edward M. Dell
Cuyahoga Community College
Cleveland, OH

D. Ross Thomson, Ph. D.
Careers by Choice
Clifton Park, NY

Kimberly Goudy
Central Ohio Technical College
Newark, OH

R. L. Whipple
Carrington College
Boise, ID

DeAnn Hurtado
Sinclair Community College
Dayton, OH

ABOUT THE AUTHOR

For over 35 years, Dr. Pattie Gibson (Odgers) has taught a variety of courses in computer applications and business systems to high school, community college, and university students in Arizona and overseas in West Berlin and Stuttgart, Germany. She received her bachelor's and master's degrees from Arizona State University and her doctorate from Northern Arizona University. She is currently an associate professor at Northern Arizona University where she works with graduate students and teaches graduate-level educational leadership and technology classes.

PART 1

The Customer Service Environment

© Kurhan/Shutterstock

© Siobhan Love

Siobhan Love, Massage Envy, Flagstaff, Arizona

Recognized recently by Massage Envy as managing one of the top-ten customer service locations in the United States, co-owner Siobhan Love is an example of a contemporary customer service provider who combines technology and the personal approach when serving clients.

Delivering a welcoming customer service environment is essential to our success. A high percentage of the population has had no, or minimal, exposure to massage, and may be intimidated by such a personal experience. From the time we advertise, to booking an appointment, to confirming, to standing and greeting customers, to providing services, and finally to thanking them when they leave, the entire experience should be welcoming. By doing so, we help customers change their view of massage as something that is simply a luxury to a view that recognizes it as a necessity for health maintenance.

1 What are the biggest challenges in customer service today?

The biggest challenge in customer service is having your employees subscribe with enthusiasm to your service approach. When this goal is achieved, business soars. So, knowing how to encourage service providers, build morale, and maintain excitement takes ongoing and creative efforts. We are highly selective of the people who want to join our environment. We look for applicants who are personable, genuine, wholesome, open, and honest with a desire to listen and learn.

2 What advice would you offer customer service representatives?

With the vast use of technology at our fingertips, it's incredibly powerful that we can get our name out there, advertise, promote, and entice customers globally. Still, one-on-one personal interactions cannot be replaced. Communications with people make the difference because connections are cultivated, not automated.

People want to be treated well. They don't just want to be acknowledged—they need to be appreciated. They are paying for a service and deserve personal recognition. So, our front-desk service reps stand up and greet customers, remember their names, thank them, ask them how their day is; and as they get to know them, inquire how their family is doing, where they're going on vacation, and so forth. You can make someone's day better just by showing sincere interest in them and you can also make huge steps toward developing a loyal customer as well.

3 To what extent do you use social media and online technologies?

We use social media, such as *Facebook* and *Twitter*, because of its ability to reach a vast audience. It provides a free and easily accessible avenue to disperse information. We use social media to promote specials, announce events, and to touch base with subscribers on a regular basis. Though its reach is somewhat interactive and superficial, it does create a reminder of our business and a memory prompt of the feeling they had the last time they experienced our services.

Online forums, opinion sites, and blogs are trickier because they are independent reviews not endorsed by the company. Everyone knows that personal views are subjective and can vary greatly. These, however, create a challenge (and an opportunity) to most businesses to ensure their quality of care is consistently high, because they never know when a negative online review will impact them harshly!

4 What technologies do you use to collect customer feedback?

In our clinic, every client who chooses to have an email address on file automatically receives an electronic comment card from us. This ensures that we receive feedback; and if necessary, we address any customer service concerns immediately one-on-one. This action prevents a negative review that may be posted in cyberspace and cannot be easily addressed. It's worth restating that personalized interaction with customers is extremely important. In my opinion, it's far easier for a disgruntled client to type vitriol into their computer about a poor experience, when they don't have a distinctive relationship established with the business.

FIRST IMPRESSIONS

How does Siobhan Love combine technology and the personal approach in her business practice? Record your impressions in your journal.

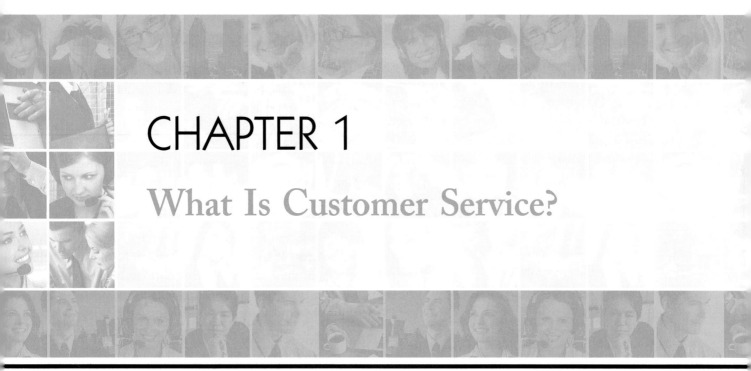

CHAPTER 1

What Is Customer Service?

There is only one boss—the customer.
And he can fire everybody in the company,
from the chairman on down, simply by
spending his money somewhere else.

SAM WALTON, FOUNDER OF WALMART

OBJECTIVES

1. Define customer service and list its goals and challenges.

2. Defend the organizational benefits of serving both the external and internal customer well.

3. List customer needs.

4. Describe the concept of social customers relative to their purchasing habits and impact on organizations.

Zappos

The shoe and clothing website Zappos.com defines customer service in its own effective way. It has built its brand and success by placing customer support as a *core strategy*. For example, customer service representatives are encouraged to take whatever time is needed, using chats and e-mail messaging for example, to help customers find the specific shoes they are looking for. To the firm's owner, Tony Hsieh, employees don't have to be passionate about shoes, but they do have to be passionate about service.

Zappos operates 24/7/365 from a 77,000 square-foot Las Vegas warehouse. It is unique among wholesale/retailers because it physically stocks vast numbers of styles and brands rather than shipping orders from specific shoe manufacturers. In that way, Zappos can assure customers of immediate delivery with a product return policy good for up to a year from purchase. Coupled with a free shipping and return policy, Zappos cultivates loyal and repeat customers.

The company is being sold to Amazon for almost a billion dollars. This selling price is a clear indication that companies like Zappos, who emphasize excellence in service, can become valuable commodities. Amazon and Zappos are two companies that use a customer service channel as an integral part of selling its products.

SOURCE: Barry Moltz, "The 10 Customer Service Trends for 2010," *Small Business Trends*, December 15, 2009, http://smallbiztrends.com/2009/12/customer-service-trends-2010.html accessed November 2, 2010.

What is customer service? It is not about fancy products or intricate corporate culture; it is about dedicated, trustworthy employees and loyal, satisfied customers. Today, with more competitors vying for customers' attention, exceptional customer service is essential to staying profitable in business. Businesses—large or small, industrial or retail, new or established—cannot survive without customers. To attract and retain them, companies listen to customers and strive hard to serve them well.

The approach in this book is to place you in the role of a service provider. In your career as a customer service representative chances are much of your on-the-job success may depend upon your ability, knowledge, and willingness to provide exceptional customer service. According to the Bureau of Labor Statistics, there is a demand for service-related jobs. Between 2008 and 2018, employment in service occupations is projected to increase by 4.1 million, or 14 percent, which is the second-largest growth rate among the major occupational groups.[1]

To help you imagine yourself in the role of a customer service provider, this book provides a variety of interactive exercises to connect your understanding of the role of customer service provider with your experience as a consumer. The development of quality customer service skills is emphasized in nearly every exercise and feature in this edition of *The World of Customer Service*. These activities are intentionally designed so that you can reflect upon issues and refine the service skills you need based largely on how you would like to be treated as a customer. For example, in responding to the *What Do You Think?* feature, you are asked to react to a

---

[1] *Occupational Outlook Handbook*, 2010-11 Edition, Bureau of Labor Statistics http://www.bls.gov/oco/oco2003.htm accessed November 12, 2010.

chapter topic and prepare short and simple journal reflections drawn from your experiences. Respond to these exercises thoughtfully and use this interactive text as practical preparation for the interactive world of customer service.

CUSTOMER SERVICE TODAY

Successful customer service involves distinct, critical components that, when merged together, produce a cohesive, efficient whole. These critical components include global considerations, the use of diverse forms of online communication media and technology, and the delivery of service that is sensitive to the needs of customers.

It is an inescapable fact of the contemporary business world that customers today demand *exceptional* customer service. To that end, a successful company, like Zappos in our opening feature, recognizes that its competitors may easily be able to copy its products, its prices, and even its promotions; but competitors cannot copy an organization's employees and the distinctive and exceptional service each employee provides.

Customer Service Defined

Even though every customer is unique, they all expect three things—a quality product, reliable timely service, and reasonable prices. In other words, customers want to receive what they feel they have paid for.

Customer service means different things to different people. In reality, however, the only perspective that matters is the customer's concept and perception of good service at the time it is needed and delivered. Some examples of good customer service are

- For a busy traveling executive, an international flight that leaves and arrives on time.

- For a harried executive administrative assistant, working with a dependable office supply store that keeps a good inventory of products on hand and delivers dependably.

- For a lonely retiree, conversation and kindness from a waitress when frequenting a neighborhood restaurant.

- For a college student entering a new school, competent and caring advice from an advisor on the best course of study.

Though there have been changes in the customer service industry, the definition of customer service hasn't changed. Comprehensively stated, **customer service** is the process of satisfying the customer, relative to a product or service, in whatever way the customer defines his or her need, and having that service delivered with efficiency, compassion, and sensitivity. That definition still stands even though social applications such as Facebook, Twitter, and blogs, engage customers in a new way.

There is a new worldview of customers at work that product or service organizations must either embrace or ignore at their peril. The **customer-centric service** worldview means that business revolves around the customer. What was once a company-controlled marketplace has become an uncontrolled, customer-directed, and transparent global environment. Whether online or offline, savvy customers have unparalleled power to research and transact with companies when, where, and how they choose.

A customer-centric customer service representative is respectful to the customer's point of view and lets the customer know that his or her point of view is heard and valued. A customer-centric organization puts customers first, is service oriented, and thoughtfully listens to, develops, and satisfies a loyal, repeat customer base.

Developing a loyal customer base isn't easy. Each time customers come in contact with an organization, they get an impression of the service and the products. Everyone in an organization touches customers. The employee's behavior and attitude affect how the customer feels about the company. As the **customer service representative (CSR)**, or frontline service provider who deals with customers on a day-to-day basis, you come to signify all that your company stands for—both good and bad. To the customer, you are the voice and personality of your organization. Customers who experience exceptional customer service will come back for more. They will be less likely to shop around as a result of how well you listen to and treat them.

Customer service is shaped by the needs and behaviors of both consumers and businesses. As the demands and characteristics of customers and businesses change, customer service continues its fascinating evolution. Thriving companies view a customer across all communication channels. For example, the following diverse forms of communication have greatly influenced this evolution.

- **24/7/365 Service Delivery** Because BlackBerry smartphones, iPhones, and other Smartphones now support a generation of consumers in this *always-on* mode, customers demand quicker response times. These new forms of communication allow customers to chat directly to service representatives, either through written or video chats, any hour of the day or night.

- **Self-Serve Approach** Customers are increasingly online. They want self-service options and demand responses in real time. In addition, social media, such as Twitter and Facebook, have grown to be an important new channel for interacting with customers and engaging customer-to-customer interactions in innovative, helpful ways. In addition to checking a company's website and its brochures, many customers research information on products and services from social networking sources, such as blogs and online user rating websites.

- **Customized Service** Technology allows companies to personalize customer website visits. For example, they welcome customers back by name and suggest items based on previous purchases. With the immediacy and personalization of this fast-paced Internet world, great customer service is only what the customer says it is at a particular point in time. Service difficulty is amplified because this standard varies from person to person. More companies are customizing shopping or service experiences either online or in person because consumers want it.

- **Growth of Communication Channels** Customers can now compliment or complain in different ways—video, audio, blog, forum, etc. With the growth of these communication channels, poor customer service experiences can be shared with the world in seconds. Customers increasingly control the kind of service they would like to receive by switching organizations, or communicating it through social channels. Tools like Facebook, Twitter, and YouTube allow customers to tell or show potentially thousands of people about pleasure or dissatisfaction with a company immediately following a service interaction. Every satisfied customer can be a booster for a company and every dissatisfied customer can be harmful.

Goals

Organizations, like people, require direction and focus to achieve stated goals. The quality of service that a customer receives is greatly influenced by an organization's goals—often identified by its mission statement and its vision of doing business. As simple as the statements "Good service is good business" or "Our customers are #1" can be, either one may say all that is necessary to represent a company's overall customer goal. Another example of a purpose statement is the Ritz-Carlton Hotel's motto: "We are ladies and gentlemen serving ladies and gentlemen." If employees at this hotel follow the motto to the letter, they provide the finest personal service and facilities for their guests who will always enjoy a warm, relaxed, yet refined hotel experience. Skills, resources, competitors, partners, and customers all need to be consulted in assessing the starting point.

Planned goals ensure that daily business decisions, actions, and behaviors are customer-focused and designed to adapt as needed to changes in customers' needs, desires, and expectations. For instance, Nordstrom, an upscale department store, consistently strives to deliver superior customer service. When helping customers, top management has empowered employees with a basic core value: use good judgment in all situations. Employees are told that, beyond this basic mandate, there will be no additional rules. Nordstrom's staff proves the company philosophy works, as it is usually ranked by *Fortune* magazine as one of the best companies for which to work.[2]

---

[2] Mike Patel, "Customer Service—Nordstrom way" http://maheshmikepatel .wordpress.com/2010/01/21/customer-service-nordstrom-way/ accessed November 12, 2010.

When companies ask employees to put themselves in the place of their customers, they are asking that the employees' efforts provide the same treatment and service that they would expect to receive if they were the customers. This is a variation of the Golden Rule, "Do unto others as you would have them do unto you." For lack of a stated mission and values statement, many companies use this as a guiding principle when serving customers.

Customer service is not new, but there appears to be much confusion as to its importance and degree of practice in today's marketplace. When organizations commit to a way of treating customers by writing down their mission statement, values, and goals, they create a corporate culture that is better understood and lived by all who work there. Figure 1.1 lists five common customer service myths and corresponding facts that speak to an organization's corporate values.

CUSTOMER SERVICE **TIP**

One way to exceed customer expectations is to promise good but deliver great! Always strive to go above and beyond what is expected.

Challenges

The Internet, mobile/wireless technologies, and social networks have created challenges for service providers because they have influenced an unparalleled shift in the balance of power from companies to their customers. Diverse global consumers, armed with instant 24-hour access to information, are not only reshaping the products that a company offers

REMEMBER THIS

Figure 1.1 Common Customer Service Misconceptions

MYTH	FACT
We are providing good service, but there is a perception outside the organization that we are not.	You may, in fact, already be providing good customer service, but you can improve it. Moreover, if the customer's perception is that you are not providing quality service, then you need to determine why that perception exists.
You can't improve service without more people and a larger budget.	It is far more costly to provide poor service than it is to provide high-quality service. Eliminating long, repetitive customer interactions and responding to customer complaints more efficiently saves time and money.
Why all the concern over customer service? If customers don't like the service we provide, they can go elsewhere.	Before they go elsewhere, customers could circulate negative commentary interpersonally or to the online community in a way that can be unfavorable for you and/or your organization.
I don't need to worry about customer service because I don't deal with the public.	You cannot provide high-quality service to your external customers until you provide high-quality service to your internal customers.
You can't provide high-quality customer service when the requirements you must implement force you to tell customers "no."	Quality customer service is not saying "yes" to every customer request. People can accept "no" if it is presented in the right way, but they cannot accept loss of dignity and loss of control.

and the distribution channels it uses, but are also demanding a higher level and quality of service than ever before.

The power shift from companies to their customers underlies the new customer economy where consumers can use social media applications to make complaints, praise companies, and open a dialogue around a particular service issue or product. Businesses must realize how the depth of their online community relationships with customers and the perceptions of those customers are linked directly to maintaining their reputations, credibility, and profit margins.

For example, in April 2010, Echo Research conducted an online survey of a random sample of 1,000 American Express consumers aged 18 and older. The survey explored specific attitudes and preferences toward customer service and revealed overall that nine in ten consumers believe that the level of customer service is important when deciding to do business with a company. Of those surveyed, the three most high-ranking factors consumers use to decide which companies they choose to do business with are: personal experience (98 percent), a company's reputation or brand (92 percent), and recommendations from friends and family (88 percent). Other survey findings said that nearly half (48 percent) of consumers always or often use an online posting or blog to get others' opinions about a company's customer service reputation and that 58 percent will spend more with companies they believe provide excellent service with the average spending 9 percent more.[3]

Because online social communications and digital technologies have changed the way people seek out services and products and choose to shop, companies must carefully craft who they are and how they want to conduct business to maintain their reputations. As a result, many businesses will have to reshape their corporate cultures and customer service initiatives to take these new forms of communication channels, opinion sharing, and shopping into account.

IDENTIFYING THE CUSTOMER

Richard Branson, British entrepreneur of Virgin brand, said, "If you look after your internal customers you don't have to worry about the external customers."[4] Branson means that while companies focus thousands of dollars on external customer service in hopes of wooing and retaining customers, little attention is being paid to the effect poor internal customer service has on overall customer satisfaction. Sooner or later the ripple effect reaches external customers. A company's commitment to internal customer service must match its company's external focus on customer care.

External Customers

External customers, the persons or organizations that purchase and use a company's products and services, are the customers whose needs we traditionally think of serving. To be successful, an organization must first identify its customers and learn as much about them as possible—including their age, gender, income level, lifestyle, and occupation. This collection of demographic information creates a **customer profile**, which explains who the customers are and what they want in terms of service. Companies identify their main customers for a very good reason—so that they can develop and market the goods and services their customers want. External customers are critically important because they sustain a company's existence.

---

[3] "Global Customer Service Barometer: Findings in the United States" *A research report prepared for American Express by Echo*, 2010, http://about.americanexpress.com/news/pr/2010/barometer.aspx accessed November 2, 2010.

[4] Stephanie Edwards, "12 Ways to Ensure Your Internal Customers Look after Your Internal Customers," *MYCUSTOMER.com*, March 15, 2010, http://www.mycustomer.com/topic/customer-experience/12-ways-ensure-your-internal-customers-look-after-your-external-customers-0 accessed November 2, 2010.

Digital Vision/Getty Images

What is the importance of understanding the customer profile?

Internal Customers

Internal customers, vendors, consultants, or departments within a company that rely on colleagues to provide the support they need to serve their own internal and external customers are as important as external customers. These customers directly impact revenue and customer retention. For example, if you work at an organization's computer help desk, your internal customer is anyone who requests your assistance in using a company-provided software application. Or if you work for a multinational corporation, you want to fully support your overseas colleagues with helpful troubleshooting service and other customer support issues. Typically, the way internal customers are treated translates into how a company is perceived by its external customers.

There is a clear link between job satisfaction and productivity. However, job satisfaction also depends on the **service culture** of an organization. This culture comprises the things that make a business distinctive and make the people who work there proud to do so. When employees of the "Top 10 Best Companies to Work For" were asked by *Fortune* magazine why they loved working for these companies, it was notable that they didn't mention pay, reward schemes, or advancing to a more senior position. Instead, these employees spoke first of the sincerity of the relationships at work, that their work culture felt like an extension of home, and that their colleagues were supportive.[5]

When colleagues support other departments with service, products, or information to help them do their jobs, everyone wins. Excellent internal customer service starts with good morale. Happy employees are productive, and customers take note. Corporate values that emphasize treating internal customers well translate to good external customer care. In companies where internal customers are often ignored or taken for granted, productivity is compromised and workflow will suffer.

A similar characteristic of external and internal customers is that they both have their own set of needs that they expect the company to meet. When service professionals take the approach—"How can I help you?" rather than "I'm here to do a job," it changes the nature of customer service. Both internal and external customers are best served when service revolves around satisfying the needs of any customer, rather than simply going through the motions that most jobs require.

WHAT DO YOU THINK
1.2

How closely do you identify with the idea that an internal customer is important? Write a journal entry explaining your response.

NEEDS OF CUSTOMERS

One of the foundations of a flourishing business is an understanding of customer needs. However, understanding customer needs is not as easy as it sounds. Customers often confuse needs with wants and expectations. By asking key questions and probing for additional information, you can help them define their needs. As emphasized by Ms. Love of Massage Envy in the Part Opener, one reason for her business's success is because after each service, customers receive a comment card that allows concerns to be addressed immediately, in a one-on-one basis.

[5] Ibid.

The reasons consumers buy vary considerably, but they typically stem from basic needs that each of us has.

1. *The need to feel welcome.* We all want to be acknowledged and welcomed warmly by someone who sincerely is glad to see us. A customer should never feel she or he is an intrusion on the service provider's workday. Little things mean a lot. Acknowledgment, name recognition, and eye contact make a person feel more important and appreciated. That first impression a customer gets from a service professional is critical. Anyone doing business with a company and is made to feel like an outsider will probably not return for future products and services.

2. *The need to be understood.* Customers need to feel that the service person understands and appreciates their circumstances and feelings without criticism or judgment. Even though emotions, customs, and language barriers can complicate communication between the customer and the service person, every effort should be made to work with these challenges.

3. *The need for fair treatment.* Customers need the assurance and confidence that they will be taken care of promptly and fairly—whether online or face-to-face. Customers want their needs addressed as quickly as possible, and not deferred because of class distinction or other discriminatory judgment. The more people or time it takes to address a customer's needs, the greater chance of customer dissatisfaction.

4. *The need for control and options.* Control, in this case, represents customers' need to feel that they have an impact on the way the service experience turns out. Customers have little patience for policies and procedures; they want to deal with a reasonable service provider who can interpret the policies for them. In addition, customers need to feel that other options are available for getting what they want accomplished. They become upset when they feel they have wasted their time and thus, accomplished nothing.

How would you prioritize your needs in a customer-provider exchange?

WHAT DO YOU **THINK**

1.3

Think about your needs as a consumer. In a brief journal entry, rank the four needs listed above in the order of their importance to you. How might your feelings influence the service *you* provide to others?

THE SOCIAL CUSTOMER

Businesses must go where their customers are and right now, customers are turning to **social media** as a customer service channel. According to Forrester Research, three in four American adults in 2010 used social tools to connect with each other compared with just 56 percent in 2007.[6]

Websites such as Facebook, Twitter, Yelp, and YouTube give customers unparalleled power to influence the way others view products and services. When consumers use social media channels to make complaints, praise companies, and open a dialogue around a particular issue, it can be a good thing. It puts the power into the hands of the

---

[6] Dan Power, "Interface: Confessions of an Active Social Networker," March/April 2010, http://www.information-management.com/issues/20_2/confessions-of-an-active-social-networker-10017314-1.html accessed November 12, 2010.

consumer and reminds companies that customers are talking to each other. What is increasingly challenging for companies, however, is to know how to handle their customer service relations through this new medium because currently there are no rules.

Today's customer profile is unlike any the business world has seen before. Customers not only know what they want, but they can tell you when and how they want it. What customers do not want is to be "managed" because the social customer consumes information in a different way. They learn about new products and brands through social channels. Figure 1.2 lists some additional characteristics of today's social customer.

The Impact of Social Media

As social media continue to grow, the ability to reach more consumers globally has also increased enabling a potentially massive community of participants to productively collaborate. When it comes to social media for business, there is no one-size-fits-all strategy. But to ensure results, a business must align this movement with its overall business objectives.

REMEMBER THIS

Figure 1.2

Characteristics of the Social Customer

- Turns to friends and online networks for advice and recommendations
- Is open and vocal about online and face-to-face buying experiences
- Is savvy, confident, and fast when using the Internet to research products to purchase
- Expects organizations to have an online presence, and wants to make contact with brands through online channels such as email, chats, or an easy-to-complete contact form
- Wants confirmation that a complaint or comment was heard, acknowledged, and taken into consideration
- Connects good and bad customer service directly to future purchasing decisions

Below is an overview of customer service social media "listening tools" in use today on the Internet:

- **Facebook** is a social networking website launched in February 2004 with more than 500 million active users as of July 2010. Users can add people as friends, send messages, and update their personal profiles to notify friends about themselves. Facebook allows anyone who declares their age as 13 or older to become a member of the website.

- **Twitter** is a popular instant messaging system that lets a person send brief text messages up to 140 characters in length to a list of followers. Launched in 2006, it was initially designed as a social network to keep friends and colleagues informed throughout the day; however, now it is widely used for commercial and political purposes to keep customers, constituents, fans, and others up-to-date. Twitter messages, or **tweets**, can be made public and sent to anyone requesting the feed, or they can be sent only to approved followers.

- A **blog** is a type or part of a website and is usually maintained by an individual with regular entries of commentary. Most blogs are interactive, allowing visitors to leave comments and messages to each other. Many blogs provide commentary or news on a particular subject; others function as personal online diaries. A typical blog combines text, images, and links to other blogs, Web pages, and other media related to its topic.

- An **Internet forum**, or message board, is an online discussion site that can contain a wide range of content, including news, gossip, and research. It reflects the expansion of media production through new technologies that are accessible and affordable to the general public.

- **Social data** consists of information about an individual's relationship to other people, groups, events, things, and concepts. This human-generated data is usually expressed in the form of very simple facts. Individually, these facts have little value but collectively, and in sufficient quantity, they can represent a richer view of customers and their purchasing environment. The value of social data is that it can be harvested from retail systems and user-generated social media activities into meaningful customer processed data using specialized software tools.

- **YouTube** is a very popular video-sharing site that lets anyone store short videos for private or public viewing. Founded in 2005, it was acquired by Google in 2006 for $1.65 billion. Within a couple years, more than 25 quadrillion bytes of videos were being streamed from the site each month. Videos are streamed to users on the YouTube site or via blogs and other websites.

- **MeasuredUp** is an example of a leading customer service resolution website where millions of connected, loyal, and involved consumers share service experiences with each other and directly with companies. The power of the collected consumer voice combines with the reach of the Internet to answer questions and encourage companies to listen to and resolve a variety of customer problems. MeasuredUp is not a place for ranting, profanity, or slander. It is a place for caring and thoughtful consumers to post reviews about great and inferior customer service.

- **Angie's List** is a review service of companies designed to take the angst out of hiring contractors. The service has grown to more than one million members in some 200 cities and serves up reviews in 500 categories, primarily home and healthcare services. No anonymous reviews are accepted and the website provides live call center support and help if a project goes bad.

- **Yelp** was founded in 2004 to help people find great local businesses such as doctors, repair shops, and restaurants. More than 33 million people visited Yelp's website in one month alone (June, 2010). Yelpers, as they are called, have written over 12 million local reviews, with more than 85 percent of them rating a business three stars or higher out of five. In addition to reviews, consumers can use Yelp to find events, special offers, or to talk with other Yelpers. Any business that

chooses to can set up a free account to post offers, photos, and message their customers.

In summary, the social customer may go to Twitter with a question, an Internet forum with a customer service query, Facebook with a compliment, or Yelp.com with a complaint.

Customers challenge companies to be aware of what is being said about them. Businesses need to learn a new way of listening to customers, and this can benefit everyone. A common thread linking all definitions of social media is a blending of technology and social interaction that creates a new level of value for both an organization and the customer it serves. Which social media process a business chooses to use depends on its ability to respond to consumers quickly and with the most accurate and relevant information.

A yet to-be-solved organizational problem is that the functions of a customer service department don't quite fit with how social media works because most customer service departments are not available 24/7/365 as social media applications are. Some credible brands, like McDonalds and IBM, are utilizing social media to reach customers and to build or maintain their reputations.

An added advantage of social communication channels is being able to unite all of these contact interactions within one customer record using social customer relationship management (CRM). Even though **social CRM** is mostly about people and processes, companies need the right tools to achieve the ability for everyone to engage and be in alignment. For example, there must be a process in place

CUSTOMER SERVICE **TIP**

Always strive to improve your overall service by focusing on the small details of each transaction. It will mean a lot to the customer and make a difference in total customer satisfaction.

by which each message is automatically routed to the right person, classified by type (question, complaint, or compliment), and studied. In addition, a CSR must take action to satisfy the customer. Finally, the company must determine the extent of the influence each concern will have on future customer exchanges.

Multichannel Customer Contact Points

Customers expect to contact a business at their convenience using their preferred method. As a customer service representative, you will serve customers through various contact points. A **contact point** is the method that a customer uses to communicate with a company. For example, customer contact occurs in person, on the phone, through written communications, and online. To the customer, it doesn't matter where the interaction takes place as long as the frontline employee, the CSR, takes ownership of the problem.

A caring, friendly atmosphere and quick resolutions to problems create *positive* points of contact. Clean, neat surroundings—whether in an

---

✔️ **MAKE IT A HABIT**

Basic Service Reminders

Don't miss a chance to make a good impression. Practice the following guidelines to help make all customer service exchanges positive.

- Conduct all service interactions with consideration and friendliness.
- Demonstrate to the customer that you are doing everything in your power to satisfy him or her.
- Don't assume you know what a customer needs; take time to listen with interest and ask the right questions.

---

office, a store, or a restaurant—say, "We pay attention to details because we value them as important to our success." Accurate invoices, prompt shipments, and returned phone calls help convey a positive impression to customers. Easy-to-navigate websites with on-demand 24/7 access to customer service representatives via chats, phone contact, or responsive e-mail communications are others. For example, at Massage Envy, Ms. Love emphasizes the importance of delivering a welcoming customer service environment. For them, it begins with standing and greeting customers at the time of service and concludes with a sincere thank you for their patronage.

Examples of *negative* points of contact include letting a business line ring five or six times before answering it, leaving the customer on hold for two or more minutes, and not replying promptly to an e-mail request for information. This translates to the customer as "We don't value your time." Long lines, out-of-stock items, and difficult-to-complete online order forms are other ways to leave an unfavorable impression about the company and its product or services.

Though the aforementioned positive and negative points of contact seem obvious, when the obvious isn't stated for the record, these important reminders have a tendency to be taken casually or not at all. Any successful company strives to make sure that all its points of contact with customers are positive ones. In the final analysis, *all* customers deserve exceptional service at each point of contact, regardless of the means they use to seek customer service.

Tiered Service

In years past, most thriving companies gave all their customers special attention, regardless of the size of their purchase. The thinking then was that a customer who makes a small purchase today might make a large purchase tomorrow. Many companies are asking themselves, "Why invest the same amount of customer service effort and expense in a one-time customer as we would in a customer who has a multimillion-dollar history with our business?" This approach to serving customers is referred to as a **tiered service system**, a concept that understands customer service to be fundamentally inter-related with a customer's actual or potential value as a consumer. Many companies use a database of customer transaction records, which have been stored and analyzed with the help of computers and customer relationship management software. The concept and use of CRM software will be discussed in depth in Chapter 4; however, the underlying principle of CRM is that every interaction with a customer is part of a larger relationship. With CRM, the company should be able to capture, maximize, and use organized meaningful reports to help analyze customer loyalty and potentially increase sales.

What does tiered service look like? Whether we realize it or not, we are already being served by this concept each time we choose to fly. Airlines typically place their customers into three tiers of service: basic, or coach-class; enhanced, or business-class; and premium, or first-class. For the customer, the good news with a tiered service system is that there are a lot more choices on price, convenience, and comfort. Also, consumers have the option to upgrade seats and request additional legroom. On the other hand, companies can invisibly identify individuals who do not generate profits for them and may provide them with inferior service.

Although tiered service exists, customers should never feel that they are getting a certain level of service because they are buying a certain level of business. All customers should feel that they are receiving the same level of customer service when it comes to assistance with problems or the handling of complaints.

WHAT DO YOU THINK 1.4

Do you use social media tools on a regular basis? If so, what tools do you use most frequently when sharing a positive or negative customer service interaction? Write a brief journal entry describing your experiences.

WRAPPING UP

It is clear that Zappos and Edward Jones (see page 16) define customer service each in a unique way. Chapter 1 presented an all-inclusive response and argument to what customer service is. With intention, a successful organization like Zappos or Edward Jones bases its service standards with the following awareness in mind: its mission and business goals, who its internal and external customers are, and how the challenges of social media and global competition might impact its existence and future growth plans. With this information, the study of the Global Customer chapter that follows will seem all the more relevant.

FOCUS ON. . .
BEST PRACTICES

Edward Jones

Edward Jones boasts on its website that it is unlike any other investment firm. Many would agree because it is most unique in how it honors the needs of both its internal and external customers.

This customer-oriented company has been named to the top ten of *Fortune* magazine's "100 Best Companies to Work For" list for eight years. That prestigious recognition doesn't just happen without client-focused guiding principles and a high regard for its dedicated associates. To illustrate the point, the investment adviser boasted that, during the recent recession, none of its 12,615 offices closed, nor were any of its employees laid off. Salaries were frozen, but profit sharing

continued. Internal customers (employees) supported the company because they felt a vested interest in its success.

In a similar way, Edward Jones meets several basic needs of its external customers. Being accessible and approachable to its clients in offices on Main Street instead of high-rise corporate structures, Edward Jones offers unparalleled customer-friendly interactions. A typical customer visit begins with a warm greeting by the branch office administrator and continues with a comfortable unhurried conversation with the financial advisor. This consulting session is fully focused on the client needs in a private, uninterrupted environment.

SOURCE: Regina Deluca-Imral, "Edward Jones Ranks No. 2 by FORTUNE Magazine in its 11th Year on Best Companies to Work For List *Ranks in the Top 10 for Eight Years*," *Edward Jones Press Release*, January 21, 2010.

SUMMARY

- Customer service is the process of satisfying a customer relative to a product or service, in whatever way the customer defines his or her need, and then delivering that service with efficiency, compassion, and sensitivity.

- The power shift from companies to their customers underlies the new customer economy, in which the depth of relationships with customers and loyalty to those customers are critical to an organization's success.

- Both internal and external customers are important because they impact company revenue and customer retention.

- Customer needs include the need to feel welcome, to be understood, to be comfortable, and to be in control.

- The social customer consumes information in a different way and learns about new products and brands through social channels.

KEY TERMS

Angie's List
blog
contact point
customer-centric service
customer profile
customer service
customer service representative
   (CSR)

external customers
Facebook
internal customers
Internet forum
MeasuredUp
service culture
social CRM
social data

social media
tiered service system
tweets
Twitter
Yelp
YouTube

CRITICAL THINKING

1. Why are organizations' mission statements for customer service different from each other?

2. How can a company successfully serve its external and internal customers?

3. In what ways do customer needs relate to the reasons people buy from certain companies?

4. To what extent do you feel social media has affected the way businesses serve customers today?

5. If you were the president of a retail organization, would you be fearful or appreciative of

receiving complaints via social media applications? Describe what actions you would take with customer-community feedback and comments.

6. Name two advantages to organizations of providing customers with multichannel contact points.

7. If you owned your own business, would you provide your customer base with a tiered service system? Defend your position.

 ## WHAT DO YOU THINK NOW?

Project 1.1

Assume you are doing a report on *best practices in serving internal customers.* Reread your responses to the *What Do You Think?* questions that you completed throughout this chapter. What are some day-to-day practices that support internal customers? What situations and practices might diminish efforts to support colleagues in an organization? What skills are required to serve internal customers well? Compile your responses, as directed by your instructor.

ONLINE RESEARCH ACTIVITY

Project 1.2   Students are Customers with Needs Too

Assume you are writing a report on higher education (universities and community colleges) meeting the needs of students in your state. Identify what you feel are five of your needs as an educational consumer. Visit the websites of at least four institutions of higher education in your state and locate each school's mission statement and vision. In addition, identify other available services those schools offer that might assist students in their decision-making process. Finally, compare and contrast your needs with each school's identity.

As a result of your research and analysis, write a brief report indicating which school best meets your needs and why. Present your findings as part of a moderated panel discussion or other activity as directed by your instructor.

COMMUNICATION SKILLS AT WORK

Project 1.3   Social Media CSR

Assume you have been asked to participate on a company task force with two co-workers to review the qualifications for a new CSR position focused on social media. Review the job description below with your team.

Job Title: Customer Service Social Media Representative

Job Description: Build rapport between the company and its customer base through exemplary customer service engagement.

Roles/Responsibilities:

- Monitor the company's social media outlets/networks (Facebook, Twitter, etc.) for customer service related inquiries, complaints, concerns

- Answer all customer service inquiries on any social networks immediately and in the company's tone (conversational, but informative)

- Organize customer service inquiries, concerns, and responses for future reference

- Track the types of questions that appear on social media

Qualifications: The ideal candidate should demonstrate the following:

- Exceptional communication skills (verbal and written)

- Attention to detail including a firm and patient demeanor

- Strong grasp of the structure, purpose, and tone of social networks

- Ability to think quickly, and formulate responses within a short turnaround time

- Ability to communicate on social networks in a professional way

- Ability to multi-task

- Strong organizational skills

- Proficient with Microsoft Office programs

- At least 3 years of high volume e-commerce customer service experience.

Working in small groups, discuss the content of this job posting, identify skills and competencies that are different from typical CSR positions, and write up your task force findings for a later discussion, as directed by your instructor. As an alternative, follow your instructor's directions to join a group and use the instructor-designated discussion board to complete the group project.

DECISION MAKING AT WORK

Project 1.4   Tiered Service—a New Approach

Richard Lee, President of Elgin Technology Products, recently returned from a Technology Conference in downtown Chicago. As a result of talking with leaders of other companies, he is now considering establishing a tiered service system, an idea he shared with the manager of the Customer Service Department.

Mr. Lee's basic thought is to reward the customers who give Elgin Technology Products $100,000 worth of business with an end-of-year "thank you payment" that reflects a 5 percent discount on all yearly purchases. In addition, those customers would receive a commitment to next-day turnaround time on the resolution of all customer service problems. Moreover, the customers who purchase $500,000 or more annually would receive a 10 percent discount and a commitment to a four-hour resolution of customer service problems. Mr. Lee has requested that you and three other CSRs share your opinion and concerns regarding this decision.

1. Name some advantages of making the decision to use a tiered service approach at Elgin Technology Products.

   _____

   _____

   _____

2. Name some disadvantages of making the decision to use a tiered service approach at Elgin Technology Products.

   _____

   _____

   _____

3. Based upon your findings, would you endorse the decision to use a tiered service approach or not?

   _____

   _____

   _____

CASE STUDY

Project 1.5 **Customer Orders Are Perfect or They Don't Pay**

Thunderbird Container Products President, Beverly Whisenhunt, stormed out of her office and said, "Customers' orders are perfect or they don't pay. That's a critical goal of ours that customers expect and we are going to deliver!" At first, those in earshot thought she must be kidding, but the seriousness with which she made that statement and her demeanor said differently. Give some thought to this pronouncement and be prepared to discuss the following three questions in a class discussion.

1. In your opinion, can a company afford to live by this statement? Why or why not?

_____

_____

_____

2. Can you think of any situations in which an organization may have difficulty honoring such a customer pledge?

_____

_____

_____

3. What are some potential benefits to the company by setting such a high standard?

_____

_____

_____

Kurhan/Shutterstock

CHAPTER 2

The Global Customer

*It is the service we are not obliged to give
that people value the most.*

JAMES C. PENNEY, FOUNDER, J. C. PENNEY STORES

OBJECTIVES

1. Discuss the impact of globalization on customer service.

2. Describe diversity in the workplace relative to serving the needs of diverse personalities in global customers.

3. Identify the four personalities of customers and distinguish among them.

4. Contrast customer service wants among the five generational groups.

5. Discuss ways to communicate effectively with disabled persons.

Craigslist

Craigslist, a website for local classifieds and forums, is an example of a company being impacted by globalization. The company's success, in part, has been due to its inclination to embrace this *customer-to-customer sales phenomenon* in the U.S. and around the world. Seventh worldwide in terms of English-language page views, the website has more than 50 million people who use this Internet site in the U.S. alone. Craigslist is also available in French, German, Italian, Portuguese, and Spanish with total users self-publishing about 50 million new classified ads each month.

Total website traffic is in excess of 20 billion page views per month.

"It's important to create an atmosphere where customers want to help each other," notes Craig Newmark, founder of Craigslist.org and a customer service rep himself. "It begins with treating customers the way you'd like to be treated, taking customer service seriously, and following through. The way we run our site encourages people to give each other a break because of that culture of trust."

SOURCE: Craigslist Factsheet, http://www.craigslist.org/about/factsheet accessed October 13, 2010.

IMPACT OF GLOBALIZATION

As simple as it may sound, best-in-class global service is all about delivering the right information in context to optimize business processes, applications, and activities that support service. In the opening feature, it is clear that Craigslist provides the right information for customer-to-customer self-service, whether on a domestic or global level. Of importance is this: If content, processes, and people are not managed accurately, a business cannot deliver the customer service expected of it, and service becomes a weakness rather than a strength. This, of course, is compounded by globalization.

As business has turned more to an integrated world market to meet its needs, the difficulties of communicating at a global level have become increasingly widespread. Any service communication channel requires transparency where customers cannot detect that the company is not directly handling, similar to face-to-face encounters.

Because rules differ among cultures about how to talk to and act toward others, service communication problems arise. For example, customers and service reps often are unsure if it is alright to look someone in the eye while speaking, to express feelings openly, or to show emotions in e-mail and live chat communications with those we don't know. When companies outsource the service function, correct cultural interactions are difficult to control and impossible to fully oversee. Customer service representatives must take care to avoid potential damage to a company's reputation if the quality of service is deficient or uncaring.

To their credit, companies can and do offer multichannel service options to mitigate service risks. For example, a mix of locations such as domestic, outsourced offshore, nearshore, and homeshore virtual agents offer choices to the customer that fit each one's unique needs in particular buying situations.[1]

---

[1] "The State of Service in Insurance," *IBM Enterprise Content Management*, May 2010, 6, ftp://public.dhe.ibm.com/common/ssi/ecm/en/iuw03006usen/IUW03006USEN.PDF accessed October 13, 2010.

Outsourcing

Outsourcing, also referred to as subcontracting, is the purchase of labor from a source outside of the company, rather than using the company's own staff. Many feel, however, that the practice of outsourcing customer service to offshore call centers may be a good idea carried too far. Critics of the practice point to a growing body of evidence that suggests faulty economics and customer dissatisfaction are forcing a rethinking of the low-cost service approach.[2] Customer resistance, combined with data security concerns and the unexpectedly high costs of managing offshore call centers, offset and dilute their promised economic benefits.

India's previous outsourcing success, for example, has diminished, and the country is now seen as a strong source for non voice-related customer care offerings. Back-office and non-voice services including keyboarded chats and e-mail messages are now delivered from this global location.[3]

Nearshoring

Nearshoring is a form of outsourcing in which business processes are relocated to locations that are low-wage, but close in geographical distance and/or time zone to the client company. A viable nearshore option could be located in North America or even a Latin American country like Argentina. As opposed to outsourcing, which refers to sourcing from low-cost countries from across the globe, nearshoring offers certain advantages such as similar time zones, cultural and linguistic affinity, geographical proximity, as well as economic, political, or historical linkages. Further, service reps from Latin American locations tend to have a high degree of customer empathy and often share a much needed bilingual capability. Bilingual online service representatives are a major driver for nearshoring in the United States because of the need to support the expanding Spanish-speaking population.

Homeshoring "Virtual Home Agents"

Imagine a work commute that is just down the hallway, a few minutes from your coffeepot and the morning news. You plug in your headset to the phone, boot up your computer, and begin taking calls from customers. After 30 minutes of call time, you move on to a scheduled break to tend to a few chores around the house. You get another cup of coffee, finish a few small household tasks, and return to your desk to begin taking calls again.[4]

The previous description appeared in an article about virtual call centers and it is a fairly good representation of a day in the life of a virtual call center agent. An increasing number of companies are moving customer service jobs out of high overhead call centers and into what is possibly the lowest overhead place in the United States: workers' homes. Companies are hiring U.S. home-based call agents as an alternative to the more expensive in-house operators or less qualified offshore call centers. This work style trend is called **homeshoring.** When compared to offshoring or nearshoring, homeshoring is less likely to risk the accent fatigue, cultural disconnection, and customer rage.

While homeshoring provides a flexible and cost-efficient domestic delivery solution for many companies, generally the type of service support delivered from at-home virtual agents involves structured programs such as customer care, order taking, and sales with well-defined processes and pre-established goals. A homeshoring agent is paid anywhere from $7 to $30 an hour and typically prefers a more flexible family-friendly schedule.[5]

Companies benefit from using homeshoring agents. They save money and report a higher worker

[2] Norm Alster, "Customer Disservice?" *CFO,* October 26, 2005, http://www.cfo.com/article.cfm/4390954/c_2984406/?f=archives accessed October 13, 2010.

[3] Brendan B. Read, "Which Shore to Land On?" *TMCnet,* June 1, 2010, http://www.tmcnet.com/call-center/features/articles/92323-which-shore-land.htm accessed October 13, 2010.

[4] Melissa Brewer, "Homeshoring Brings Legitimate Work-at-Home Jobs Into American Homes," http://www.worldwideworkathome.com/articles/homeshoring.html accessed March 22, 2011.

[5] Ibid.

retention rate as well as more satisfied customers when they contract with virtual agents who do not require work space or paid benefits. In addition, phone and broadband technology now make it simple for companies to forward their calls to home-based workers and allow only need-to-have access rights to internal corporate database systems.

A drawback for home agents is they are often left out of the social safety net. Freelancers don't have access to affordable insurance, are taxed more than traditional employees, and have limited access to benefits such as unemployment insurance, retirement plans, and unpaid wage claims. The upside to this movement, however, is the rise of homeshoring employers. Homeshoring has paved the way to legitimate work from home that allows flexibility for a whole new workforce that includes work-at-home parents, elder caretakers, military spouses, and people with unique medical needs or disabilities. Forrester's 2010 survey of contact center decision makers found that 35 percent of companies

had plans for expanding their virtual home agent program.[6]

CULTURAL DIVERSITY AND THE GLOBAL CUSTOMER

Culture is defined as a system of shared values, beliefs, and rituals that are learned and passed on through generations of families and social groups. Most individuals' cultural make-up is simultaneously shaped by several dissimilar elements, such as ethnicity, family, religion, and economic status. Culture affects a person's perception of the world. More important, during customer interactions, it often defines what behavior is acceptable and unacceptable.

It is particularly essential to understand that the meaning of "good service" has different interpretations in different cultures. Understanding colleagues from different cultures makes for a more cohesive and effective organization. Internal customers, like external customers, have their own unique needs and perspectives. Strategically aligning products and services to meet those needs will reap benefits. The more service providers know about their customers and culture, the better customer relations will

WHAT DO YOU THINK

2.1

Survey two or three family members and friends to see if they would like to work as a home-agent and why. From your discussions, record in your journal some pros and cons of working with customers out of your home.

Ethics / Choices

Suppose you have a co-worker who tells culturally-slurred jokes. They are meant to be funny, but, in fact, are offensive to you and other co-workers. Would you ignore the issue, talk about it with the offender, or discuss it with your manager? Explain.

In what ways is a diverse global workforce good for customers, employees, and the organization?

---

[6] Elizabeth Herrell, "Contact Center Manages Embrace Home Agents as Smart Move," *Forrester Blogs*, http://blogs.forrester.com/elizabeth_herrell/10-05-24-contact_center_managers_embrace_home_agents_smart_move accessed October 13, 2010.

be and the more sensitive to others the workplace will become. Organizations and their employees who are aware of cultural differences definitely have a competitive advantage.

Because language barriers and cultural misunderstandings can get in the way of effective communication and create complexities in customer situations, one could ask, What role does culture play in customer service? It is accepted that customer service representatives will interact with people of diverse cultural backgrounds every day; and while it is impossible to know about every element of a person's culture, keep in mind that each internal or external customer should receive the same courteous, professional, and knowledgeable service.

Our cultural values provide a subconscious view that we use to function and interact with others. We begin to learn this view at a very early age, even before we acquire language skills. It guides our reflexive behavior by providing us with guidelines on how to respond in a wide range of situations—how formal to be, how close to stand to someone, what physical contact is appropriate, how much eye contact to maintain, how to demonstrate respect in writing and face-to-face, and so forth.

A manifestation of one's own culture is that it is often taken for granted and accepted as the norm, not examined and questioned. This means we are often unaware of the filter through which we are looking at others. This presents the possibility of service-related problems because people from diverse cultures encode and decode messages differently. These differences increase the chances of misunderstanding, especially nonverbal behaviors and concepts of time, space, and authority, which can be particularly troubling during customer service encounters.

Nonverbal Behaviors

Cultural differences in nonverbal behaviors are a common source of misunderstandings and conflict in the workplace. For instance, many Westerners like to make eye contact, interpreting it as an indication of interest and honesty. Moreover, they also show friendliness through relaxed body language. When these behaviors do not happen, it can sometimes be interpreted as shiftiness, coldness, or disinterest. However, in Eastern cultures the opposite is true. Eye contact shows that you see yourself as equal or are being belligerent. Additionally, constant eye contact with a superior is considered rude because it may be seen as defiance or a challenge to authority.

Being aware of these nonverbal nuances will help reduce negative impressions in intercultural communications with customers. Low-context cultures such as the United States and Canada tend to give relatively less emphasis to nonverbal communication. People in these settings tend to place less importance on the unspoken word than on the literal meaning of words themselves. In high-context settings such as Colombia, however, understanding the nonverbal components of communication is relatively more important than receiving the intended meaning of the communication as a whole.

Concept of Time

The perception of time is one of the central differences between cultures. In the West, time tends to be seen as quantitative, measured in units that reflect the march of progress. It is logical, sequential, and present-focused. Conversely, in the East, time is treated as if it has unlimited continuity, an unraveling rather than a strict boundary. For example, business meetings will often run longer and later than Westerners are accustomed to when conducting negotiations in Eastern countries.

Concept of Space

Another variable across cultures has to do with ways of relating to space. Crossing cultures, we encounter very different ideas about appropriate personal space. North Americans tend to prefer a large amount of space. Europeans, on the other hand, tend to stand closer to each other when talking, and are accustomed to smaller personal spaces. The difficulty with space preferences is not that they exist, but the connotations that are attached to them. For instance, if someone is accustomed to standing or sitting very close when they are talking with another, they may see the other's attempt to create more space as evidence of coldness, condescension, or a lack of interest. In contrast, those who are accustomed to more personal space may view attempts to get closer as pushy, disrespectful, or threatening. Neither is correct, they are simply different.

Concept of Authority

Authority is the power or right to give commands, enforce obedience, take action, or make final decisions. How a given society views authority can significantly affect business-related communication because perceptions of authority figures can shape how a message will be received. For example, David Victor observes in his article "Cross-Cultural/International Communication" that "in a relatively decentralized business environment—as exists in many highly centralized U.S. companies—people generally pay attention to a person based on how convincing an argument he or she puts forth, regardless of that person's rank or status within the organization or society at large."[7] In contrast, highly centralized cultures such as China believe high rank equals high respect. Therefore, messages from high ranking officials are taken as truth, regardless of whether individuals agree or disagree.

Serving Diverse Customers Well

As companies expand across the globe, challenges in customer service grow. In order to avoid cultural collisions with customers—when emotions, habits, or judgments taint service efforts—a customer service representative (CSR) needs to be aware of how communicating effectively with different cultures plays a role in the service encounter. One suggestion is for CSRs to identify their own cultural differences and be conscious of not stereotyping customers. **Stereotyping** happens when people categorize individuals or groups according to an oversimplified standardized image or idea. Because stereotyping can lead to poor interactions that result in misunderstandings and prejudgments, it strongly hinders positive customer service encounters.

It is the responsibility of the CSR to understand each customer, regardless of any cultural differences

or accents. Accents can be hard to understand, but the responsibility for understanding what is being said rests with the CSR. When serving customers with a spoken accent, apologize to them when you do not understand what they are saying. Be sure to speak to them slowly and clearly. Repeat back, or **paraphrase** what they have said to you using other words for clarification. Or, if necessary, ask them to repeat what they have said. It is as important for a listener to attempt to understand a heavy accent as it is for the other person to make strides toward improving his or her English skills. Because some cultures consider feedback or criticism damaging to one's reputation, CSRs might paraphrase often.

To communicate effectively with other people, we must know them as individuals—their unique background, personality, preferences, and style. Customer service interactions can be complex under the best of conditions. Issues of language, race, gender,

---

✅ **MAKE IT A HABIT**

Cross-Cultural Communication Techniques

For more effective communication with domestic and global customers and colleagues, consider the following:

- Use a variety of communication methods (written, visual, and verbal) to get your message across.
- Err on the side of formality. Most cultural groups value formality, and it will demonstrate respect on your part.
- Make an effort to pronounce names and titles correctly. If you are not sure about proper pronunciation, ask.
- Respond to what is being said, not how it is said.
- Never make a derogatory comment about any culture, generation, or disability.

---

[7] David A Victor, "Cross-Cultural/International Communication," *Encyclopedia of Business*, 2 ed., http://www.referenceforbusiness.com/encyclopedia/Cos-Des/Cross-Cultural-International-Communication.html accessed October 13, 2010.

religion, age, or disability can complicate communication efforts. A significant point for understanding diversity is for CSRs to recognize that it is reciprocal. That is to say, if someone is different from you, then you are different from them. Accepting the diversity of others is expressing your desire for others to accept your diversity.

To be more specific relative the major ethnic groups, consider,

- *Hispanics* Recent statistics show the Hispanic American population is growing at a rate of four times that of the general population. The 2010 Census revealed that over the past 10 years, the Hispanic population has increased from 35.3 million in 2000 to approximately 50.5 million in 2010.[8] The purchasing power of Hispanics is expected to reach 1 trillion dollars by 2013.[9]

- *Asians* No one Asian subgroup makes up more than 25 percent of the total U.S. Asian population, and each has a more distinctly different set of cultural values, beliefs, and attitudes making Asian consumers more difficult to target as a separate shopper segment. As a group, however, Asians tend to have more education and higher incomes than the general population. In 2009, 14.5 million Americans—4.7 percent of the country's population—claim Asian ancestry, which makes the group a powerful force in the U.S. consumer market. The Selig Center projects that the nation's Asian buying power will climb from $509 billion in 2009 to $697 billion in 2014.

- *African-Americans* Although most African-Americans share a common cultural heritage, they are, by definition, native citizens and make up part of the broader culture of the United States. The Selig Center projects that the African-American buying power will rise from $910 billion in 2009 to $1.1 trillion in 2014.[10]

Maximizing the Potential of Global Diversity

Creating and sustaining a diverse workforce and a diverse customer base are competitive advantages. Diverse ideas come from diverse people, and diverse revenue streams come from diverse customers. It does not matter if the diversity is race, age, gender, sexual orientation, ethnicity, physical ability, religion, education, appearance, or any other characteristic.

Sensitive companies that provide a good cross-cultural employee training program find it to be very helpful. The content of this training program might include an explanation of the differences between cultures, as well as formal manners and etiquette to follow when serving international customers. How CSRs perceive the needs of customers may depend on their own cultural, personality, and generational perspectives.

The previous discussion about the shift in purchasing power in the United States provides further evidence for the importance of cultural diversity. As the diversity of the American population increases, the future of multicultural growth opportunities will be very exciting to businesses. Businesses that take the extra steps to effectively communicate with multicultural customers will have a clear competitive advantage over those who do not.[11]

WHAT DO YOU THINK

2.2

Describe a customer service encounter you have experienced or observed where the service provider did an outstanding job in serving a culturally diverse customer. Conversely, describe a service encounter where the service provider was insensitive to the needs of the customer.

---

[8] US Census Bureau, http://2010.census.gov/news/releases/operations/cb11-cn125.html accessed April 8, 2011.

[9] Octavio Orozco, "The Hispanic Market," *Multicultural Marketing News*, January 28, 2010.

[10] Jeffrey M. Humphreys, "The Multicultural Economy 2009," *Georgia Business and Economic Conditions*, http://www.terry.uga.edu/selig/docs/GBEC0903q.pdf accessed October 13, 2010.

[11] Elisabete Miranda, "Multicultural Markets," *Multicultural Marketing News*, January 28, 2010.

CUSTOMER PERSONALITIES

Even with the wonders and complexities of global communication, the CSR still has to contend with variables that are intrinsic to the human personality. Though the term **personality** can be defined in different ways, relative to customer service, it relates to the pattern of collective character, behavioral, temperamental, emotional, and mental traits of a person. Personality is another dimension of the challenge of diversity issues when serving customers well. Today we know more about basic human personality types than ever before. We also know how each personality type should be handled. When CSRs apply this knowledge on a regular basis, customers will feel they have been treated properly.

People often feel they do not belong to any one personality group, but each of us has one dominant personality style that defines our behavior. Although every customer is different, as Peter Bender notes in his article "How to Deal with Difficult Customers," most can be categorized into one of four groups: *analytical, driver, amiable,* and *expressive.* Here are some basic characteristics of each personality style along with suggestions for how best to serve each one.[12]

Analytical   Driver

Amiable   Expressive

Photodisc/Getty Images

Put yourself in the role of a customer at a restaurant or a department store. Which personality type do you prefer to serve you? Why?

Analytical

People with an **analytical personality** are known for being systematic, well organized, and deliberate. They value numbers and statistics, love details, and tend to be introverted. These individuals appreciate facts and information written and presented in a logical manner. They enjoy completing detailed tasks and take the time to analyze and compare their choices before making a purchasing decision. They believe the more thought they put into it, the happier they will be with their decision. Others may see the analytical person as being cautious, structured, and someone who does things "by the book."

Because this personality type often works with numbers and technology, they seek careers in engineering, computer science, finance, purchasing,

quality control, and accounting. When working with analytical customers, a CSR needs to provide facts and work with them in step-by-step fashion when delivering service.

The Driver

Those with a **driver personality** want to save time, value results, love being in control, and doing things their way. They are extroverted and may show little or no emotion. They are called drivers because they are the people who make things happen—they take tremendous pride in getting tasks and objectives completed. The driver thrives on a challenge and the internal motivation to succeed. They are practical people who can do a lot in a relatively short amount of time. They usually talk fast and get right to the point. Others often view them as decisive, direct, and pragmatic.

These dominant risk-takers quite often end up at the top of an organization. Business owners and doctors often fall into this personality category. As

[12] Peter Urs Bender, "How to Deal with Difficult Customers," *Professional Selling,* http://www.peterursbender.com/articles/difficult.html accessed October 13, 2010.

customers, drivers will tell you exactly what they want, and they do not want to hear a lot of "fluff." When you tell them what you will do for them, they expect you to follow through and do it quickly.

The Amiable

The **amiable personality** type wants to build relationships, loves to give others support and attention, values suggestions from others, and fears disagreement. These people tend to display a lot of emotion. Amiables are dependable, loyal, and easygoing. They like things that are non-threatening and friendly. They dislike dealing with impersonal details and cold hard facts. Often described as warm and sensitive, they can be perceived as wishy-washy.

Amiable people gravitate toward professions such as nursing, teaching, and jobs that require teamwork. They like to work in groups, are very family-oriented, and resist sudden changes. Amiables want sincerity from a salesperson, and they appreciate a stable environment in which to buy. One of their worst fears is to buy from a disreputable operation and to be taken advantage of.

CSRs will find that this personality tends to be the most challenging because their cautious nature keeps them from getting too enthusiastic about anything. They tend to be factually driven so when working with these clients, give them a lot of information and do not pressure them to make a decision. Remember, when serving this personality type, be vigilant about keeping appointments, staying on schedule, and honoring commitments because the amiable personality likes everything to be predictable and planned. They want to know how things are going to be handled.

The Expressive

The people who have **expressive personalities** value appreciation and a pat on the back, love social situations, like to inspire others, and are extroverted, readily showing emotion to others. People of this type are usually identified as the life of the party and are very outgoing and enthusiastic with a high energy level. They can be great idea generators, but may not have the ability to see an idea through to completion.

Often thought of as a talker, overly dramatic, impulsive, and manipulative, expressive people are great communicators and are attracted to professions such as sales and marketing. They are comfortable with people and spend a fair amount of time "shooting the breeze" in order to develop trust. They tend to be disorganized and dislike details. More often than not, they are slow to reach a buying decision.

Figure 2.1 recaps in table form characteristics of each personality type.

REMEMBER THIS

Figure 2.1 Personality Characteristics

ANALYTICAL	DRIVER	AMIABLE	EXPRESSIVE
• controlled	• action-orientated	• patient	• verbal
• orderly	• decisive	• loyal	• motivating
• precise	• problem solver	• sympathetic	• enthusiastic
• disciplined	• assertive	• team player	• convincing
• deliberate	• risk-taker	• emotional	• impulsive
• cautious	• forceful	• considerate	• influential
• diplomatic	• competitive	• empathetic	• charming
• systematic	• independent	• persevering	• confident
• logical	• determined	• trusting	• optimistic
• conventional	• results-orientated	• congenial	• animated

SOURCE: Don Straits, "The Toughest Question in the Interview," All Business, *http://www.allbusiness.com/print/1605-1-22eeq.html* accessed October 13, 2010.

Here are some tips for your own personality type when dealing with others who are different than you:

- *Analyticals* should speak and smile more. Show appreciation and personal interest. Relax. Share information and be more open to others.

- *Drivers* must slow down when dealing with other personality types. Take more time to listen. Try to hold back from dominating and learn when to relinquish some control. Show more patience and be more relaxed.

- *Amiables* need to be more assertive in customer situations. Talk more, listen less. Take control and take some risks.

- *Expressives* should listen more and slow down. They should write things down and set specific goals. Check details and remember to stay calm. Learn to focus.[13]

WHAT DO YOU THINK

2.3

Out of the four personality types just described write down the one you most identify with. Given your personality type, in what ways should you adapt your service skills to other personality types?

GENERATIONAL DIFFERENCES

Though generational differences are not universal among people in the world, it is still helpful to have an awareness of a customer's generation and to know that generation's service preferences. These are two steps that lead to excellent customer service. Understanding and appreciating the factors that shape each generation can help with everything from recruiting new employees and motivating seasoned ones to serving a generationally diverse customer base around the world.

At no time in our history have so many and such different generations been asked to work together. The once linear nature of power at work, from older to younger, has been dislocated by changes in life styles and health, an increase in longevity, as well as the demands of technology and a digital knowledge base.

Whether a CSR or consumer is located in Asia, Europe, or America, each individual has been influenced by different formative events of his or her generation. As such, each brings a unique set of core values, skills, and expectations to the job or marketplace. These generational differences can result in a synergistic explosion of productivity or the opposite—a downward spiral of miscommunication and misunderstanding.

Good service must be seen *from a customer's point of view*. In service interactions, what you do, how you do it, how well it must be done, and proving you can do it again are all based on who the customer is. To that end, each generation tends to have its own definition of service. What might seem like excellent customer service to one person might be offensive to another, particularly if they are from different generations.

Understanding these generational differences is critical to CSRs who are willing to adapt their personal styles to meet their customers' needs. These understandings have the promise of creating harmony, mutual respect, and joint effort where today there is often suspicion, mistrust, isolation, and employee turnover. There are presently over 309 million people living in the United States. They can be divided into the following five generations: the Mature Generation, Baby Boomers, Generation X, Generation Y, and Generation Z.

CUSTOMER SERVICE **TIP**

By examining customer service through the perspectives of the different generations, you can apply specific customer service techniques that will be successful in each generation's context.

---

[13] Ibid.

Mature Generation

The oldest population group is referred to as the **Mature Generation**. The Matures, born prior to 1946, comprise in excess of 60 million people within the United States. They grew up in the midst of war-time shortages and economic depression of the 1940s. To some, their work ethic and desire to do the right thing by others make them unique among generations that follow.[14]

Matures grew up learning the value of a dollar. Even now, they remain conservative spenders, opting to do without rather than spending impulsively. When they decide to purchase an item, they generally save up the money to pay for it in cash.

Baby Boomers

The **Baby Boomer Generation**, born between 1946 and 1964, came of age in the midst of tremendous economic expansion, learning to use all the convenience-oriented products that came on the market during their youth. Because of their generation's size, approximately 80 million strong, Boomers have a significant influence on every aspect of society. They currently make up the majority of the political, cultural, industrial, and academic leadership roles in the United States.

Boomers have always put in long hours because of how closely they associate their occupation with their identity. Even as they edge into retirement, predictions are that most of them will still want to work after they reach retirement age. Baby Boomers were the first credit-card generation and many used it extravagantly.

Generation X

The U.S. Census Bureau estimates **Generation X,** those born between 1965 and 1981, to be some 50 million strong. They "work to live," not "live to work," as the previous generation does. Because many of them came from homes where both parents worked, they have been the most unsupervised generation and have developed into self-sufficient adults. They were

the first generation to expect diversity and to fully accept women in positions of power in the workplace.

Generation Xers operate as people "who walk the talk." They are verbal, globally aware, street smart, process driven, and technically adept. They want respect for their expertise, loyalty in relationships, and products that are modern.

Having watched their Baby Boomer parents put in long hours, Gen Xers have developed a different perspective about work. They do not necessarily equate productive work with long hours. Instead, they look for ways to work smarter, resulting in fewer hours but greater productivity.

This generation views training and development as a means for enhancing their versatility in the marketplace—as an investment in their future with *any* employer, not just the present organization. They believe that a job is a contract and the burden is on the organization to keep them engaged and growing. If that doesn't happen, they will move on to another job that is more challenging for them.

Having come of age after the chaos of the sixties and seventies, coupled with watching their parents spend extravagantly, Generation Xers have chosen the more conservative paths of saving and spending prudently. They value time off, which provides the work-family balance they seek. Finally, they look for an enjoyable atmosphere where work is not taken too seriously.[15]

Generation Y

Generation Y (also called Millennials) presently account for nearly 85 million people in the United States. Born between 1981 and 1990, this generation is one of the most unique groups. They have been highly nurtured by family and others and the Internet is their medium for communicating, entertaining, and learning.

Millennials live in an era of technology and rapid change. As the Millennials have entered the

---

[14] U.S. Census Bureau, http://quickfacts.census.gov/qfd/states/00000.html accessed October 13, 2010.

[15] Emily McRobbie, "Generational Differences are Important." (presentation, Coconino Community College Employee Development Day, Flagstaff, AZ, October 30, 2009.)

REMEMBER THIS

Figure 2.2 Generational Differences

MATURE GENERATION	A Mature is patriotic, loyal, fiscally conservative, and has faith in institutions. These customers tend to struggle with technology and typically need more attention than others.
BABY BOOMERS	A Baby Boomer is idealistic, competitive, questions authority, desires to put their own stamp on things, and challenges institutions. These customers are independent with a "can-do" attitude. They like to dig in and overcome obstacles all on their own.
GENERATION X	A Generation Xer is resourceful, self-reliant, distrusts institutions, and is highly adaptive to both change and technology. These customers have very strong opinions and are very in-tune with issues regarding relationships, community, and the environment.
GENERATION Y	A Generation Yer is confident, ambitious, and very technologically sound. These customers can be impatient and need information quickly as evidenced by their use of technological instruments and their ability to multi-task with ease.
GENERATION Z	A Generation Zer is more self-directed and processes information at lightning speed. As a result, they are ushering into society novel approaches to thinking, communicating, and learning.

SOURCE: Reprinted, in part, with permission of Emily McRobbie.
ADDITIONAL SOURCE: "2010 Report: Generation Analysis," *Sparxoo,* http://www.slideshare.net/sparxoo/2010-generation-trend-report accessed August 10, 2010.

workforce, employers have discovered that "fun" and "stimulation" seem to be the operative words for rewarding this generation. Employers embracing these desires have been able to maintain lower turnover rates and achieve higher productivity.

As customers, Millennials are usually known as those that need instant gratification. Once they decide they want something, they usually make a pretty quick decision to get it—especially with technology purchases, because they are very techno-savvy.[16]

Generation Z

The newest wave of customers is from **Generation Z** (also called the Silent generation, iGeneration, and Net generation). They were born after 1990 and into a time when technology was ruling the world. They are estimated to number more than 25 million strong and growing. The majority of their communication takes place on the Internet, and they show very low verbal communication skills. Most of their formative years are spent in cyberspace. They are used to instant action and satisfaction due to Internet technology and their extensive use of various social networking tools.

According to the California Teacher's Association website, Generation Zers prefer to communicate online—often with friends they have never met. They cannot imagine life without cell phones or social networking websites. They prefer computers to books and want instant results. They are very collaborative and creative. It is predicted that they will change the workplace dramatically in terms of work style and expectations. These are the children of Generation X parents, who came of age during the greatest technological leap in history.[17]

Figure 2.2, above, recaps in table form characteristics of each generation.

---

[16] Ibid.

[17] Sherry Posnick-Goodwin, "Meet Generation Z," *California Teachers Association Magazine,* http://www.cta.org/Professional-Development/Publications/Educator-Feb-10/Meet-Generation-Z.aspx accessed October 13, 2010.

Serving Different Generations

It is a major challenge to serve multiple generations all at the same time. Specifically, when serving the newest customers in Generations X, Y, and Z, some unique service reminders are in order. First, these generations tend to be unforgiving about poor customer service, expect 24/7/365 service, and are prepared to negotiate service relationships. When getting their needs met, they believe that if they do not ask, then they will not receive.

On the whole, the younger generations prefer to conduct business and make purchases online or by phone instead of face-to-face. Because they are in constant communication with others, using cell phones, PDAs, and other electronic Internet-based devices, they have high consumer awareness and use this understanding to obtain what they need or desire.

In contrast, this concept of "customer service" can take a different twist when working with the senior market that consists of the older Mature and Baby Boomer generations. These consumers are typically more loyal, but simultaneously, more demanding. They want less noise and fewer visual stimuli in their on-ground shopping experience. Many prefer not to shop online and are often not very computer savvy.

Customer service representatives should be sensitive to the special needs of some global seniors. Many retirees struggle with hearing and vision loss. Their mobility may be restricted, they may be in pain, and it may take them a bit longer to do things. Moreover, they may be more resistant to asking for help outside of their family and friends.

In addition to physical challenges, countless retirees may suffer emotionally from a lack of significant social contact. While no one expects CSRs to wear the hat of therapist, it is important to understand the importance of spending a little extra time with senior customers. Service providers should not brush off seniors or cut off conversations with them. Keep in mind that a senior's trip to the bank or to the store may provide his or her only social contact for the day. It takes so little to be kind to others and it can mean so much.

WHAT DO YOU THINK
2.4

Out of the five generations just discussed, which generation do you represent? Given your characteristics, record how you might adapt the delivery of your services to other generations.

CUSTOMER SERVICE TIP

In delivering great customer service, create a customer experience in a way that is unique to that person and isn't the same as the next customer's.

THE DISABLED CUSTOMER

Dissimilar cultures react to disabilities in different ways. Regardless, it is important to ensure that the dignity of persons with disabilities is respected when services are provided. A **disability** is a condition caused by an accident, trauma, genetics, or disease, which may limit a person's mobility, hearing, vision, speech, or mental function. Specifically, as noted by the Americans with Disabilities Act, an individual with a disability is a person who:

- has a physical or mental impairment that substantially limits one or more major life activities;

- has a record of such an impairment; or

- is regarded as having such an impairment.[18]

Discrimination against customers with disabilities is often unintentional. It may stem from a general lack of awareness that many of us have about disabilities. Consequently, it is important for companies to plan ahead to meet the requirements of their customers with disabilities. Wherever necessary

---

[18] Wisconsin Department of Health Services, http://www.dhs.wisconsin.gov/disabilities/physical/definition.htm accessed October 13, 2010.

What suggestions can you give a co-worker to enhance a service encounter with disabled customers?

and reasonable, service providers should adjust the way they offer their services, so that people who are physically challenged can use them in the best way. It is perfectly acceptable to consult with them about how they might best be served. Often, minor measures that are embedded in common sense work wonderfully. One example is to practice patience and to allow more time to deal with disabled customers.

Understanding Disabilities

The Americans with Disabilities Act and the efforts of many disability organizations have made strides in improving accessibility in buildings, increasing access to education, opening employment opportunities, and developing realistic portrayals of persons with disabilities in television programming and motion pictures. However, progress is still needed in communication and interaction with people who have disabilities. Non-disabled individuals are sometimes concerned that they will say the wrong thing, so they say nothing at all—thus further segregating people with disabilities.

Etiquette considered appropriate when interacting with disabled people is based primarily on respect and courtesy without being condescending. Outlined below are several lists of tips to help service providers when communicating with persons who have disabilities.

Communicating with Physically Disabled Persons

- When introduced to a person with a disability, it is appropriate to offer to shake hands. People with limited hand use or who wear an artificial limb can usually shake hands. (Shaking hands with the left hand is an acceptable greeting.)

- If you offer assistance, wait until the offer is accepted. Then listen to or ask for instructions.

- Do not be afraid to ask questions when you are unsure of what to do.

Visually Impaired Persons

- Speak to the individual when you approach him or her.

- State clearly who you are; speak in a normal tone of voice.

- When conversing in a group, remember to identify yourself and the person to whom you are speaking.

- Never touch or distract a service dog without first asking the owner.

- Tell the individual when you are leaving.

- Do not attempt to lead the individual without first asking; allow the person to hold your arm and control her or his own movements.

- Be descriptive when giving directions; verbally give the person information that is visually obvious to individuals who can see. For example, if you are approaching steps, mention how many steps.

- If you are offering a seat, gently place the individual's hand on the back or arm of the chair so that the person can locate the seat.

Hearing Impaired Persons

- Gain the person's attention before starting a conversation (i.e., tap the person gently on the shoulder or arm).

- If the individual is lip reading, look directly at the individual, speak clearly (in a normal tone of voice), keeping your hands away from your face.

Use short, simple sentences. Avoid smoking or chewing gum.

- If the individual uses a sign language interpreter, speak directly to the person, not the interpreter.

- If you are telephoning, let the phone ring longer than usual. Speak clearly and be prepared to repeat the reason for the call and who you are.

Mobility Impaired Persons

- If possible, put yourself at the wheelchair user's eye level.

- Do not lean on a wheelchair or any other assistive device the customer may be using.

- Do not assume the individual wants to be pushed—ask first.

- Offer assistance if the individual appears to be having difficulty opening a door.

- If you are telephoning, allow the phone to ring longer than usual to allow extra time for the person to reach the telephone.

Speech Impaired Persons

- If you do not understand something the individual says, do not pretend that you do. Ask the individual to repeat what he or she said and then repeat it back.

- Be patient. Take as much time as necessary.

- Try to ask questions which require only short answers or a nod of the head.

- Concentrate on what the individual is saying.

- Do not speak for the individual or attempt to finish her or his sentences.

- If you are having difficulty understanding the individual, consider writing as an alternative means of communicating, but first ask the individual if this is acceptable.

Learning Disabled Persons

- If you are in a public area with many distractions, consider moving to a quiet or private location.

- Be prepared to repeat what you say, verbally or in writing.

- Offer assistance completing forms or understanding written instructions and provide extra time for decision-making. Wait for the individual to accept the offer of assistance; do not "over-assist" or be patronizing.

- Be patient, flexible, and supportive. Take time to understand the individual and make sure the individual understands you.

Service Animals

Many people with disabilities use service animals. Although the most familiar type of service animal is a guide dog used by the blind, service animals are assisting people who have other disabilities as well. Many disabling conditions are invisible. Therefore not every person who is accompanied by a service animal appears to be disabled. Currently, a service animal is not required to have any special certification or identification as such.

A service animal is *not* a pet. According to the Americans with Disabilities Act, a **service animal** is any animal that has been individually trained to provide assistance or perform tasks for the benefit of a person with a physical or mental disability, which substantially limits one or more major life functions.

Remember when serving a person who is accompanied by a service dog that you should not touch the service animal, or the person it assists, without permission. In addition, do not make noises at the service animal as it may distract the animal from doing its job. Finally, avoid trying to feed the service animal, as it may disrupt his or her schedule.

WHAT DO YOU **THINK**

2.5

How comfortable are you with the tips to help service providers when communicating with persons who have disabilities? Respond in your journal.

FOCUS ON. . . BEST PRACTICES

Burger King Corporation

Burger King Corporation received the *Profiles in Diversity Journal's* 2010 Diversity Leader Award, which recognizes companies for their commitment to diversity and inclusion communication practices. BURGER KING® is dedicated to recruiting, retaining, and developing its employees from diverse backgrounds, as well as creating a workplace where everyone can thrive both personally and professionally. Its diversity and inclusion efforts are built on a four-pillar strategy, encompassing its workforce, community, restaurant guests, and operators/suppliers.

"As we globalize our processes and procedures to ensure consistency, we still need to remain compliant with local laws [and] rules around the globe," said Marlene Gordon, vice president and assistant general counsel for Burger King Corporation (BKC). The company's diversity initiatives and commitment to flexibility are not new concepts; rather, these values are at the core of the company's culture and are reflected in its inclusion mission statement: "We value, honor, and respect differences in our employees, customers, franchisees, and suppliers."

Operating more than 12,000 restaurants worldwide, approximately 90 percent of BURGER KING® restaurants are owned and operated by independent franchisees, many of them family-owned operations. In 2008, *Fortune* magazine ranked BKC among America's 1,000 largest corporations and the company was recently recognized on the top 100 "Best Global Brands" list.

SOURCES: Michelle Miguelez, "At Burger King, Women and Minorities Can Have It Their Way," http://www.diversity-executive.com/article.php?article=785 and Michelle Miguelez, "Burger King Corp. Receives 2010 Diversity Leader Award from *Profiles in Diversity Journal*," http://www.businesswire.com/portal/site/home/?permalink/?ndmViewId=news_view&newsId=20100408006725&newsLang=en accessed July 31, 2010.

WRAPPING UP

Mindful of the cultural diversity of today's market, Chapter 2 presented exceptional customer service ideas and concepts needed to serve several types of internal and external consumers through global media. At the same time, the chapter presented tips relevant for one-on-one service to customers with distinctive personalities, customers belonging to multi-generational groups, and disabled persons. As an example of best practices in customer service, Burger King is featured above. This global corporation is widely recognized as one that serves diversity well. The information in this Global Customer chapter is a good foundation for understanding how best to deliver Exceptional Customer Service, the topic for Chapter 3.

SUMMARY

- Globalization of customer service through outsourcing, nearshoring, and homeshoring are three trends whose benefits most businesses cannot afford to ignore in today's competitive global economy.

- Creating and sustaining a diverse workforce and a diverse customer base are competitive advantages to any business enterprise.

- Identifying personality types and then interacting with each individual as he or she would like to be treated is another aspect of diversity. The four types of personalities are analytical, driver, amiable, and expressive.

- Understanding generational differences allows service providers to adapt their personal styles to serve global customers with respect to the customer's individual set of core values and expectations. The five generations in today's marketplace include the Matures, Baby Boomers and Generations X, Y and Z.

- Whenever necessary and reasonable, service providers should adjust the way they provide their services to customers with disabilities so that people who are challenged can still receive the best possible service.

KEY TERMS

amiable personality
analytical personality
authority
Baby Boomer Generation
culture
disability
driver personality

expressive personalities
Generation X
Generation Y
Generation Z
homeshoring
Mature Generation
nearshoring

outsourcing
paraphrase
personality
service animal
stereotyping

CRITICAL THINKING

1. In your opinion, what service factors contribute to the global success of Craigslist?

2. If you were the owner of a business that needed to provide customer agents through either outsourcing or homeshoring, which would you choose and why?

3. Why is diversity in the workplace deemed advantageous to businesses like BURGER KING®? In what ways can diversity be challenging to an organization?

4. In your own words, give a simple description for each of the four personality types. Think of people in your life who fit these personalities and the different ways you interact with them based on their personality type.

5. If you were a guest service agent at a fine hotel in your area, how would your personal service approach be different when serving each of the five generations of customers?

6. Describe an experience you have had or have heard about where a person with disabilities was served in an exemplary fashion.

WHAT DO YOU THINK **NOW?**

Project 2.1

Assume you are doing a report on *spotlighting global companies that serve diverse customers*. Reread your responses to the *What Do You Think?* questions that you completed throughout this chapter. What are some thoughtful service techniques and practices that serve customers best regardless of a CSRs personality or generation? What situations and practices should be avoided when serving the global customer? What skills are needed to serve diverse customers around the world? Compile your responses, as directed by your instructor.

ONLINE RESEARCH ACTIVITY

Project 2.2   Homeshoring Hiring Issues

Many companies are still working through the best employment strategy to use when hiring dependable homeshoring virtual agents with good communication skills. Consider the following examples of two people who are interested in applying for this position.

- Rosie has over 25 years of customer service and administrative experience. She has a home office with high-speed Internet, a state-of-the-art phone service, and most everything else she needs to work from home. However, she has been fired from her last three jobs because of excessive absences due to caring for her elderly parents. She is fluent in Spanish.

- Matt has muscular dystrophy, which robs him of motor skills and his ability to hold down his last job as a technical data clerk. His physical challenges prevent him from working outside his home, but he has excellent communication skills. He sees working as a homeshore representative as an opportunity to be productive and earn money for his family by taking customer service, technical support, and inbound sales calls from his home.

Conduct research to learn what the best qualifications for an online service representative are. Working with two other classmates, discuss the following questions and report your findings, as directed by your instructor. As an alternative, follow your instructor's directions to join a group and use the instructor-designated discussion board to complete the group project.

1. Given these two persons who show interest in a homeshoring position, evaluate each one's strengths and weaknesses relative to a largely unsupervised position of working at home.

   _____

   _____

   _____

2. What skills and factors should be considered when evaluating a person for a homeshoring position?

   _____

   _____

   _____

3. To what extent do you think the concept of homeshoring will change the type of person who applies for these kinds of positions?

   _____

   _____

   _____

COMMUNICATION SKILLS AT WORK

Project 2.3   Communication Styles among Generations

Younger generations seem more detached in their communication styles. A great deal of the differences among communication styles can be attributed to the development of electronic technology. Brainstorm with one or two students and jot down your first ideas as you answer the following questions.

1. What impact are generational variations in communication styles having on the workplace?

   _____

   _____

2. How should employers deal with these differences effectively?

   _____

   _____

3. List your ideas that are critical to serving all generations of customers well.

   _____

   _____

DECISION MAKING AT WORK

Project 2.4   Free Personality Test for CSR Position

Many employers look for specific personality types to fit certain roles. For a CSR position, for example, they might look for someone who is an Amiable and has these general tendencies: cautious and thoughtful; hesitant until they know people well, then affectionate and caring; very literal and aware of the physical world; uncompromising about personal standards; diligent and conscientious; organized and decisive.

What is your personality type? Go to www.cengage.com/marketing/gibson and find the Web links for Chapter 2. Visit any of the websites listed there for a free assessment of your personality type. After you have determined your personality type, do the following:

1. Assume you are a CSR interacting with each of the following personality types in a customer service situation: a) analytical, b) driver, c) amiable, and d) expressive. Use the information covered in the chapter to decide how you would react, based on your own personality type, to each of the personality types in a customer situation when the customer is returning a faulty product and wants cash back, not credit toward a future purchase. Your company's policy gives you the authority to make that decision.

2. Prepare a one-page synopsis in which you summarize these four situations. Be prepared to discuss your ideas in class before submitting your report to the instructor, if directed.

Here is an example: You are the CSR and you are an Expressive. Your customer is an Analytical. As an Expressive, you really want to understand your customer as a person. You like to get enthusiastic about things. However, that's the wrong approach with an Analytical. You will need to be as systematic, thorough, deliberate, and as precise as you can in your approach. Provide analysis and facts.

CASE STUDY

Project 2.5   A Complaint from a Disabled Customer

At Juniper Computer Works, customers seldom complain because customer service is a top priority. However, recently the president of the company, Mr. Walter Marcellus, received a complaint in writing from a person who is disabled. Mr. Marcellus knows that he not only must respond, but perhaps change policies and procedures in the company regarding serving the disabled in more appropriate ways. Mr. Marcellus has asked for a focus group to be formed to give him advice on handling the complaint and what steps the company should take at this time.

> In part, the complaint read,
>
> Today I was at your store and wanted to purchase a new laptop computer. I never write companies when small incidents occur (concerning my disability and being confined to a wheelchair), but I feel that today's behavior by your sales staff warrants this letter. I chose to inform you, the president, so that others in my circumstance at your place of business will not be so offended.
>
> I felt very patronized when, after asking questions of Joanne, your service/sales representative, she responded in almost a child-like voice—not once but three times! Then she proceeded to lean on my wheelchair as she was demonstrating the laptop to me. I felt it was more appropriate for her to use a chair; so when I suggested she do so, she said, "Oh, this will only take a minute or so more" and then continued to lean over me for another five minutes!
>
> I am incensed enough to write this letter! By the way, after leaving your store I purchased my laptop from another store within the hour.

Analyze the case and determine:

a) if the customer has a legitimate complaint,
b) what Mr. Marcellus' response should be to the customer, and
c) what recommendations as far as training, policies, and procedural changes you might make to Mr. Marcellus.

Be ready to participate in a class discussion as directed by your instructor or to submit a case analysis, if requested.

Kurhan/Shutterstock

CHAPTER 3

Exceptional Customer Service

*They may only call once in their life, but
that is our chance to wow them.*

TONY HSIEH, CEO, ZAPPOS

OBJECTIVES

1. Explain the relationship between customer expectations and customer perceptions.

2. Cite examples of customer *first impressions*.

3. Describe the three customer turnoffs.

4. Discuss the importance of customer loyalty.

5. Discuss the traits and skills CSRs should possess.

Ritz-Carlton Hotels

The Ritz-Carlton does not "hire" employees, as other organizations do; the hotel "selects" new members for the Ritz-Carlton team. Every day at the chain's 73 properties in 24 countries, all 38,000 Ritz-Carlton employees participate in a 15-minute "lineup" to talk about one of the "basics." For example, Basic #14 states "Use words such as 'Good morning,' 'Certainly,' 'I'll be happy to,' and 'My pleasure.' Do not use words such as 'OK,' 'Sure,' 'Hi/Hello,' 'Folks,' and 'No problem.'" The "lineup" ritual makes the hotel one of the few large companies that sets aside time for a daily discussion of its core service values.

Moreover, if you are employed by Ritz-Carlton, the hotelier will spend several thousands of dollars to train you. First, you will go through a two-day service introduction to the company values including the "credo" and the 20 Ritz-Carlton "basics." Employees are then required to take a 21-day course that emphasizes specific job responsibilities, for example, the 28 steps used by a bellman when greeting a guest. To reinforce these teachings, the hotel requires each employee carry a plastic card imprinted with the credo and the basics, as well as the "employee promise" and the following three steps of service.

Step 1: A warm and sincere greeting. Use the guest's name.
Step 2: Anticipation and fulfillment of each guest's needs.
Step 3: Fond farewell. Give a warm good-bye and use the guest's name.

With all this training, it is not surprising that employees are empowered by top management. Simon F. Cooper, president of the Ritz-Carlton Hotel Company, explains the commitment to empowerment in this way: "Every single Ritz-Carlton staff member is entrusted, without approval from their general manager, to spend up to $2,000 on a guest. And that's not per year. It's per incident. Though the option doesn't get used much, it displays the deep trust we have in our staff's judgment."

SOURCES: Bill Lamphton, "My Pleasure"-The Ritz-Carlton Hotel PART II, *Expert Magazine*, November 4, 2010 http://www.expertmagazine.com/EMOnline/RC/part2 .htm; About Us: Gold Standards, http://corporate.ritzcarlton.com/en/about/goldstandards.htm; Rober Reiss, "How Ritz-Carlton Stays At the Top," Forbes.com, November 4, 2010 http://www.forbes.com/2009/10/30/simon-cooper-ritz-leadership-ceonetwork-hotels.html; and Duff McDonald, "Roll Out the Blue Carpet How Ritz-Carlton Can Teach You To Serve Your Customers Better," CNNMoney.com, May 1, 2004 http://money.cnn.com/magazines/business2/business2_archive/2004/ 05/01/368262/index.htm accessed November 11, 2010.

CUSTOMER PERCEPTIONS

Exceptional customer service is obviously provided at Ritz-Carlton hotels, but remember: Exceptional service ultimately is in the eye of the beholder—the customer. How does the customer determine whether a company has provided exceptional customer service? It usually depends on two factors: the customer's expectations and perceptions. **Customer expectations** are the beliefs about service a customer has *before* a transaction. Typically, a customer forms expectations from several sources: Internet social media (i.e., Facebook, YouTube, Twitter, blogs), print/TV/Internet advertising, previous experience, word of mouth, and the competition.

Customer perceptions in contrast, are the opinions created about service *during and after* a transaction. Customers' perceptions are based on how actual service measures up to their expectations. If customers get more than they expected, the end result is *exceptional* customer service. However, if customers get anything less than what they expected, they perceive a performance gap; in that gap lies customer disappointment. Disappointed customers will leave an organization and take their business elsewhere, and poor service is responsible for much of the disappointment experienced by customers.

According to a study by RightNow Technologies, 73 percent of customers leave because of poor customer service. Another recent study conducted by the Rockefeller Corporation is more specific. It reported that 68 percent of customers leave because they think the business does not care about them. In dealing with the question as to why businesses lose customers, a study conducted by the Small Business Administration (SBA) notes that "the perception that members of the sales staff don't care ranks as the leading factor." The study notes further that "nearly 70 percent of those polled in the SBA study indicated that the perception of a non-caring staffer led customers to leave and buy from other businesses." By comparison, product dissatisfaction ranked second, with only 14 percent of those polled.[1]

The Value of Exceptional Customer Service

In practice, what does exceptional customer service really mean? Mahatma Gandhi once said in reference to how to serve others, "A customer is the most important visitor on our premises and he is not dependent on us. We are dependent on him. He is not an interruption in our work. He is the purpose of it. He is not an outsider in our business. He is our business. He is part of it. We are not doing him a favor by serving him. He is doing us a favor by giving us an opportunity to do so."[2]

If you know what success is, and why it is important, then you have a much higher chance of succeeding. Delivering an exceptional customer service experience is no different. Understanding what exceptional customer service is and what it is not is important to make clear for any business. Figure 3.1 on page 44 compares the types of service experiences customers have based on three aspects—product, service standards, and people.

Exceptional customer service is a mindset that defines each company's culture. It is pervasive, visible to others, and everyone's responsibility. Although this unity of purpose begins with hiring and training the right people, it also requires organizations to keep the basic company functions in superior shape so that CSRs do not get bogged down with cleaning up problems, correcting errors, or being on the defensive with customers. Figure 3.2 on page 45 suggests actions companies can take to improve performance by applying solid approaches to customer service.

Service is not easily managed, because it involves many variables. Everything from needs, wants, and personalities to technological issues make global management a considerable challenge. Therefore, when focusing on serving customers in the best way, remember the following truths:

- Customer service happens instantaneously, either right in front of the customer or at a distance through the use of technology.

- Service must be individualized for each customer. It cannot be standardized or routinely applied universally, such as the use of scripts online or at call centers.

- Different customers have different needs; further, the needs of the same customers continuously change.

CUSTOMER SERVICE TIP

If a company doesn't take care of its customers, some other company will.

[1] Ann Barr, "The Number One Reason Why Customers Leave," *ENX Magazine*, http://www.enxmag.com/2010%20months/AD%2021001/article_abarr_The%20Number%20Ine%20Reason%20Why%20Customers%20Leave_jan2010.htm accessed November 4, 2010.

[2] Cited in Karin Fowler, "Customer Service Tips with Karin Fowler," Center for Business Industry and Labor, May 2010 Newsletter, http://www.cbil.org/May_news10.htm accessed November 4, 2010.

Figure 3.1 Types of Customer Service Experiences

ASPECT	NEGATIVE EXPERIENCE	PERFECT EXPERIENCE	EXCEPTIONAL EXPERIENCE
	Where expectations were not met Result: Customer went to competitor	Where expectations were fully met Result: Customer experienced nothing negative	Where expectations were fully met and something special was added Result: Customer received 10 percent over Perfection—and didn't expect it!
Product	• Did not have product in stock • Stocked only low-end products	• Had the right product of good quality • Received good value for the money	• Offered extra information of value to customer • Went the extra mile • Received a relevant free offer (discount, coupon) with the product
Service Standard	• Could not find anyone to help • Didn't feel they cared about what customers needed	• Were quick and efficient	• Were both personal and appropriate • Provided immediate solution to concerns
People	• Were joking around together instead of helping customers • Noted careless dress and grooming practices	• Liked the experience and the people • Were professional, courteous, and respectful	• Remembered name from a previous visit • Made a check-in phone call to follow up • Used previous likes and needs to satisfy current purchase

CSRs need be reminded of delivery level on a regular basis by asking themselves—In my role,
• what actions will trigger a negative customer experience?
• what actions will create a perfect experience?
• what is the value-added, unexpected experience that I might provide?

• Complete customer service requires others in your organization to support you; it requires customer service teamwork, with everyone committed to the same goal.

Critical First Impressions

According to an old saying, "You never get a second chance to make a first impression." Nowhere is this more applicable than in business situations, because how you initially communicate with people is key to your overall and continued success. In general,

CUSTOMER SERVICE TIP

Customers with high expectations—sometimes referred to as tough, demanding customers—make a business better. The secret is to use the situation as an opportunity to maximize customer retention and improve customer services.

Figure 3.2

Actions That Advance Extraordinary Approaches to Service

- *Decide who you are and what you can deliver.* It is important to know what you can and cannot provide in alignment with the company's mission statement and values.
- *Decide who your customers are and what they want.* It may be that what you think customers should value might not really be what they value.
- *Deliver more than you promise.* Make sure you give your customers more than they request, and ensure it is something they will value.
- *Treat your employees as you expect them to treat your customers.* Treat your employees with respect. Make them feel special. The result is that they will treat customers the same way. In business, this idea is referred to as the *mirror principle*, which says, your employees won't treat customers better than you treat them.

consumers spend their money where they are treated well.

Successful companies examine and evaluate their customer service program regularly to establish a baseline standard for serving customers. A **baseline standard** is the minimum level of service it takes to satisfy customers under ordinary circumstances. Here are some examples of practices that constitute a baseline:

- Greet all customers just after they enter your business.
- When possible, use a customer's name.
- When asked, walk the customer to the product and place the item in his or her hand.
- Always return voice and e-mail messages within 12 to 24 hours of receipt or sooner.

Moment of truth is a term coined by Jan (pronounced *Yon*) Carlzon of Scandinavian Airlines Systems (SAS) in turning around his company as a result of a tremendous loss of profits in the early 1980s. Simply put, a **moment of truth** is an episode in which a customer comes in contact with any aspect of the company, however remote, and thereby has an opportunity to form an impression. This moment of truth happens in a very short time period, from 7 to 40 seconds. That is the amount of time you, as a CSR, have to make a good impression on your customer. It is this impression that will guide the rest of the service encounter.

If the moment is favorable, the whole interaction will be pleasant. If it is not, a positive customer relationship has been tarnished. Carlzon's idea is that, if his company's 10 million passengers had an average contact with five SAS employees, the company had 50 million unique, never-to-be repeated opportunities, or "moments of truth." With these moment-of-truth events and supportive employees, over the course of two years the company recovered from an $8 million loss to a profit of $71 million.[3]

Keep in mind that a positive first impression is not going to be effective in the long run if a subsequent negative experience eclipses it. The best way to maximize the value of a positive first impression is to reinforce it with favorable experiences throughout the course of future interactions.

Though typically not acknowledged, positive first impressions are influenced by customer service representatives' personal habits. While it seems an obvious point, when a CSR's hair is groomed, hands and fingernails are clean, clothing is appropriate and fresh, then these general actions mirror professionalism on the job. Moreover, when CSRs interact with customers online and their technical skills clearly demonstrate attention to detail, accurate forms processing, and a pleasant voice during conversations—these practices also send a positive impression to customers.

Indicative of the age of quick response time that we live in, returning calls promptly, delivering products or services quickly, and using modern 24/7 technology to decrease response time are always

[3] Jan Carlzon, *Moments of Truth*, New York: Ballinger Publishing Company, 1987, 3.

CUSTOMER SERVICE TIP

Undeliverable promises can do more harm than saying "no" to a customer. Always honor the commitments you make to customers.

smart business moves. Each of these actions helps to create superior first impressions because newer generations of customers simply are not willing to wait.

Empowerment

Empowering employees with the resources and trust to solve customer concerns is a critical component to making a great first impression. This is a cornerstone of the Ritz-Carlton customer service plan. Defined as giving somebody power or authority, **empowerment** must follow a top-down model that conveys authority through the ranks to front-line service professionals. It enables employees to make administrative decisions based on corporate guidelines. When employees can do whatever they have to do on the spot to take care of a customer to that customer's satisfaction, that is empowerment. If the customer doesn't win, then the company loses.

One significant benefit of empowerment is the elimination of nearly all multi-level problem solving that involves management. Scores of managers talk about empowerment, but many have difficulty putting it into practice. Too often, they don't really understand what empowerment is. For example, many managers believe empowerment means giving employees the authority to make a decision to take care of the customer—as long as the action the employee takes follows the rules, policies, and procedures of the organization. True empowerment means that employees can bend the rules to do whatever they have to do (within legal bounds) to take care of the customer.

Empowerment is an important aspect of legendary customer service for any business. Employees at the Ritz Carlton are allowed to spend up to two thousand dollars without consulting with a supervisor to resolve a customer problem. Having a team of empowered employees who are afraid to make a decision is as bad, if not worse, than not having an empowerment program at all. When employees make a customer-related decision, the greatest concern for many of them is they will be reprimanded—or worse, fired—for making what management sees as a bad decision.

For empowerment to work, employees should know they will not be fired if they make an error and that it is okay to make mistakes in the process of working to win customer satisfaction. Once empowered, CSRs have the responsibility to exercise that authority when the need arises. Ultimately, an empowered employee has far-reaching effects in keeping a customer who would consider going elsewhere for the product or service. It is of little value to talk service unless employees are also empowered to deliver exceptional service and rewarded for doing so.

Customer Turnoffs

Attracting replacement customers is an expensive process because it costs many times more to generate new customers than it does to keep existing ones. Unfortunately, few companies even track customer-retention rates, much less inquire about what issues might be driving their customers away. Could it be fear about discovering the answers that prevent businesses from ever asking the question "What turns you off as a customer?"

Ethics / Choices

Time after time, when entering the employee break room, you overhear other CSRs talking about how bad the management is at your company—specifically, your manager. What is your reaction to this situation? Would you enter the discussion to express your personal views, would you ignore the discussion, or would you try to reason with your co-workers and advise them against spreading negative thoughts? Explain.

If asked, customers would probably cite three categories of turnoffs.

1. *Value turnoffs.* When a customer says, "I didn't get my money's worth on this product," this is a value turnoff. Value turnoffs include inadequate guarantees, a failure to meet quality expectations, and high prices relative to the value perceived of the product or service.

2. *System turnoffs.* These irritations arise from the way a company delivers its products or services. When transactions are unnecessarily complicated, inefficient, or troublesome, customers experience system turnoffs. For example, employees who lack the knowledge to answer customer questions and organizations that have just one person capable of fulfilling a key function are symptomatic of system failures. So are voicemail menus that are unnecessarily complicated and time-consuming. Slow service, lack of delivery options, cluttered workplaces, unnecessary or repetitive paperwork requirements, and inadequate reordering processes are additional examples of system turnoffs.

3. *People turnoffs.* These are the turnoff occurrences most often associated with poor customer service. Examples include showing customers lack of courtesy or attention, using inappropriate or unprofessional behavior or language, and projecting an indifferent attitude. In short, any behavior that conveys a lack of appreciation, care, or consideration for the customer is a people turnoff. Of the three

What can you do to show customer appreciation?

CUSTOMER SERVICE **TIP**

Don't pass blame. When a customer calls with a problem you personally did not create, don't rush to point out that, "I didn't do it," or "It's not my fault." Instead of dodging the issue or blaming someone else, immediately apologize for the customer's inconvenience and take speedy action to resolve it.

turnoffs just discussed, people turnoffs are the most serious concerns to business because once customers feel unappreciated or disrespected, their loyalty is lost. Customers who return to these businesses after being treated poorly generally do so only when there are no other alternatives available.

Customer-centric organizations make every effort to avoid customer turnoffs in their quest for customer loyalty.

WHAT DO YOU **THINK**

3.1

What business-based situations and actions turn you off as a consumer of products and services? Record your responses.

EARNING CUSTOMER LOYALTY

As we have noted in Chapter 1, profound changes have transformed the business world. Ask most managers what is different in today's economy and they will tell you that markets are more crowded with global competitors, and it is harder than ever to attract and retain customer attention as buyers who spend do so with increasingly limited disposable income.

Interestingly enough, a momentous inverse shift has occurred—we have, in effect, entered an age of

✓ MAKE IT A HABIT

Exceptional Service Reminders

To provide top service interactions that promote customer loyalty, make these practices spontaneous:

- Neglect other duties temporarily if you sense you need to spend extra time with a customer in need.
- Realize you have as much to do with the tone of a customer transaction as the customer does, so smile and receive each customer warmly.
- Always go the extra mile and give unexpected value with the service you provide.

customer scarcity. Customers have become the most precious of all economic resources to businesses. Earning and keeping their loyalty is essential to successful companies.

Customer loyalty can't be bought; it must be earned. **Customer loyalty** occurs when an organization retains its best customers as a result of finding, attracting, and intentionally retaining customers who regularly purchase from them. Earning trust and relationship building is at the heart of customer loyalty.

The best way to survive in the current marketplace is to build a wide base of loyal customers, by

What does a loyal customer look like and expect?

tailoring the shopping experience, whether online or in person, to support customer-oriented behaviors and policies as much as possible. According to Fred Reichheld, author of *Loyalty Effect*, a mere 5 percent increase in customer retention can result in a 75 percent increase in customer value.[4]

In companies across America, a disconnect between expectations and reality may be driving away customers. Incredibly, the disappointments that customers experience are often the result of failed expectations that the company has experienced within itself. For example, customers are routinely disillusioned because many businesses fail to meet their promised deadlines, fail to back up their products adequately, or provide inconsistent product service and support after the sale. Clearly, customer loyalty is not earned in these ways.

Customers tend to stay with organizations that enable them to feel valued and appreciated, even if an organization cannot always respond to all of their needs and problems. Most people shift from one supplier to another because of dissatisfaction with service, not price or product offerings. It is the service provider's responsibility, therefore, to manage the emotions in customer service exchanges.

In summary, there is an equation for keeping customers. It's not exactly a secret, considering the multitude of books on the topic. It is as follows: Take a good, first reaction with the customer; add in reliability, a quick response time, quality services and products, plus empathy; and the result is a satisfied customer. Take away any of these factors and customer loyalty will begin to decline.

WHAT DO YOU THINK 💡

3.2

What reasons justify your loyalty to a particular business? Make a list of your responses.

---

[4] Frederick Reichheld, *The Loyalty Effect: the hidden force behind growth, profits, and lasting value*, Boston: Bain & Company, Inc., 1996, 56.

Figure 3.3 Tips to Earn Repeat Business

Ask questions	Never make assumptions about what customers expect in terms of quality and service.
Be honest	For long-term success, honesty is not just the best policy; it's the only policy.
Fix the problem	When a mistake occurs, give your customers two things: an apology and a solution to the problem at no expense to the customer.
Learn from the competition	Pay attention to the service provided by competitors; then try to improve on that level when you are dealing with your customers.
Back up your company's promises	Nothing ruins credibility more than when customer service representatives promise what their company cannot deliver.
Offer "one-stop" service	Customers do not like being passed along from one person to another. Always try to take care of the problem personally and immediately.
Build an emotion-friendly service culture	To deal effectively with customers' emotions, employees must be aware of the full range of their own emotional states—both positive and negative.

Figure 3.3 lists some tips that are useful to earn repeat business from customers.

WHO IS RIGHT FOR CUSTOMER SERVICE?

For a customer loyalty program to be effective, a business must factor in the performance of its front-line employees. Superior service doesn't just happen; it is a process. Next to a company's product, excellence in customer service is the single most important factor in determining the future success or failure of a company. Regardless of what a company does to make a profit in terms of the product or service it provides, the company is also in the business of providing customer service.

If you look at companies that are not doing well or have gone out of business, one of their common threads is failure to deliver superior customer service. A look at today's successful companies will show that they took the necessary time to listen, understand, and then deliver what their customers said they wanted. More importantly, they are believers in the value of hiring the right people and providing customer service training for not only frontline employees, but for management and all other support workers as well. Top organizations carefully select people to fill the position of customer service representatives because CSRs *count* in these companies.

Who is right for customer service? A reasonable response is that any and all employees who are committed to a company's mission are right for customer service, but employees with a very specific skill set are right to be customer service representatives.

The Role and Traits of CSRs

The CSR's primary service focus is always to resolve the customer's problem as quickly and completely as possible. This requires exercising judgment; possessing knowledge of the product, customer history, company information, and competitive data; and using that judgment and knowledge along with common sense.

When hiring customer service professionals, companies should look for a *helping attitude*. You can teach anyone almost anything, but the feeling of customer service has to come from within a person. First-rate CSRs intuitively sense what irritates their customers. For example, seemingly minor issues such as the way a carton is labeled or a product is packaged *are not minor*, if they bother the customer.

The most important task in hiring CSRs is to select individuals who fit in with the company's customer service culture and have a demonstrated skill and interest in working with the public. Companies look for a variety of character traits, abilities, and experience levels for customer service jobs. The profile for an exceptional CSR includes the following characteristics:

- *Initiative* Takes the initiative to resolve issues before they become problems; ensures that customer needs are met

- *Objectivity* Is open-minded; is respectful to others; treats others equally and fairly; tolerates different points of view

- *Positive attitude* Is optimistic; maintains a cheerful attitude; looks for positive resolutions to problems

- *Problem solving* Provides appropriate solutions to problems; capably handles customer requests; finds positive resolutions to problems

- *Relationship building* Is friendly and courteous; easy to talk to; tactful and diplomatic; respectful and considerate

- *Resilience* Is open to criticism; feelings are not easily hurt; tolerates frustration well

- *Resistance to stress* Works effectively under stressful conditions; remains calm; copes well when under pressure

- *Responsiveness* Looks for speedy solutions to problems; goes the extra mile to please the customer; responds quickly and effectively

- *Sensitivity* Shows an understanding of and an interest in customers' needs and concerns

A customer service representative can work in a variety of settings and have any number of job titles. For instance, a CSR might work at a help desk, with customers at a counter face-to-face; on the phone in the role of telemarketing; or on the Internet in a multi-contact, technology-infused center that provides immediate assistance and technical information to internal and external clients. Regardless of the setting or job title, the CSR's role, in general, is to answer questions, solve problems, take orders, resolve complaints, and share customer concerns with management.

Service Duties and Skills

Although the responsibilities of a CSR are many and varied, most companies write the job description to include the following duties:

- Provides in-house support for salespeople whenever a customer requires information or assistance

- Provides communication between levels of management and customers

- Represents the customer's interests, rather than those of a department within the company

- Helps develop and maintain customer loyalty

- Handles customer complaints and strives to have the company set them right

- Alerts upper management to trends or conditions within the company's products or services that lead to customer dissatisfaction and recommends solutions to problems

Figure 3.4 identifies the critical skills CSRs need as well as the tools and technology they use when applying those skills.

Ethics/Choices

Assume you are answering a customer's inquiry about a product. After an amicable conversation with you, the customer realizes she cannot afford your product and thanks you. You know that a competitor offers the same product in her price range. What do you do?

WHAT DO YOU THINK

3.3

Which service skills, shown in Figure 3.4, are the most difficult for you? Describe why you chose the ones you did.

REMEMBER THIS

Figure 3.4   Service Skills and CSR Tools and Technologies

FUNDAMENTAL SERVICE SKILLS	TOOLS AND TECHNOLOGY
Know how to: • build rapport, uncover needs, listen, empathize, clarify, explain, and delight customers. • handle customer complaints, irate customers, and challenging situations. • avoid misunderstandings, manage expectations, and take responsibility. • work in teams and build internal cooperation and communication within the organization. • communicate well in writing, and speak effectively to others to convey accurate information. • show a positive customer service attitude and actively look for ways to help people.	Tools: • Autodialing systems • Wireless telephone systems • Wireless telephone headsets • Multi-line telephone systems Technology: • Contact center software • Customer relationship management software • Electronic mail software • Enterprise resource planning software • Network conferencing software

FOCUS ON. . .
BEST PRACTICES

Loyalty Program Award Recipients

Customer loyalty programs are experiencing a resurgence. Organizations that offer these programs, as part of their customer loyalty strategy, hope to increase sales and reinforce their brands by encouraging consumers to concentrate all or most of their related purchases on the company's product. The net result of these programs is to encourage customer loyalty through such marketing strategies as reminder mailings, cross-sell and up-sell offers, and discounts on future purchases.

The COLLOQUY Loyalty Awards is a prestigious competition that rewards innovative customer retention strategies. Two of the top winners in 2010 were Godiva and Hyatt.

• Godiva Chocolatier's Godiva Chocolate Rewards Club program provides a creative way to reward and retain customers. In addition, the Rewards Club allows Godiva to track and analyze customer activity. Since May 2009, its numbers have exceeded 2 million, and more than half of Godiva's sales come from Rewards Club members. Records indicate that Rewards Club purchases are 20 percent higher than those made by non-Loyalty Club customers.

• Hyatt anchored its Hyatt Gold Passport by offering generous perks, including free Internet service, and suite upgrades. In addition, Hyatt has empowered its employees to provide exceptional customer service by providing guests with complimentary dinners, laundry services, and massages. Overnight stays had risen by 41 percent in 2009 over 2008 among members.

SOURCE: "Citi, Hyatt and Godiva among winners of the first ever COLLOQUY Loyalty Awards honoring outstanding innovations in the loyalty industry," September 17, 2010 http://www.colloquy.com/breaking_view.asp?xd=7580 accessed November 1, 2010.

WRAPPING UP

Keeping in mind the insightful experiences each of us have had with exceptional customer service, Chapter 3 emphasized the important relationship between customer expectations and initial perceptions, and emphasized further how these first impressions affect the economic success of organizations and their products. In contrast, the chapter also discussed what turns customers off and how those turnoffs might affect customer loyalty. Companies like Godiva and Hyatt pride themselves in providing much sought-out customer loyalty programs to counter these turnoffs and support their best customers. Clearly, these and other companies recognize that customer attraction and retention can only occur when a company has an aggressive and comprehensive strategy in place. Prepare now to see how businesses use crucial bits of information to create their Customer Service Strategy, the subject of Chapter 4.

SUMMARY

- Customer expectations are what a customer wants before a transaction; customer perceptions are created during and after a transaction.

- The best way to maximize the value of a positive first impression is to reinforce it with favorable experiences throughout the course of future interactions.

- Three customer turnoffs relate to value, system, and people.

- The depth of relationships and loyalty to customers are critical to an organization's success.

- Regardless of the setting or job title, a customer service representative's primary duties are to answer questions, solve problems, take customers' orders, and resolve complaints.

KEY TERMS

baseline standard   customer loyalty   empowerment

customer expectations   customer perceptions   moment of truth

CRITICAL THINKING

1. Why are customer perceptions one of the most critical aspects of exemplary customer service? Do you think guests of the Ritz-Carlton have a preconceived notion of the quality of service they might expect to receive? Discuss some reasons why.

2. Think of a business you've purchased from recently that resulted in an exceptional customer service experience. What made that experience exceptional? Does that business provide a loyalty program? If you have first-hand knowledge, what is your opinion about loyalty programs?

3. Do you agree with the statement "you never get a second chance to make a first impression"? Why or why not?

4. Describe a local business that you regard yourself as loyal to and then explain why.

5. Of the three types of customer turnoffs—value turnoffs, system turnoffs, and people turnoffs—which do you feel is the most often violated by organizations? Why? Compared to other hotel chains, why might the Ritz-Carlton have fewer people turnoff situations to deal with?

WHAT DO YOU THINK NOW?

Project 3.1

Assume you are writing a report about *the skills CSRs must have to provide exceptional customer service.* Reread your responses to the *What Do You Think?* questions that you completed throughout this chapter. What are sure-fire techniques and practices that provide superior customer service? What situations and practices might provide easy traps for mediocre or inferior customer service? What skills are necessary to be truly outstanding in your profession? Compile your responses, as directed by your instructor.

ONLINE RESEARCH ACTIVITY

Project 3.2   Social Media's Effect on Loyalty

Visit a website such as Amazon or Barnes and Noble and locate three recent books that discuss the effects of social media on customer loyalty and retention. Prepare a one-page report summarizing three pieces of key information from each book. (Often the websites have a section for each book that gives an Overview or Editorial Reviews of the book that will provide the information you need.)

COMMUNICATION SKILLS AT WORK

Project 3.3 **Moment of Truth Examples**

Look at the list of customer-oriented industries below and write down specific actions a customer service professional can make to improve a moment-of-truth experience as it relates to each of the four industries. For informal research, ask another adult if they have had a moment-of-truth experience in the past week and if so, have them describe it. Be prepared to share your findings and written ideas as part of an in-class or online discussion.

1. Hotel (e.g., Holiday Inn Express)

_____

_____

2. Restaurant (e.g., Chilis)

_____

_____

3. Retail store (e.g., Walmart)

_____

_____

4. Airline (e.g., Southwest Airlines)

_____

_____

DECISION MAKING AT WORK

Project 3.4 **Customer Turnoffs Discussion**

You are sitting in the company lunchroom with two other CSRs, Doug and Christine. Doug is relating a troublesome customer problem he has just experienced and is asking how you and Christine would have handled it. You discuss it, then the discussion moves to other examples of situations that turn customers off and how each of you would handle those situations. Listed below are three major customer turnoffs, which are not specific to a particular industry.

1. Waiting on the phone while the CSR is processing a purchase order and hearing others in the background laughing and socializing

2. Red tape—such as refunds, credit checks, and adjustments on account

3. A company's failure to stand behind their products or services

Upon your instructor's direction, pair up with a classmate and role play each of the given situations that can turn customers off. In a class discussion, be prepared to state how you, representing a specific company, might address each scenario in a positive way. As an alternative, follow your instructor's directions to join a group and use the instructor-designated discussion board to complete the group project.

CASE STUDY

Project 3.5   **The Mirror Principle**

Helen Harrison, marketing director of a major manufacturing plant on the East Coast, was driving back from an early morning Chamber of Commerce meeting and was reflecting on a statement made by the breakfast speaker. The speaker described the mirror principle by saying, "Your employees won't treat your customers better than you treat your employees." Given the increasingly fragile employee morale, decrease in sales, and increase in customer service complaints at the plant over the past six months, Helen is wondering if this is what is happening at her company.

1. If you were Helen, in what ways would you translate your feelings into an action plan for improvement?

_____

_____

2. What steps would be included in your action plan to turn around these problematic customer service issues?

_____

_____

CHAPTER 4

Customer Service Strategy

However beautiful the strategy, you should occasionally look at the results.

WINSTON CHURCHILL, ENGLISH STATESMAN

OBJECTIVES

1. Describe customer service strategy and its relationship to a SWOT (strengths, weaknesses, opportunities, and threats) analysis and a strategic plan.

2. Connect the importance of data warehousing to the efficiency of a customer relationship management strategy.

3. Identify the major components of a customer service infrastructure.

4. Discuss the changing role of CSRs as it incorporates additional marketing and sales activities.

Amazon

Amazon.com, a Fortune 500 company based in Seattle, Washington, is one of the top global leaders in e-commerce. Jeff Bezos started Amazon.com in 1995, and per their website, today "offers everything from books and electronics to tennis rackets and diamond jewelry." Operating sites in the United Kingdom, Germany, France, Japan, Canada, and China, Amazon maintains over 25 fulfillment centers around the world.

The online giant is obsessed with providing quality service to consumers and targets two strategic goals: the satisfaction of a customer and efficient corporate growth. Its marketing strategies are near-legendary, because Bezos has noted: "Start with customers and work backwards … Listen to customers, but don't just listen to customers—also invent on their behalf … Obsess over customers."

These goals were backed by an unexpected business philosophy—Bezos expected to operate at a loss for 4 to 5 years. In "Marketing Strategies of Amazon.com" Melvin Ram notes that, "despite its massive growth, Amazon.com remains relentlessly focused on the consumer. Out of 452 company goals in 2009, 360 directly affected the customer experience."

According to *Small Business Notes*, "Amazon.com offers a personalized shopping experience for each customer, book discovery through Search Inside The Book, convenient checkout using 1-Click Shopping, and several community features like Listmania and Wish List that help customers discover new products and make informed buying decisions."

SOURCES: Melvin Ram, "Marketing Strategies of Amazon.com," June 22, 2009 http://www.webdesigncompany.net/amazon-com-marketing-strategies accessed December 10, 2010. *Small Business Notes.* http://www.smallbusinessnotes.com/history/corporatestories/amazon.html accessed December 10, 2010.

CUSTOMER SERVICE INTELLIGENCE

Whether you are an international corporation like Amazon.com or a sole proprietorship, a strong customer service strategy is important and is often what separates the successful organizations from the rest. In a business-model sense, many organizations consider customers strategic assets. As such, most companies regard assets (customers) as items that must be protected and their value maintained and even maximized over time.

When companies identify their essential customer service standards early in the process of gathering customer intelligence, these standards provide a basis for measuring results. Figure 4.1 on page 58 provides examples of general customer service standards, as well as those for external and internal customers.

With these standards identified, organizations next need to identify who their customers are, and what their customers want so they can develop a customer service strategy that fulfills those customer expectations. While the elements of good customer service are generally in place at most organizations, a strategy is needed to pull them together. In order to formulate that plan, it is necessary to conduct an in-depth preliminary analysis of the company's strengths and weaknesses.

Figure 4.1 Customer Service Standards

TYPE	STANDARDS
General	• Make it a goal to exceed the expectations of all customer groups.
	• Proactively anticipate customer needs.
	• Be accountable to service commitment.
	• Be aware of communication style (i.e., audible voice, eye contact); always communicate professionally.
External Customers	• Greet customers courteously and professionally.
	• Listen actively to customers' requests and take prompt action in response.
	• Respond to website questions/requests within 24 hours during normal business hours.
	• Conclude encounters with customers courteously and professionally.
Internal Customers	• Interact with colleagues courteously and professionally.
	• Work to resolve issues with colleagues through direct discussion that results in agreed-upon solutions.
	• Be considerate, cooperative, and helpful to every staff member.
	• Be unilaterally accountable for addressing inappropriate behavior and comments.

SOURCE: http://thethrivingsmallbusiness.com/articles/customer-service-standards/ accessed November 10, 2010.

SWOT Analysis

A **SWOT analysis** is a formal review of a business organization's strengths, weaknesses, opportunities, and threats that ultimately contributes to a comprehensive strategic plan. It provides information that is helpful in matching the firm's resources and capabilities to the competitive environment in which it operates. As such, a SWOT analysis is vital to have when formulating a strategic plan because an organization's strategy will be more successfully implemented if a business organization can correlate internal strengths and weaknesses with external opportunities and threats.

The SWOT analysis begins with specifying the objective of the business venture or project, such as *providing unparalleled customer service.* With that objective in mind, identify internal and external factors that are favorable and unfavorable to achieving that objective.

• *Strengths:* These are characteristics of the business that give it an advantage over others in the industry. A firm's strengths are its resources and capabilities that can be used as a basis for developing a competitive advantage. Examples of customer service strengths include: strong brand names, superior service reputation among customers, the addition of Customer Relationship Management (CRM) that improves service and product promotion, and low product returns (below 5 percent).

• *Weaknesses:* Characteristics or deficiencies that place the organization at a disadvantage relative to others are termed weaknesses. The absence of certain strengths, for example, may be viewed as a weakness. Each of the following may be considered a weakness as well: a weak brand name, poor service reputation among customers, and a recent defective product that caused increased customer complaints.

• *Opportunities:* The external environmental analysis may reveal certain new opportunities for increased sales and growth or occasions to make improvements in products or processes. Some examples of such opportunities include: customers unsatisfied with a major competitor's products, arrival of new technologies, and a competitor no longer in business.

- *Threats:* Changes in the external environment may present challenges to the business that hurt its ability to profitably serve customers. Some examples of threats include: shifts in consumer tastes away from the company's products, the emergence of substitute products, and changes in state or Federal tax laws.

Figure 4.2 illustrates the four components of a SWOT analysis.

Forward-thinking companies conduct a SWOT analysis in an effort to answer the following questions *before* they write the strategic plan document.

- Where is the business trying to get to in the long-term (i.e., 5–10 years)?

- In which markets should a business intentionally choose to compete?

- How can the business successfully outperform the competition in those markets?

- What types of resources (financial, skills, technical competence, facilities, and personnel) and organizational infrastructure are required to compete profitably?

- What external environmental factors (positive and negative) affect the businesses' ability to compete?

Figure 4.2

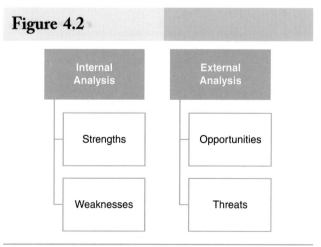

SWOT Analysis Framework

Levels of Management

Businesses typically have three levels of management—top, middle, and lower or supervisory. The skills required at each management level are similar, but they are applied differently because the activities performed by each are different.

Top Management   Typical job titles for this level are president, vice president, and superintendent of schools. These managers focus on long-range strategic decision-making that sets the tone and vision for the future in terms of new products, new markets, new facilities, etc.

Middle Management   Department heads, branch managers, and deans fit in this category of managers. They implement the strategies that have been determined by top management with intermediate-range tactical decisions.

Lower Management   Individuals in these positions include supervisors, department chairs, call center managers. They make daily decisions that ensure specific jobs are performed that meet the organization's objectives. In the past, traditional managers typically developed these plans with limited input from subordinates. However, in organizations that use the strategic planning process, this trend has changed.

Formulating Strategic Plans

Typically, a **strategic plan** for any organization has an easy-to-follow structure that includes the following elements relative to customer service:

- Objectives: Broad statements describing the targeted direction of customer service

- Goals: Service objectives that are quantified and stated in terms of a specific time period

- Strategies: Statements of how the service objectives will be achieved and the methods employed to achieve those objectives

- Tactics: Specific steps to be taken to implement the strategies and identify who is responsible for their completion

- Performance Indicators: Measures of customer service performance that show progress in meeting the goals and also monitors service and the degree to which quality customer service is delivered

Having a well-thought-out customer service strategy is the foundation for a strong service culture. Without one, management and employees often flounder, lacking a roadmap to guide them.

With these comprehensive elements in mind, a business organization must consider the following as a means of formulating and implementing the strategic plan:

1. *Identify service goals:* Create specific goals and standards for achieving customer satisfaction so employees understand and promote the target organizational objectives.

2. *Share the vision and goals:* Employees need to understand what the vision and goals for customer service are and what their responsibility is to achieve them. For example, an organization that shares a customer service vision with employees and customers is very different from an organization that does not share them, but leaves front-line employees untrained and unprepared for dealing with both routine and sensitive customer issues.

3. *Hire right:* When hiring employees, carefully screen candidates to ensure they possess the disposition and skill set needed to support a strong customer service environment. Most employers realize that essential service skills can be taught, but attitude cannot.

4. *Train service providers:* Make time to train all employees in the best practices for serving customers. It is helpful to role play various service exchanges, such as: how to respond to customer complaints, how to be responsive to customers on the phone and in person, and how best to meet customer needs by applying the organization's customer service standards.

5. *Solicit customer feedback:* Customer needs must be assessed because organizations can't meet the needs of their customers without a good understanding of what those needs are. Soliciting customer feedback through customer focus groups, surveys, or comment cards helps to develop a comprehensive plan to meet and exceed customer needs. Feedback survey instruments will be more fully discussed in Chapter 7.

The strategic plan provides the basis to determine how another business strategy—Customer Relationship Management—should be put into operation.

WHAT DO YOU THINK
4.1

Have you or someone you know ever worked for a company that either conducted a comprehensive SWOT analysis or created a strategic plan? What was that experience like? Do you feel these strategic activities improve the delivery of service to customers? Record your ideas in your journal.

How would you summarize the importance of a strategic plan and how it supports customer service?

CUSTOMER RELATIONSHIP MANAGEMENT

To implement customer service strategy, a business organization must have data about itself and about its customers as well. Customer satisfaction and customer loyalty are quickly gaining ground as reasons to get a customer relationship management system up and running. In an economy that sees demand leveling off, making the most of the customers a company already has is essential. In fact, to most businesses, maintaining or improving customer satisfaction and loyalty can be more important than reducing budgets.

Working hand-in-hand with a strategic plan, **customer relationship management (CRM)** is a business strategy that integrates the functions of sales, marketing, and customer service, using technology and massive databases of information. It is all about understanding customer needs and leveraging that knowledge to increase global sales and improve service in a more personal way.

The customer focus that CRM brings to a company is the direct result of the electronic world and the Internet. Few other approaches can offer companies the unparalleled opportunity to personalize services, provide consumers multiple choices for customer support, and track customer satisfaction.

The use of CRM in corporations is on the rise. According to Forrester Research in a study published in July 2010, "Fifty-six percent of the 455 large organizations we recently surveyed in North America and Europe have already implemented a Customer Relationship Management (CRM) solution—and many of these companies plan to invest more to upgrade their tool set. An additional 20 percent have plans to adopt a CRM solution within the next 12 to 24 months."[1]

Briefly, how does the CRM system work? Rather than only collecting, analyzing, and reporting on customer information, CRM allows electronic measures to be taken automatically on the basis of analyzing customer information. For example, if the CRM system detects a customer problem, it can be programmed to immediately send the customer an e-mail message, alert a CSR to call the customer and personally follow up on the problem, and access the billing system to set up a credit on the customer's next invoice.

Purpose of CRM

Companies justify their CRM investment cost by recognizing that strong, lasting relationships with customers encourage recurring revenue, which offsets the cost. CRM software is relatively simple to use, and there are many benefits; however, implementing it requires massive cultural changes in most organizations. CRM is more than technology; it involves a change in philosophy and attitude.

To be effective, CRM needs to be viewed by organizations as an all-encompassing business strategy—a customer-centric philosophy of doing business that affects every consumer touch point. When companies want to implement a successful CRM strategy, they need to consider thoroughly what each element of implementation means—knowledge management, database consolidation, and channel and systems integration.

- *Knowledge management:* At the heart of CRM implementation is the careful acquisition and secure storage of information about each customer, as well as the analysis, sharing, and tracking of this knowledge.

[1] William Band and James Kobielus, "Customer Service Platforms Enable Integrated Multichannel Experiences," The Forrester Wave™: CRM Suites Customer Service Solutions, Q3 2010," *Forrester*, July 2010, 2 http://www.microsoft.com/presspass/itanalyst/docs/07-19-10CRM.PDF accessed December 10, 2010.

- *Database consolidation:* This involves consolidating customer information from any form or type of contact into a single database. The goal is to have all interactions with a customer recorded in one place and readily accessible to employees on a need-to-know basis when serving customers in marketing, sales, and support activities.

- *Channel and systems integration:* Merging information so it is readily accessible, secure, and easily updated just makes good business sense. The organized and complete snapshot of customer information allows CSRs to respond to customers in a consistent and expert manner through the customer's channel of choice. That channel may be via e-mail, a phone conversation, or an online video or text chat.

Benefits of CRM

Customer relationship management allows a company to collect information about customers, such as account history and prior questions or complaints they have had. Once that information has been collected, it can be analyzed using CRM software, and the company can more accurately gain insights into how to serve each customer better. In addition to a greater awareness of each customer's interests and problems, the biggest benefits CRM companies experience are less customer attrition, better service results, and increased customer loyalty.

Moreover, with the ability to collect important data from customers that identifies their buying habits, including preferences and frequency, CRM systems give businesses a closer look at their customers' wants and needs. Businesses can then provide better customer service solutions. Through a CRM system, CSRs have detailed, factual, and current information about their customers readily available

Golden Pixels LLC/Shutterstock.com

What aspects of CRM seem most useful for providing effective customer service?

on their computer screen as a result of data warehousing and data mining.

Data Warehousing and Data Mining

Data warehousing works in conjunction with and enhances the value of customer relationship management systems. This coordinated, enterprise-wide approach to data integration enables cross-functional analysis, and secure storage and management of critical business processes.

Specifically, a **data warehouse** provides a common location for all crucial business data regardless of the data's source. This makes it easier to report and analyze information than it would be if multiple data sources, such as sales invoices, order receipts, and general ledger charges, were used separately to retrieve information.

Setting up a large company-wide system like this is necessary prior to the application of data mining. By its very nature, **data mining** is the process of extracting *patterns* from data located in the data warehouse.[2] Mining is an essential tool that transforms data into business intelligence giving companies that use it an informational advantage. Its ability to identify patterns among customers

CUSTOMER SERVICE **TIP**

Successful companies don't use technology to replace human relationships, but only to enhance them.

---

[2] Duane Sharp, "From Data Warehousing to Data Mining," *Suite 101®.com*, February 5, 2009, http://www.suite101.com/content/from-data-warehousing-to-data-mining-a93631 accessed December 10, 2010.

targets, for example, the customers most likely to respond to an upcoming mail campaign or to purchase a new product about to be launched.

Data mining works because it utilizes several data analysis and modeling methods to detect specific patterns and relationships in data. This helps companies understand what customers want based on previous purchases and also forecasts what they may buy. Other benefits of data mining include:

- Better business decisions based on a solid fact-driven understanding of specific customer behaviors

- Profitable customers that can be identified quickly and, therefore, better served with specific loyalty programs

- Marketing messages for new and improved products that can be targeted to customers more effectively and thereby, significantly reduce direct marketing expenses

Preferred Customers

Around the turn of the twentieth century, an Italian economist named Vilfredo Pareto created a mathematical formula that described the unequal distribution of wealth in his country. Pareto's formula stated that eighty percent of the nation's land was in the hands of twenty percent of the population. Later, in the 1930s and 40s, a business writer named Joseph Juran applied Pareto's formula to business in what he called the 80/20 Rule, noting that twenty percent of something is often responsible for eighty percent of the results, thereby making the distinction between "the vital few and the trivial many."[3]

While some question the correlation that claims eighty percent of sales comes from twenty percent of clients, CSRs know from careful study of data that a core group of customers are often responsible for a large percentage of sales. It is prudent customer service strategy to encourage and reward that group through preferred customer benefits. Members of

preferred customer groups often receive special newsletters, have exclusive first picks at new items and sale items, and accumulate reward points that translate into discounts, travel tickets, and other free gifts. Author and consultant Ron Ackerman notes that, "Success begins when management actually cares enough about this customer group to get actively engaged."[4] Leadership encourages preferred customer strategy to insure "internal and external communication that motivates customer centric behavior from all corners of the organization." A "gold card member" in a diners club might move to the front of a line and receive the first table available on a Friday or Saturday night because the management knows who he or she is. Such treatment encourages continued if not increased sales.

WHAT DO YOU **THINK**

4.2

How do you feel about special treatment for preferred customers? Can a company go too far in rewarding them? Record your response in your journal.

SERVICE INFRASTRUCTURE

In addition to housing customer data in one place, there are other service infrastructure components that customers also expect to be in place. Customers look for companies with solid reputations that are supported by a well-designed customer service strategy and infrastructure. Clear service standards, like those noted in Figure 4.1 on page 58, and a strategic plan to achieve them require decision makers to take the next step to evaluate and develop a framework, or **service infrastructure**.

To establish a service infrastructure, begin with the fundamental challenges to which every

[3] http://management.about.com/cs/generalmanagement/a/Pareto081202.htm, accessed January 30, 2011.

[4] http://ezinearticles.com/?Preferred-Customer-Strategy—Crisis-in-Execution&id= 5438693, accessed January 30, 2011.

Ethics / Choices

What should corporations and their employees do to be more socially responsible (acting to benefit society) to the community from which they operate and profit? Should social responsibility be a part of a company's long-range customer service strategy? Do customers expect it to be?

What risks are there to organizations when they underestimate the power of *one unhappy customer?*

service-oriented business must respond. These include concerns about: hiring the best people, providing a quality management team for support, ensuring transparent communications throughout the organization, and consistently monitoring service policies and procedures. Part of this effort is for companies to spend the time and effort needed to assess and provide the best facilities, tools, CSRs, and needed ongoing training that meets strategic customer service goals.

Facilities and Service Tools

Organizations honor their customer service strategy when they ensure that the service location and facilities are adequate and that the needed equipment, such as communication devices and software, are up to date in the customer contact center.

The contact center must be modern because it is an essential point of any organization from which all customer contacts and interactions are managed. It is also an integral part of the company's customer relationship management system. Contact center representatives don't just communicate on telephones. In addition to calling, today's customers also initiate communication with companies by emailing, visiting websites, instant messaging, and even blogging.

Just as the role of the contact center has expanded into a source of intelligence for the whole organization, the scope of expectations on the part of the customer has expanded as well. With all these expectations, a service advantage of CRM software is that it tracks service issues from the moment customers report them until they are resolved. This tracking requires no human intervention; it produces immediate and current information.

Customer Service Life Cycle

One strategic use of Internet technology involves use of the **Customer Service Life Cycle (CSLC)**, a concept that encourages companies to think in terms of differentiated involvement with the customer during distinct stages of use of a product. A recent article by Gabrielle Piccola and Bonnie R. Spalding outlines those stages as: *the requirements phase*, in which a customer realizes the need for a service or product and begins to research specific qualities about it; *the acquisition phase*, in which the customer orders, purchases, and receives the product or service; *the ownership phase*, in which the customer deals with any issues that arise from usage; and *the retirement phase*, in which the customer retires the product in some way, evaluates usage, and perhaps thinks about further purchases. CSLC reminds companies that customers have distinct needs at each one of these stages, and creative Internet strategy that responds to those needs provides quality customer service and increases retention.

Some of the examples that the authors note include a creative response to the requirements phase made by the arrangement between Denny's Restaurants, Fairfield Inns, and Mapquest. When customers type in a destination, they can click the box that indicates the Denny's or Fairfield Inn en route to their destination. Discovering the availability of these establishments is a useful supplement to the customer's travel research. Likewise, Four Seasons Hotels offers an interactive website that allows prospective or potential customers to investigate the facilities of one of their establishments. Viewers can zoom in and have a closer look at rooms, restaurants, and banquet, meeting, and recreation facilities.[5] While critics argue that the stages sometimes overlap, CSLC is another reminder that that creative Internet service is becoming more and more essential to cutting edge customer service.

CSRs and Training

Implementing customer service strategy means putting the right people in place, who are trained in the latest communication devices and digital technologies. For example, with the popularity of wireless communication devices, businesses reach their customers through Smartphones and other telecommunication gadgets.

When communicating with customers, CSRs use e-mail, text-based Internet chatting (the ability to hold a real-time conversation over the Web by typing back and forth), **voice-over Internet protocol** (**VoIP**, the ability to have a real-time verbal conversation over the Internet), and push technology (the ability to send a customer a specific image over the Internet directly to the customer's computer screen).

Savvy customers who need help from a CSR expect more, because they have already covered the simpler, more basic answers and solutions on their own through the electronic avenues provided to them on the company's website. This makes it very important to keep CSRs well trained in the latest service technologies and to pay careful attention when hiring and training service professionals.

Online CSRs, sometimes referred to as **e-reps**, require top skills, and these skills need continual updating through training programs. Of particular note is training in oral and written communication skills to conduct real-time, verbal- and text-based conversations with customers. Accurate and fast keyboarding skills are necessary so they can respond quickly to customers without making careless typographical, spelling, or grammatical errors. In addition, skills in multitasking (a component of work efficiency) are critical because reps frequently respond to several customers at once in the online, real-time chat mode.

✔️ MAKE IT A HABIT

Pride and Personal Responsibility

At the end of the workday, feel good in knowing that you have made a sincere effort to:

- Perfect an aspect of your oral or written communication skills.
- Learn an additional work technique to streamline your productivity.
- Support customer service objectives and strategic plans in the best way you can.
- Put your best foot forward as you demonstrate high standards of professional service and communication with each customer interaction.

WHAT DO YOU THINK

4.3

Describe the CSR you'd like to become and the service infrastructure you'd need to support your efforts. Record your thoughts.

MARKETING AND SALES

In the service of implementing the goals of a customer service strategic plan, the role of a customer service representative has taken a more hands-on involvement with company marketing and sales activities. To increase the selling of products and services requires a concerted effort by everyone involved in the sales team. Two examples of this are up selling and cross selling, both of which contribute to the direct profitability of the company.

---

[5] http://www.entrepreneur.com/tradejournals/article/79382268_3.html, pp. 1, 3, accessed February 1, 2011.

Up Selling and Cross Selling

Today, more CSRs are adding up selling and cross selling to their existing duties, since many organizations realize now more than ever before that the contact center is the primary touch point for consumers. As such, one of the primary goals of customer service is not only to satisfy and retain customers, but also to close a sale, thereby increasing revenue and customers at the same time.

Although up selling and cross selling have been in practice for years, when done right, these are two of the least expensive and most effective techniques businesses can use to increase sales. **Up selling** refers to an improved sale. When you persuade the customer to buy a more expensive product compared to the one he or she asked for, that is up selling. For example, think of the last time you were in a retail store that sold television sets. It becomes easier for the floor sales person to upgrade your purchase decision because you were able to quickly compare the resolution and visual quality of many TVs at one time and perhaps be swayed to buy a more expensive one. The purpose of up selling is to position higher priced products in a good/better/best progression.

Cross selling, on the other hand, is when the sales person promotes products related to the one ordered; thus selling an extra product in the process. In other words, when you cross sell, you offer the customer a product or service related to whatever he or she is already buying. Cross selling can be as simple as the waiter asking if you want an appetizer or salad to go with your main entrée. Or when you buy a book at Amazon.com, the site automatically lists and shows photos of other books purchased by people who bought the book you just ordered.

Both techniques seek to build on an existing customer base, rather than bring in new customers. Both methods also encourage customers to spend a little more, and that results in boosting overall sales. Two advantages of using up selling and cross selling techniques are: (a) they are relatively inexpensive because no advertising or other promotion gimmicks are used or needed and (b) there is no need to hire new people for promotion because regular service staff (CSRs) can promote new products along with the ones they are already servicing.

It is important to note that many cross-selling opportunities arise naturally. For example, if you are selling a baseball glove, you can also offer a bat, balls, and other sports clothing and accessories. Busy customers appreciate being told about additional products or services that might better meet their needs or about new items that were not offered in the past. The key to successful cross selling and up selling is to focus efforts on meeting the customer's needs, rather than simply pushing more products on consumers.

WHAT DO YOU THINK

4.4

Describe the last time you either upgraded a product or bought an additional product you didn't expect to buy as a result of up selling or cross selling. Record your experience in your journal.

WRAPPING UP

Regardless of the industry in which a company is classified, all of its employees are in the business of customer service. If a company cannot give customers the appropriate information, response, or resolution within a reasonable time frame, service and pricing won't matter. Chapter 4 has presented a conceptual way to achieve a high-level of service throughout an organization by developing a well thought out *Customer Service Strategy*. Conducting a SWOT analysis, developing a strategic plan, employing CRM complete with data warehousing capabilities, and carefully designing a customer service infrastructure in organizations are steps that serve customers well, make a profit, and promote a solid reputation.

Infrastructures are run by people, and so it is time now to examine the personal skills that a CSR must demonstrate to ensure that those structures function effectively. *Essential Customer Service Skills*, the topic of Part 2 chapters begins with a focus on *Critical Workplace Skills*.

Comcast

Service technicians must exercise great care when responding to in-home service calls and corporate America must take note. Comcast, for example, got some unwanted large-scale publicity when a YouTube video was broadcast to the world and captured a service technician asleep on a customer's couch. As a result, company executives revisited the biggest U.S. cable company's business plan and quickly created some new strategies in an effort to improve Comcast's image.

According to an article in *Multichannel News*, one strategy was "deploying new software—'Grand Slam'—that gave customer-service agents and field technicians the ability to recognize and diagnose problems in every device in the customer's home. The software also lets technicians and customer-care agents determine whether the problem is isolated to one customer or is more widespread." Another initiative called MOSS—Make Our Supervisors Successful—gives supervisors of CSRs and technicians special training and a new focus as employee coaches. As the article describes, "MOSS is designed so that 60% to 70% of a supervisor's time is dedicated to coaching and empowering front-line employees to be more successful."

Companies must be ever vigilant to customer concerns that can pop up instantly. They must be quick to apply whatever strategies are needed to minimize customer dissatisfaction. With a *living* customer service strategic plan that reflects an understanding of customers and the current business environment, the job is easier to do.

SOURCE: K. C. Neel, "Comcast Empowers Customer-Care Crews: Listening to Front-Line Employees Leads to Bottom-Line Satisfaction Gains," *Multichannel News*, July 12, 2010, http://www.multichannel.com/article/454631-Comcast_Empowers_Customer_Care_Crews.php accessed December 10, 2010.

SUMMARY

- Having a well-thought-out customer service strategy is critical to creating a strong service culture.

- A SWOT analysis helps a business organization prepare for formulating a customer service strategy by providing information about a company's strengths, weaknesses, opportunities, and threats.

- Customer relationship management (CRM) is a business strategy that enables the implementation of customer service strategy by analyzing the functions of sales, marketing, and customer service, using technology and massive databases of information.

- Data warehousing works in conjunction with and enhances the value of customer relationship management systems because it provides a common data location for all crucial business data regardless of the data's source.

- To establish a service infrastructure, begin with the fundamental challenges to which every service-oriented business must respond: staffing, quality management, transparent communications, and the latest service policies and procedures.

- The role of a customer service representative has expanded by adding cross selling and up selling activities.

KEY TERMS

cross selling

customer relationship
   management (CRM)

customer service life cycle
   (CSLC)

data mining

data warehousing

e-reps

service infrastructure

strategic plan

SWOT analysis

up selling

voice-over Internet protocol
   (VoIP)

CRITICAL THINKING

1. What do you think about CEO Jeff Bezos' controversial approach to starting Amazon.com? Why was the approach successful?

2. What are the service advantages to customers when a business sets its goals and strategies based on the findings from a comprehensive SWOT analysis? In your opinion, can students use the SWOT analysis successfully as applied to school and work decisions (i.e., selecting a particular job or a particular course of study)? Explain.

3. Defend an organization's right to collect customer data. Are there limitations companies should impose on the protection and use of this information? Discuss.

4. Forecast what you think the customer service infrastructure will look like in five years. Evaluate your prediction with regard to how it will change the way customers are served and how CSRs will perform their ever-growing list of duties.

 ## WHAT DO YOU THINK NOW?

Project 4.1

Assume you are doing a report entitled, *"The Best Uses of Customer Service Data: A Business Strategy."* Reread your responses to the *What Do You Think?* questions that you completed throughout this chapter. What are some decisive uses of a SWOT analysis and CRM in serving customers? What specific situations and practices should be monitored more carefully when using CRM strategy? What kind of infrastructure would best serve customers? Compile your responses, as directed by your instructor.

ONLINE RESEARCH ACTIVITY

Project 4.2   Abuses of Data Warehousing

Research a number of websites and locate several articles on the abuses of data warehousing and data mining. As a result of your research, present your findings in a class discussion, as directed by your instructor.

COMMUNICATION SKILLS AT WORK

Project 4.3   Strategies and Customer Service Life Cycle

Work in a group with five classmates. Assume that you are part of a management team for a new company that manufactures and installs home security systems. Brainstorm and develop a customer service strategy for this new company that integrates a projected customer service life cycle for its product. Develop a chart presentation that contains these two items about your company and present it to the class either in discussion or panel format, as directed by your instructor. As an alternative, follow you instructor's directions to join a group and use the instructor-designated discussion board to complete the group project.

DECISION MAKING AT WORK

Project 4.4   Up Selling and Cross Selling Dilemma

"But I don't want to sell anything—that's not why I became a CSR!" exclaimed Hillary. Hillary was reacting to a recent service department meeting, where her manager told CSRs that they were to begin up selling and cross selling products as a part of taking phone orders starting next week. As an incentive, the top two CSRs in product sales will get a $150 gift certificate to a first-class restaurant in town and be recognized in the monthly newsletter. Unfortunately, it appears that Hillary is not the only CSR who is upset. Management is appropriately concerned that morale may go down as service attitudes become increasingly negative.

For this activity, form a decision-making group and brainstorm a multi-step strategy to promote this new sales approach with CSRs. You will need to be as systematic, thorough, deliberate, and precise as you can in your approach. Evaluate also the manner in which Hillary's organization announced this added responsibility. Provide analysis and facts in a class discussion or written report, as directed by your instructor. As an alternative, follow you instructor's directions to join a group and use the instructor-designated discussion board to complete the group project.

CASE STUDY

Project 4.5   Establish a Knowledge Base

The customer service department is often separated from the rest of the company, training and operating in a "silo" rather than as a company-wide service system. (The term "silo" is an idea that each department in an organization is independent from the others and operates accordingly.) Management has determined that this situation is not in sync with identified customer service goals and strategies. You have been asked to serve on a task force, charged with developing a plan to "turn the situation around."

Brainstorm with several students as many ideas as you can to improve this "silo" impression. After your group comes up with at least two ideas that have merit and address the problem, present your plan as part of a panel discussion. As an alternative, follow you instructor's directions to join a group and use the instructor-designated discussion board to complete the group project. Submit your project as a group-developed paper.

For example, one way is to establish a company wiki where all departments can contribute customer service knowledge and real-time lessons learned.

PART 2

Essential Customer Service Skills

Al Smith, Vice President of Customer Service, Lexus Division, Torrance, California

Responsible for all activities in the parts, service, and customer satisfaction departments for Lexus, Al Smith joined Toyota in 1990 and has held a number of management positions at Toyota's corporate headquarters in Torrance, California.

We have a philosophy and a covenant at Lexus that speaks to building the best cars in the industry, building the best dealer network in the industry, and treating each customer as a guest would be treated in our home. We also believe that every customer we have deserves special attention because he or she has made a commitment to us by purchasing a Lexus, and we should reciprocate by providing the best customer experience. We also understand that customers are our best advocates.

1 For Lexus, what are the biggest challenges in customer service today?

Our customers have high expectations of us from the relationships we've built over the 20 years we've been in business. As you might expect, those expectations have evolved and our operations have changed to meet and hopefully exceed their expectations. Lexus customers know that they are able to make a phone call to Lexus, or visit their dealer and get great service. But, today, they should also be able to text us, chat with us, or connect via social media. Most of the challenge, I would say, is just managing the customer relationship in a dynamic environment or the "new normal."

2 In light of the "new normal", is Lexus hiring a different type of call center rep?

We don't think we need to hire a different type of person, but we do need to learn how to give our people more leeway to use good judgment. We expect our associates to have the *courage* to challenge the rules sometimes. They are trained to treat each contact according to the circumstance of that particular situation. We have over 35 people answering calls and five of these associates are supervisors. I'd prefer 35 people with the mindset of our supervisors, willing to go all out for our customers. It's a matter of hiring those persons who want to go the extra mile to support the customer—those who are patient enough to listen and understand the circumstance and bold enough to challenge protocol in advocacy of the customer.

3 What advice would you offer customer service representatives?

There are some people who can turn hostile situations into productive conversations by leveraging their calming demeanor. They can effortlessly diffuse most situations. So, when selecting team members we look for those traits. Soft skills are very important in customer service roles. We can teach them the hard skills, but it is the soft skills that make the difference in our business, quite frankly. At Lexus, we do extensive training for all of our associates. They learn techniques on how to diffuse a situation, how to speak confidently and compassionately; and how to interact with customers to seek the most positive outcome possible.

4 Any additional comments?

From the standpoint of delivering exceptional customer service, we launched a new service organization at Lexus last year, our Social Media Team. The Team's direction is *pro-active customer service*. Under normal operating approaches, we wait for customers to contact us—and we react to the circumstances presented. However, this particular team is tasked with *reaching out to the customer*. Through social media channels, for example, team members watch, they listen, and they understand what the concerns of customers are. At the right time, they will intervene and introduce themselves as Lexus representatives, and then seek to resolve any issues that they hear about on the Web.

FIRST IMPRESSIONS

What are some of the traits that Al Smith admires in a customer service representative? Record your observations in your notebook.

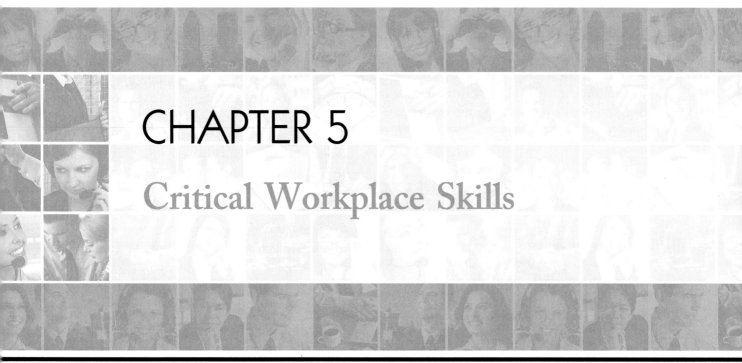

CHAPTER 5

Critical Workplace Skills

*Time is the coin of your life. It is the only
coin you have, and only you can determine
how it will be spent. Be careful lest you
let other people spend it for you.*

CARL SANDBURG, U.S. BIOGRAPHER AND POET

OBJECTIVES

1. Identify techniques to better organize and manage time.

2. Discuss the importance of understanding and managing stress.

3. Understand the difference between positive and negative stress.

4. Define anger management and list ways to control it in the workplace.

5. Describe the benefits to customers of the teamwork approach in organizations.

Google

Why shouldn't work be challenging and fun at the same time? It was those concepts that Google built its company culture around. As a result, the Googlers, as they are called, enjoy their jobs in a creative, team-oriented environment with minimum stress.

According to Google's website, here are a few things you might see in a Google workspace:

- Bicycles or scooters for efficient travel between meetings; dogs; lava lamps; massage chairs; large inflatable balls.

- Laptops everywhere—standard issue for mobile coding, email on the go, and note-taking.
- Foosball, pool tables, volleyball courts, assorted video games, pianos, Ping-Pong® tables, and gyms that offer yoga and dance classes.
- Healthy lunches and dinners for all staff at a variety of cafés.

How would you like to work at Google?

SOURCE: The Google Culture, http://www.google.com/corporate/culture.html accessed December 10, 2010.

TIME MANAGEMENT

How well we deal with time- and stress-related issues is a reflection of our attitudes, beliefs, behaviors, and organizational skills. Setting priorities and keeping them straight is a challenge in this fast-paced world. When CSRs learn to manage their time and stress levels, they not only increase their productivity, but they also improve their overall attitude and well-being.

Webster's Dictionary defines *time* as "the period between two events or during which something exists, happens, or acts." We have the ability to use time in constructive ways. Rather than letting time control work situations and outcomes, CSRs can be in charge of it by applying smart time management techniques. In general, **time management** consists of identifying activities that must be completed, and then prioritizing those activities so that the most important ones are accomplished first. CSRs should not attempt to squeeze more activities into an already overloaded schedule, instead, they should plan well and use the time they have in the most effective way.

Time management is an application of self-management. To manage ourselves, we need to examine our work habits, our environments, and how we manage our time and organize our workload. Do we manage time or does it manage us?

Effective time managers find that the key to controlling how they use time is to record important tasks and appointments, rather than keep everything in their heads. Using an electronic device such as a personal digital assistant (PDA) or Smartphone can help organize a busy schedule. A **personal digital assistant (PDA)** is an electronic hand-held personal organizer. Although Smartphones have largely taken over the handheld computing space, PDAs are still

Ethics / Choices

Have you ever set unrealistic time frames for yourself, or have others pressed you to complete a rush project? What do you think prompts us to behave in this way and then experience stress in work situations?

Stockbyte/Getty Images

Why is good time management one of the most important skills for customer service representatives to master?

used for personal and work uses. A **Smartphone** is a mobile phone that combines the functionalities of a PDA and cell phone with Internet connectivity capability.

Time Management Tips

When you schedule your time wisely, you control your life and can get more done each day. Effective time management has important health benefits, too. By managing your time more wisely, you can minimize stress and improve your quality of life. On its website, the Mayo Clinic discusses several time-saving strategies.

Plan and prioritize tasks Planning your day can help you accomplish more and feel more in control of your life. Write a to-do list, putting the most important tasks at the top. Keep a schedule of your daily activities to minimize conflicts and last-minute rushes. Remember that time-consuming, but relatively unimportant, tasks can consume a lot of a service professional's day. Prioritizing tasks will ensure that you spend your time and energy on those tasks that are truly important to you.

Say "no" to nonessential tasks Consider your goals and schedule before agreeing to take on additional work. If possible, look at your to-do list and consider what can be delegated to someone else.

Take the time you need Doing work right the first time may take more time upfront, but doing a job too quickly will result in errors, and usually the time spent making corrections will end up taking more time overall.

Limit distractions Block out time on your calendar for big projects. During that time, close your door and turn off your Smartphone, pager, and e-mail alert.

Take care of yourself Get plenty of sleep, eat smart, exercise regularly, and take breaks. A healthy lifestyle can improve your focus and concentration, which will help improve your efficiency so that you can complete your work in less time. Too much stress can derail your attempts at getting organized. When you need a break or a short walk, take one. Do some quick stretches at your workstation. Take a day or two of vacation to rest and re-energize.[1]

Time Wasters

Poor time management can interfere with everything you do. For CSRs, it limits the number

---

✔ MAKE IT A HABIT

Organizing Your Time

When organizing your time, ask yourself:

- What do I want or need to do that I am currently not doing?
- What do I want or need to complete that I have not yet completed?
- What do I want or need to start that I have not yet started?

Then, list the tasks from highest to lowest priority: first, highest priority to complete; second, important to complete; and last, nice to do in spare time.

---

[1] "Time management: Tips to reduce stress and improve productivity," 2010, http://www.mayoclinic.com/health/time-management/WL00048/METHOD=print accessed December 7, 2010.

REMEMBER THIS

Figure 5.1   Time Management Quiz

YES	NO	QUESTIONS
☐	☐	1. Do you carry scraps of paper with to-do items listed on them?
☐	☐	2. Do you have trouble focusing on the task you are doing because you are thinking of other things that need to be done?
☐	☐	3. Are you often behind schedule and routinely in a catch-up mode?
☐	☐	4. Have you started many projects that you cannot seem to complete?
☐	☐	5. Do you feel overwhelmed when you walk into work and look at your desk and work space?
☐	☐	6. Do you have so many small items on your mind that you get easily distracted from your important work activities?
☐	☐	7. Are you often remembering other priorities left undone at home while you are at work and vice versa?
☐	☐	8. Do you arrive home feeling unfulfilled in your job, so tired that you want to escape?
☐	☐	9. Do you feel that you cannot take time for physical fitness, recreation, or just plain fun?
☐	☐	10. Do you find that during and after your workday, your stress level is so high that you have trouble relaxing?

If you answered *yes* to more than two or three of these questions, you may be showing symptoms of poor time management. The question then becomes: Do you control your time or does it control you?

of customers they are able to serve in a day. It also influences the time they have available and need to fully handle customer concerns and problems. To eliminate time wasters, be honest with yourself.

How effective a time manager are you? Find out by taking the short quiz in Figure 5.1.

From time to time, CSRs get themselves into time management trouble without intending to. The reasons frequently include:

- *They can't say "no."* Be honest about your commitments. Use your schedule to explain why you can't comply with all requests for your attention. Keep in mind that you should probably say "no" to someone if the request is a last-minute one that requires an immediate response, skills that you do not have, or more time than you can reasonably provide.

- *They are buried in paperwork.* Schedule a specific time for doing paperwork and stick to it. Try not to look at the same piece of paper twice; deal with it the first time.

- *They procrastinate.* Getting started can often be the hardest part of doing anything. Once you have started, however, you gain momentum, which makes it easier to keep going. **Procrastination**, the act of putting something off, comes in many forms, as described in Figure 5.2. on page 76 If you suffer from this tendency, admit it, analyze it, and make a commitment to conquer it. The enormity of the task could be causing you to stall. Attack the task by taking baby steps at first, and you'll be on your way to more effective time management.

In a busy customer contact center, some eight-hour workdays seem to be only about five hours long. When you are deeply involved in serving customer needs, you may ask yourself, "Where did the time go?" It feels as if you have accomplished only part of what you set out to do during the day.

REMEMBER THIS

Figure 5.2 Procrastination

FORM OF PROCRASTINATION	JUSTIFICATION	CURE
Not wanting to do the task	Because procrastination usually involves something we don't want to do, we fill our available time with smaller, easier, and more comfortable projects. We avoid tasks, issues, and problems that are uncomfortable to us.	Tackle your biggest project first instead of getting the little ones out of the way. The little ones will be easy to take care of in your spare time.
Interrupting yourself	You may be interrupting yourself by getting another cup of coffee, stopping to talk with someone, making a quick phone call, or answering e-mail messages.	Set a time frame for the task you are doing and seat belt yourself to the chair.
Making the project too big	It is easy to procrastinate when the job seems too big to even get started.	Divide your project into smaller parts; then set realistic goals to accomplish each one.
Convincing yourself of defeat	Why bother trying when you are doomed to fail? Negative self-talk, such as, "I wouldn't be able to do that job anyway," is at work here.	When you start to think of a negative message, replace it immediately with a positive thought like "I know I can do this; I will get started now."

Effective time management is a challenge for everyone every day, but it only improves (and becomes a habit) with concerted effort and regular practice. Don't become trapped by rationalizing it away, by telling yourself a job wasn't that important anyway or that it was too much work. When that happens, and it will sometimes, make it a habit to look back at your original to-do list and remember why you put this particular goal on the list in the first place. Finally, take a moment to feel good about yourself as you cross that item off the list!

Though not easily recognized, the final outcome for "letting projects slide" is a loss of self-esteem. As our esteem decreases, so does our motivation and energy. This, in turn, feeds future procrastination and begins an unproductive negative cycle. When you take on a task, make it a practice to honestly commit to completing it.

WHAT DO YOU **THINK**
5.1

Evaluate your attitude toward time and how you manage it—both personally and professionally. Record your thoughts.

CUSTOMER SERVICE **TIP**

Enjoy what you're doing while you're doing it. The results will show on your face and in your attitude with customers, supervisors, co-workers, family, and friends.

ORGANIZATIONAL SKILLS

While time management is something everyone should practice, professionally or personally, a CSR needs to be particularly organized, especially today, given the complexities of the job. To be successful, CSRs must control *how* they spend the hours they have on the job. Developing effective organizational skills is one tool that can help add more time to our busy lives and ensure less stress on the job.

Lack of organization can result in mishaps, such as losing critical information and experiencing frequent customer misunderstandings. The organizational skills you apply toward planning each day provide a framework for your productivity. More important, they direct the demands on your attention and give you a sense of control.

People who manage their time well tend to be organized and in control of their workload. What makes some people appear organized and not others? Organized people are inclined to do nearly all of the following activities as a matter of routine:

- *Prepare a monthly schedule.* At the end of every month, calm your mind of incessant "things to do" lists and make a schedule of events and significant deadlines for the next month. Use the schedule to highlight or mark off duties as they are accomplished. There is mental satisfaction in knowing a task is completed and acknowledging that you met an important goal.

- *Prepare a file folder for each item on your schedule.* Make notes on a particular project and immediately file them in the proper folder to save time and not have to search for them later. Frustration dissipates when you know that you have everything you need in one place when you need it.

- *Rely on technology.* Use your Smartphone, PDA, tablet PC, or computer as an electronic assistant. There are several good personal information management programs, such as Microsoft Outlook®, which allow you to track and schedule your activities, take notes, manage meetings, and so on.

- *Organize your work area.* Keep visible paperwork to a minimum, keeping only what is needed for the moment on your desk. Arrange your desk and paperwork so it flows in a logical sequence. For example, place important items first, left to right, in a semi circle on your desk. Disorganized personal space is a very big time waster. As you work, you may have to reorganize your work area every so often throughout the day. Doing this may give you a fulfilled feeling that things are getting finished.

- *Manage your communications.* If you need to focus on a special project and not be interrupted, let your voicemail become your secretary. Return calls every two or three hours and keep a log of messages and their disposition so you do not have to rely on your memory to remember the details. You will instantly know if the task is completed or if there are still follow-up actions required.

A good sense of organization makes CSRs more efficient. If one of your main sources of stress is the sheer number of things that need to be done, getting organized should help you feel more in control. Not being able to find important documents is a major time buster and stress inducer.

Which types of technology do you use to stay organized?

STRESS MANAGEMENT

We live in an interesting age. Regardless of age, gender, position in life, and income, each of us experiences stress. People have never before experienced the amount of change, as well as the number of challenges brought about by those changes, that we encounter every day. That can be said for CSRs in particular, because of the tempo at which they must work and the uncertainties of how best to resolve the next customer call or email, which may have come from a far corner of the globe.

One way to better understand stress is to compare stress levels to blood pressure. High blood pressure or low blood pressure can be problematic, but blood pressure cannot disappear completely. The same is true with stress. When left unattended, stress can be harmful to your emotional and physical health. For example, too much stress can lead to. sleep problems, general anxiety, and feelings of frustration. Conversely, without an edge, you can become apathetic and dull. Effective stress management means finding the right balance between too much and too little stress, and then maintaining that balance at each stage of your life.[2]

What triggers your stress response? Except for major catastrophes, few events are stressful in themselves. Stress arises when you *perceive* a situation as demanding. For example, your morning commute may make you anxious and tense because you worry that traffic will make you late. Others may find the trip relaxing because it allows more time to enjoy music or quiet time while they drive.

Stress is a basic component of most customer service jobs. To understand it better, another way to look at causes of stress in a customer service environment is in terms of a *lack of something*. It can be that CSRs, for instance, feel a lack of control, lack of effective leadership, lack of continuity in performance of tasks, and lack of confidence or self-esteem. Figure 5.3 explains each one in more detail.

---

[2] http://www.mind-gliding.co.uk/extra/KSAP.htm accessed December 15, 2010.

REMEMBER THIS

Figure 5.3

Causes of Stress

- Lack of control
  The inability to get things done, get others to co-operate, satisfy customers' needs, and assimilate and organize the workflow manifests in a feeling of lack of control CSRs sense on the job.

- Lack of effective leadership
  Managers often unknowingly contribute to CSRs' stress level through poor communications, unwillingness to delegate, failure to respond to inquiries and requests, changing priorities at the last minute, and perceived disrespect.

- Lack of continuity in performance
  When CSRs' job priorities change and others redesign workflow processes without their input, they find it difficult to complete a task in progress and this do-again mode builds resentment and stress.

- Lack of confidence or self-esteem
  CSRs who feel empowered have been trained in the tools to deal with stress. As a result, customers are served by more confident service providers who have a higher self-esteem and are more efficient.

CUSTOMER SERVICE TIP

Working with positive stress and getting rid of negative stress can be considered a "facelift for the mind."

The Effects of Stress

There are psychological, philosophical, and behavioral effects of stress on workers—especially CSRs. According to the American Psychological Association in 2009, "Sixty-nine percent of employees report that work is a significant source of stress and 41 percent say they typically feel tense or stressed out during the workday." Perhaps more important to businesses is the finding that "Fifty-one percent of employees said they were less productive at work as a result of stress."[3] Stressed-out workers cost organizations dearly in diminished productivity, employee turnover, and increased medical, legal, and insurance fees.

On a philosophical level, managing stress means learning how to be flexible and how to adapt to new events. Observations show that *how* people deal with change and other situations is what makes some people feel out of control and stressed. Among the effects of stress are loss of focus and attention, tight and tense muscles, and a conscious choice to take shortcuts or bypass procedures.

Finally, behavioral patterns that indicate stress are a decline in job performance, sloppy work habits, poor housekeeping, irritable and quarrelsome behavior, alcohol or drug use, an uncooperative attitude, and general negativity. In countless organizations, these effects of stress show up as worker burnout and negative office chatter.

Burnout According to BusinessDictionary.com, **burnout** is a "feeling of physical and emotional exhaustion, due to stress from working with people under difficult or demanding conditions."[4] Worker burnout is one of the most common reasons why employees quit their service-industry jobs. Psychological exhaustion and decreased efficiency result from overwork and prolonged exposure to stress. Ironically, the more you enjoy your work and the more seriously you take the task of serving customers well, the more vulnerable you may be to the effects of burnout.

Burnout produces feelings of hopelessness, powerlessness, cynicism, resentment, and failure, as well as stagnation, fatigue, and reduced productivity. These reactions can result in levels of depression or unhappiness that eventually threaten a service professional's health and relationships, both personal and professional.

Burnout is associated with situations in which a person feels

- overworked,
- underappreciated,
- confused about expectations and priorities,
- concerned about job security,
- overcommitted with responsibilities,
- resentful about duties that are not commensurate with pay,
- pressure to work at optimum levels—all the time.

To guard against burnout, try these four tips:

1. *Don't take work too personally.* Keep in mind that when customers lash out, their frustration is over the difference between what they want and what they are getting; it is not about you personally.
2. *Don't take problems home.* Give complete attention to your job while you are at work, but leave concerns at work when you go home.
3. *Get help from others.* Remember that your co-workers are going through stressful situations also. It helps to talk over these situations together.
4. *Focus on the good news.* When customers approach you with problems, remember that most of them will become satisfied once you've handled their complaints to the best of your ability.

Negative Office Chatter Negative office chatter is a time waster and stress inducer. Time spent complaining about work, the boss, co-workers, and customers affect your attitude and that of others. Try to avoid those situations because people tend to absorb negativity through constant repetition. Staying positive can lessen stress and can be accomplished by agreeing not to talk about work at lunch and refraining from excessive complaining.

Managing Stress

When stress on the job is interfering with service professionals' ability to work, care for themselves, or direct their personal lives, it's time to take action. Part of managing stress is setting attainable goals

---

[3] "Fact Sheet: By the Numbers," *Psychologically Healthy Workplace Organization*, American Psychological Association Practice Organization, 2010, 1, http://www.phwa.org/dl/2010phwp_fact,_sheet.pdf accessed December 9, 2010.

[4] http://www.businessdictionary.com/definition/burn-out.html accessed December 8, 2010.

In what ways can negative office chatter create a stress?

and not taking on too many commitments at one time. People need to enjoy the process of living, not just be directed by the goal of getting through each day. Most people who are stressed out have very unbalanced lifestyles because they are frustrated they cannot accomplish everything they want to do.

Exercise and staying physically fit rejuvenate us and help to counteract the loss of concentration caused by stress. CSRs who manage stress effectively make time for relaxation activities and humor each day. In addition, they have developed their own stress management plans from some of the tips that follow.

Stress Management Tips How would you assess Google's commitment to provide challenging work that is also fun and near stress free? As you've already read, Google's culture provides a choice of ways to cope positively with stress in the workplace. Below are a few more to include in your personal stress management plans.

- *Pay attention to yourself.* Identify the factors that cause stress in your life so you can change or better manage them. Make a list of the situations, relationships, and events that are stressful for you. Once you have a stress awareness checklist, you

can begin to make decisions about which ones need immediate attention.

- *Don't try to control everything.* Focus on the situations that you can control and let go of those you cannot. For example, you can control your reaction to an angry customer, but you cannot control whether the customer is angry.

- *Alter your lifestyle.* Know when to say "no." Do not procrastinate. Plan for and prioritize tasks. Avoid demanding perfectionism of yourself. Use time-saving tools and technology to your advantage.

- *Change your thinking.* Substitute positive thoughts for negative ones. "I don't know how to do this, but I can learn" is better than "I can't." Drive away anxiety-producing thoughts. Give yourself a pep talk by focusing on your good qualities.

- *Create an outlet.* Exercise, do yoga, perform aromatherapy, or practice meditation. Know how to relax, play, and get silly by regularly taking physical and mental breaks. Nurture and develop your spiritual life by not neglecting matters of the soul. For many people, it brings a sense of inner peace, balance, and helps counteract the effects of stress.

Relaxation A fundamental part of any stress management program is relaxation. It is a much needed activity for overstimulated bodies and minds. Stress causes tense muscles, shallow breathing, increased heart rate, and elevated blood pressure. Relaxation reverses those effects.

Ethics / Choices

You and others affectionately call a co-worker "last-minute Sam." Sam has a good heart and means well, but he always completes his projects at the very last minute, stressing out himself and others. Some workers don't let Sam's pattern of work bother them. What would your reaction be if Sam were a colleague of yours? Would you allow his behavior to affect you?

Relaxation refers to a state of being, is self-initiated, and causes physiological and psychological changes. People relax differently, but doing what works for you is the key to making this technique successful. Simple relaxation tools like those mentioned below can help calm, de-stress, and better control angry feelings.

- Breathe deeply, from your diaphragm.

- Slowly repeat a calm word or phrase such as "relax," or "take it easy." Repeat it to yourself as you breathe in deeply.

- Visualize a tranquil experience, from either your memory or imagination.

- Perform non-strenuous, slow yoga-like stretches to help relax your muscles and feel calmer.

Humor Do you feel better at work when you are in the midst of happy colleagues? Most people do. A well-balanced life requires laughter and fun. One of the top ways CSRs can deal with stress is through humor. Exposing yourself to humor and determining the nature of your own sense of humor is the initial step in using this approach to cope with stress.

When you laugh, it helps reduce muscle tension, release anger, deal with the unexpected, and increase your sense of overall joy. What can be done to promote the spirit of a more humorous workplace? Here are some ideas that companies provide to lessen stress through humor:

1. *Sponsor weird apparel days.* Wear silly hats, funny T-shirts, outrageous ties, and so on.
2. *Celebrate holidays.* Dress up for Halloween or coordinate a holiday meal.
3. *Hold "match the baby picture" contests.* Display childhood pictures of employees and see how many co-workers can correctly match babies with adults.
4. *Organize lunch-hour board game tournaments.* Whether you choose chess, a card game, or Scrabble®, a midday diversion activity can help workers cope better.
5. *Participate on an intramural sports team.* Compete for fun against other departments in regular golf, volleyball, or other no-contact events.

Aside from humor and laughter being great stress busters, they also

- make possible a more positive motivational environment,

- are great for team building,

- enhance relationships and communication,

- ignite creativity.

Positive versus Negative Stress

Not all stress is bad. There is such a thing as positive stress, which people every so often need. **Positive stress** is a force that motivates and energizes you rather than makes you anxious and frustrated; therefore, you can channel its energy into productive results. For example, suppose you have been asked by your supervisor to train your peers in a customer-service script that you developed for a new product. You might feel stress in the form of increased energy as you anticipate training others, but it is the positive kind because it propels you to do your best. In contrast, **negative stress** decreases productivity and comes from worrying about things you have no power to change.

Stockbyte/Getty Images

Do you think that competing for fun promotes unity among co-workers?

So, how do we get rid of unwanted stress?

- *Don't worry.* By recognizing that sometimes you worry about things you can do nothing about, it's easier to channel your worry into something productive. For example, you cannot stop snow from falling on a workday morning, but you can leave home 20 minutes early on those days to arrive safely and more stress free.

- *Set goals.* Focus your energy in a positive direction instead of feeling defeated by negative self-talk. Stop getting mentally and emotionally strained if you are unhappy in your job, and take action to change it.

- *Finish unfinished business.* Make plans to complete an unfinished task or decide to drop it altogether, and stop causing yourself stress over it.

- *Resolve conflicts.* Apologize to a friend, family member, classmate, or co-worker that you've disagreed with. This is the kind of negative stress that can keep you up at night.

WHAT DO YOU THINK

5.2

Describe the behaviors of someone you know who is under stress. To what extent do you think a person's organizational skills have on minimizing or escalating stress? Record your responses in your journal.

ANGER MANAGEMENT

Anger is a natural emotion, but when it gets out of control and turns destructive, it can lead to problems— problems at work, in your personal relationships, and in the overall quality of your life. Angry people have a tendency to speak in colorful terms that reflect their inner thoughts. When you become angry, your thinking typically gets exaggerated and overly dramatic.

Angry people also are inclined to demand things such as fairness, appreciation, agreement. Everyone wants these things, and we are all hurt and disappointed when we don't get them, but angry people demand them, and when their demands aren't met, their disappointment becomes anger.

It is quite understandable that, at times, an irate customer can make a CSR angry. When that happens, how do you recognize what is happening, and more importantly, what do you do to manage anger once it starts to build? **Anger management** is a process of learning to recognize signs that you are becoming angry, and taking action to calm down and deal with the situation in a positive way. Anger management doesn't try to keep you from feeling angry or holding it in. Anger is a healthy, normal emotion when you know how to express it appropriately.

For example, if you often find yourself getting angry at work, you need to first look at the possible causes for your anger and who is responsible for your feelings. Perhaps you stayed up too late and are tired or you have a critical deadline to meet and feel anxious about it. The first thing to do if you sense you are becoming heated in a discussion is slow down and think through your responses. Don't say the first thought that comes into your head, instead, hold back and think carefully about what you want to say. At the same time, listen carefully to what the other person is saying. Always take your time before responding.

It's natural to get defensive when you're criticized, but don't fight back. CSRs have to adhere to this advice especially because the nature of the job is that the customers can become irate and spark your anger, but, in the interest of all of the goals of customer service, you cannot respond in kind. The risk of lashing out is particularly real, however, when you bear the brunt of customer criticism, perceive a lack of support by superiors and co-workers, and experience the empty feeling that you are alone in the struggle. As an alternative, listen to what the customer's underlying words may be saying. The message might be that this person feels unappreciated and taken for granted. Remember the longstanding caution about having your mind in gear before engaging your mouth and making a real effort to think before you speak.

Compromise, when you feel it is possible. If problems can't be resolved without tempers and hostility, sometimes leaving the scene of anger can be the best action you can take. Recall that you can't control other people's actions but you can control your own and influence them to be less angry.

WHAT DO YOU THINK

5.3

When you are angry, what steps do you take to manage it? Record your thoughts in your journal.

TEAMWORK

What do you think of when someone mentions the word *teamwork*? Sports teams most often come to mind, but other situations involve teamwork as well. Consider the movie industry. When producers make a movie, they have to put together a new team that includes actors, sound and light crews, makeup artists, wardrobe staff, and directors, among others. All the members of the team are needed to create the finished product, a successful movie.

Similarly, taking a team approach to customer service means working together as a group with common expectations and goals. Although companies focus thousands of dollars on external customer service in hopes of attracting and retaining customers, little attention is being paid to the effect poor internal customer service has on overall consumer satisfaction. It all starts within the organization. Sooner or later the ripple effect reaches out to influence customers.

As noted in Chapter 1, internal customer service refers to service directed toward others within the organization. It refers to building a level of responsiveness, quality, communication, teamwork, and morale. To help strengthen internal customer

service orientation, CSRs should follow these basic rules.

- *Never complain within earshot of customers.* It gives them the impression your company is not well run, shaking their confidence in you.

- *Never complain to customers about another department's employees.* Who wants to patronize a company whose people cannot get along with each other?

- *Strive to build bridges and compatibility between departments.* This can be done in the course of cross training, joint picnics, off-site gatherings, as well as day-to-day niceties.

What does teamwork show customers? A good team approach shows buyers that the company is organized and that everyone is moving toward a common goal of satisfying the customer. It also means that because of shared ownership, no team member will allow the failure of one member because the entire team will fail. When team members are accountable to each other, customers know that the final objective of the team is their satisfaction.

Teamwork Communication

Communication is one of the most important elements of a successful team. For a team to be effective, its members must communicate with each other so everyone can stay informed and work as a unit. Whenever a team is put together, issues such as different personalities, management styles, and company hierarchies arise. Many times, exchanging honest, open feedback is more difficult with someone you

What makes a team's efforts worthwhile and fun?

Ethics / Choices

Your company encourages employees to work in teams. Brent is a fellow CSR with whom you have worked before. On numerous occasions, you have noticed that he has a poor attitude. To you, it appears that he is always angry and seems to put others down without realizing his words may be offensive and insulting. Most of your co-workers simply ignore Brent and try to have as little to do with him as possible. What would be your approach with Brent?

work with than with your customers. This might be because the message you have to share with a fellow worker is not a positive one.

To maintain good working relationships, any negative feedback you offer a co-worker should be focused on a specific task, not on his or her personality. To be constructive, any criticism you offer should be accompanied by a positive suggestion on how to improve the task. By the same token, if a teammate is doing something well, be sure to mention it. Again, focus your comments on the task. An effective customer-centric environment fosters forthright feedback and values honesty.

Benefits of Teamwork

When customer service is built with organizational teamwork as its foundation, many benefits result. One of the most important benefits is that teamwork helps break down walls that can sometimes exist between departments within organizations. Teamwork can also provide new ideas and a new slant on customer problems. Finally, teamwork can create a more effective method for delegating work and any follow-up actions that must be taken, thereby reducing stress and increasing productivity.

Because no one is an expert on everything, people need to gather knowledge from others. People who work together tend to learn things faster and retain information longer than do individuals

REMEMBER THIS

Figure 5.4

Teamwork Strategies That Promote Service

1. *Support your teammates with information.* Share what you know freely with your co-workers. Use huddles—brief, informal meetings—instead of formal meetings when time is limited.

2. *Discuss new policies.* Discuss any new policies with your team and jointly create a way to explain changes to your customers in a positive way. Sometimes, using a script can ensure that everyone is consistently following the same plan.

3. *Identify areas for improvement.* Let the ideas flow without judgment in a brainstorming session. The craziest ideas sometimes turn out to be the ones that work best.

4. *Show pride in yourself and your co-workers.* Celebrate others' successes. Let the customer know you are proud of yourself, your co-workers, and your organization.

who work alone. Teamwork creates a **synergy**, which means that the combined effect of individual efforts is greater than their individual efforts alone. With synergy, problem solving becomes more effective, and better organizational decisions tend to be made. Figure 5.4 provides some strategies that team members can adopt to deliver exceptional customer service.

WHAT DO YOU **THINK** 5.4

Recall the best team you've ever been on (sports, work, group project). With that experience in mind, record your recollections of what made it fun and purposeful.

FOCUS ON. . .
BEST PRACTICES

Addressing Workplace Stress

The top workplace issues that affect worker stress, as reported by a recent study entitled "Stress in the Workplace" are: health care costs, absenteeism, and workplace safety. Though these stress issues are unavoidable, employers nonetheless must recognize them and provide a workplace that offers possible solutions to counter these on-the-job stressors.

Specific findings from the survey revealed that "66 percent of employers have implemented at least four programs intended to reduce stress. Twenty-two percent have established eight or more programs." The top four employer-provided programs identified are: employee assistance programs, flexible work schedules, work/life balance support programs, and leadership training on worker stress.

SOURCE: Ed Gadowski, Employers Using an Arsenal of Tools to Combat Workplace Stress: Survey, July 8, 2010, online http://www.buckconsultants.com/buckconsultants/Portals/0/Documents/PUBLICATIONS/Press_Releases/2010/PR-Workplace-Stress-2010Survey-070810.pdf

WRAPPING UP

Though critical workplace skills are many in number, this chapter discussed those that will assist workers involved with customer service, especially CSRs. To be successful, a good attitude, the ability to manage time, and the ability to organize priorities are keys to reducing job stress. Understanding and applying techniques to control time, management of tasks, as well as anger management are key in building positive and productive team interactions on the job. These points underscore the fact that personal skills, used individually and collectively, allow workers to respond quickly and effectively to customer-related problems, and they ready students to learn about on-the-job *Problem Solving*, the topic of Chapter 6.

SUMMARY

- Time management is not about squeezing more activities into an already overloaded schedule, but about prioritizing and completing those activities in a less stressful way.

- Being organized allows you to be able to quickly find what you need when you need it.

- Positive stress can motivate and energize a person; whereas, negative stress often makes a person feel anxious and frustrated.

- Anger management is the process of learning to recognize signs that you are becoming angry, and taking action to calm down and deal with the situation in a positive way.

- A good team approach shows that the company is organized and that everyone is moving toward the common goal of doing everything possible to satisfy the customer.

KEY TERMS

anger management
burnout
negative stress
personal digital assistant (PDA)

positive stress
procrastination
relaxation
Smartphone

synergy
time management

CRITICAL THINKING

1. Describe the behavior of a person who procrastinates doing a job or handing in a class assignment on time. Based upon your description, what remedies might you suggest to help that person be more productive?

2. Why are organizational skills important? How can you usually identify a person who exhibits these skills? What observable characteristics does the person possess?

3. Reread the *Focus on…Best Practices* feature on page 85 describing health care costs, absenteeism, and workplace safety as they affect worker

stress. Evaluate the merits of the programs businesses offer to defuse worker stress.

4. Recall a situation when you experienced positive stress that served you in a beneficial way. Explain why you think it helped you become more effective in the workplace.

5. In your opinion, is showing anger at work ever acceptable? Explain.

6. What are two ways a CSR benefits from contributing to team efforts at work? Why do you think some service professionals prefer to work alone rather than in a team?

 ## WHAT DO YOU THINK NOW?

Project 5.1

Assume you are doing a classroom presentation on *escalating stress-related problems in the workplace*. Reread your responses to the *What Do You Think?* questions that you completed throughout this chapter. What are some service attitudes and practices that reduce stress in the workplace? What service factors should be monitored to alleviate stress-producing customer situations? Which skills should CSRs possess that minimize a stressful personal and professional life? Compile your responses, as directed by your instructor.

ONLINE RESEARCH ACTIVITY

Project 5.2   Anger Management Seminars

Research a number of websites and locate several anger management consultants who provide onsite anger management seminars. Write a short paper that compares the content offerings of any three of these workshops.

COMMUNICATION SKILLS AT WORK

Project 5.3   Time-Management Suggestions

Respond to the following items with a personal example of either how you have implemented or how you would implement each suggestion. After you have identified your examples, compare and contrast your suggestions with other students, as directed by your instructor.

TIME-MANAGEMENT SUGGESTION	A PERSONAL EXAMPLE
1. Start with the most worrisome task	
2. Complete deadline work early	
3. Know your capacity for stress	
4. Stay organized	
5. Get physical	
6. Have fun	

DECISION MAKING AT WORK

Project 5.4   How to Motivate an Unenthusiastic Teammate

During a weekly team meeting, you notice that one of your co-workers is quieter than usual. He acts as if he does not care to be involved in the team's weekly sessions.

Respond to each of the following statements by role playing with another student what you might say to a team member who suffers from a lack of motivation. As an alternative, follow your instructor's directions to join a group and use the instructor-designated discussion board to complete the group project.

1. Acknowledge your teammate's value.
2. Discover the source of the problem.
3. Stress the importance of team harmony.

CASE STUDY

Project 5.5   Organizational Skills

You had planned on getting to work early to finish an important project that is due today, but your car won't start. You know you have the mechanic's number somewhere, but you can't remember where you put it. After searching all the logical places, you still cannot locate it. Now that you will be late, you will not have time to finish your project, which was assigned to you two weeks ago. You start to panic, and the clock keeps ticking.

First, indicate three organization-related problems in this scenario. Then, provide a technique or suggestion that would either eliminate each problem or reduce the its effects.

CHAPTER 6

Problem Solving

For every failure, there is an alternative course of action. You just have to find it. When you come to a roadblock, take a detour.

MARY KAY ASH, FOUNDER, MARY KAY COSMETICS, INC.

OBJECTIVES

1. Describe the steps involved in solving customer complaints.

2. Identify reasons that customers complain and describe the process for solving those problems.

3. List the conflict management styles and strategies to use when solving customer problems.

4. Discuss how a customer win-back plan is a necessary component for dealing with dissatisfied customers.

BUSINESS IN *ACTION*

JetBlue

Proactive problem solving is part of JetBlue Airways success and customer service strategy. The company's Customer Bill of Rights ensures that if a JetBlue traveler is inconvenienced in his or her travels, there is a published customer-oriented resolution in most cases. Available at the company's website, some sample entries in JetBlue's Rights include:

1. JetBlue will notify customers of delays, cancellations, and diversions.
2. All customers whose flight is cancelled by JetBlue will, at the customer's option, receive a full refund or reaccommodation on the next available JetBlue flight at no additional charge or fare.
3. For customers whose flight is delayed 3 hours or more after scheduled departure, JetBlue will provide free movies on flights that are 2 hours or longer.
4. Customers who are involuntarily denied boarding shall receive $1,000.

When a major airline stands behind these public commitments, the problem-solving issues with customers are greatly diminished and help CSRs do their job more professionally as they interact with customers who complain.

SOURCE: http://www.jetblue.com/about/ourcompany/promise/index.html accessed December 15, 2010.

UNDERSTANDING COMPLAINTS

Customer complaints can be a real challenge. Because businesses are complex, it simply is not possible to do everything right all the time. Many things can go wrong. Some issues, such as weather that slows down product delivery, are beyond an organization's control, as the JetBlue feature illustrates. Yet, there are reasons customers complain. To be successful in their role, CSRs must be comfortable with the complaint-handling process their company expects them to use.

Why Customers Complain

Customers complain for a host of different reasons. Some may not feel well, while others may just have angry dispositions. The most common reason, however, is because the expectations customers have when purchasing a product or service are not met. It only takes one unsatisfied person to shatter a perfectly good day at work for everyone, but, more importantly, dissatisfied customers can steer prospective customers away from your company.

Even when confrontations do not happen in person, the result is the same. Endless customer service e-mail loops and other service irritations frustrate customers and cost companies in reputation and profits. The result is, that once again, dissatisfied customers often take their business elsewhere.

A call to a service rep that is completely resolved on the first call is referred to as a **first-call resolution (FCR)**. If the customer does not call back about the same problem for a certain period of time, consider the resolution successful.

When customers do not articulate their complaints, they can manifest in many negative ways: unpaid invoices, lack of courtesy to front-line service reps, and negative word-of-mouth statements. As previously discussed, an unhappy Internet customer can now reach thousands of potential customers in a few keystrokes. So, smart companies are proactive. They head off bad press before it happens by making it easy for customers to complain, and then they address those complaints seriously and quickly.

Further, they establish firm guidelines regarding customer response times and stick to them.

Disagreement versus Conflict

Today's best customer service is not something that can be faked: it involves being personable and sincere. That is why when dealing with customer complaints, distinguishing whether or not it is a disagreement or conflict is vital. In general, disagreements occur between people who have different opinions about an issue. Disagreements do not necessarily have to be resolved. You can, for example, agree to debate for the fun of it or even agree to disagree.

A conflict, on the other hand, involves a more serious clash of values, perceptions, or ideas. Conflict can jeopardize productivity in terms of one's relationships at work and dealings with customers. Although most of us dislike being a part of conflict situations, it is smart for CSRs to realize that good can sometimes be brought about by conflict. For example, conflict can:

- foster a more profound understanding of another person's ideas and personality.

- promote a deeper understanding of one's self, one's motives, and one's effect on others.

- bring about a meaningful transformation in one's own behavior and style of communication.

- foster more meaningful and productive relationships with others.

If the conflict involves a company policy or practice, a positive result can involve a change in practice or procedure.

Not all conflict, however, is good. If conflict escalates with customers, the situation could result in accusations and threats when parties get angry and blame each other. Two possible customer service results that emerge from heightened conflict are:

- General issues replace specific issues as the problem goes from a person being angry over a specific behavior to wanting to sever the service relationship completely.

- Concern for self turns into retaliation, and the primary interest becomes hurting the company or getting even.

As noted, conflict begins because the product or service the customer purchased did not meet his or her expectations. Figure 6.1 illustrates from the Better Business Bureau's website the most common

REMEMBER THIS

Figure 6.1 Causes and Complaints

COMPLAINTS	CAUSES
Product Service	• Poor product quality
	• Maintenance difficulties
	• Inadequate or poor repair work
	• Goods/services delivery delays
	• Failure to fulfill product or service warranties
	• Incompetent or discourteous employees
Accounting	• Billing errors
	• Failure to provide timely refunds and adjustments, as promised
Sales Practice	• Deceptive or inaccurate advertising
	• Advertising products that are unavailable or in limited supply
	• Misleading or false representations by sales staff

SOURCE: http://louisville.bbb.org/article/effective-customer-relations--bbb-advice-on-customer-service-and-complaints-8173 accessed December 11, 2010.

complaints that deal with product service, accounting, and sales complaints.

Recognizing that unresolved complaints pose a threat to consumer confidence and the climate of the American marketplace, the **Better Business Bureau (BBB)** has dedicated itself to playing a leadership role in the resolution of consumer-business disputes. The BBB is a recognized third-party complaint handling mechanism in the United States.

Above all, the BBB believes consumers and businesses alike are best served if they can resolve their disputes independently. However, if the matter is not resolved, the BBB will attempt to bring about a resolution by facilitating two-way communication between the parties through mediation. **Mediation** is a process used to resolve differences between two parties conducted by an impartial third party for the purpose of bringing about a settlement or agreement. The decision of the mediator is not binding, however, as arbitration is.

Arbitration is a legally binding process that begins when both parties sign an agreement permitting the arbitrator to conduct a fact-finding hearing and make a final decision. This alternative to a formalized court ruling is expedient, more cost effective, consistent with most state laws, and confidential. After determining the facts, the arbitrator renders a decision, which can be in favor of the business, the consumer, or some compromise solution.

What are the benefits of using an unbiased third person to resolve differences between two parties?

The Complaint-Handling Process

It is always best when customers and the business can resolve complaints satisfactorily between them. The foundation for doing this and for maintaining customer goodwill in organizations is the publication, promotion, and practice of using a sound **customer relations policy**. The best complaint-handling systems are structured from a customer relations policy and must operate simply, effectively, and quickly to everyone's mutual benefit. Moreover, the policy manual and related procedures must be in writing and support all forms of communication exchanges and media used, such as e-mail, chats, and a variety of social media in addition to face-to-face and phone interactions.

A customer relations policy should demonstrate a strong commitment to customer satisfaction and encourage customers to communicate their concerns. In addition, the policy should spell out how, when, where, and by whom complaints and questions are handled in the company. One person within the company should have the ultimate authority and responsibility for customer relations, although *all* employees—especially CSRs—should know the guidelines as stated in the policy and how to implement them. At a minimum, a customer relations policy should:

- encourage customers to express their concerns using any available media or communication source.

- cover issues surrounding the business's advertising, social media sites, sales promotions, displays, selling methods, pricing, warranties, deliveries, returns, and refunds.

- emphasize proper training of employees in customer relations matters.

- conform to federal, state, and local laws and regulations.

What should a company do to encourage customers to complain and how should those complaints be handled? The answer lies in making it easy for customers to give honest, regular feedback and then making sure they receive prompt and effective responses to that feedback. Businesses that treat every complaint as the key to developing a better way of doing business thereby allow customers to feel safe enough to complain in a timely manner.

Service responses to complaints must provide specific and realistic feedback about what the next steps will be in response to their complaint. They must also be professional and courteous in manner. For example, will you research why the problem happened and how it can be resolved? Will you discuss it with your colleagues to prevent a similar situation from happening again? When will you respond to the customer? Will your response be in writing, by phone, or by e-mail? Set a reasonable timeframe for the resolution, and be sure to thank the customer sincerely for helping you improve the way you serve customers.

Customer complaints are never easy to hear. If a shift is made from being defensive to being creative, however, complaints can become advantageous. Thriving companies take these basic steps to completely and systematically process customer complaints.

Screen and log in information
Start the procedure by screening the customer call, electronically logging in the date the complaint is received, and recording all pertinent customer information.

Listen
A disgruntled customer wants to know that someone is willing to listen. Being quiet, paying attention, and listening carefully to what the customer is saying—without being distracted or sounding impatient—are important. Try not to interrupt, as doing so may cause the customer to argue, withdraw, or simply hang up or walk away. Give a sense that you are an "active listener." Repeat or paraphrase the concern or complaints that the customer has shared with you such that he or she has a definite sense that you have heard and understood the issue. At an appropriate time during this initial contact, remember to thank the customer for bringing the problem to your attention.

Empathize
After having the opportunity to express dissatisfaction, the customer wants to know that someone understands and cares about the situation on an emotional level. Make certain that the customer realizes that you understand, not just the specifics of the complaint, but the customer's feelings about what has happened. Find ways to respond with empathy and acknowledge the customer's feelings (upset, frustrated, disappointed). If possible, tell the customer how long it will take to satisfy the complaint, especially if a delay might occur, and acknowledge that, while this might add to their frustration, he or she is not forgotten, and a resolution is underway.

Solicit Feedback
Try to get the customer to explain how the problem happened. By asking the customer for feedback on how the problem occurred, you convey concern and a willingness to understand the problem in order to arrive at the best solution. Another way to get feedback is to ask, "What do you think would be fair in this situation?" It will appeal to the customer's sense of justice and feeling of involvement in trying to resolve the problem.

Apologize
The customer wants to hear that you are sorry about the problem or inconvenience, even if you are not necessarily the one to blame. You can apologize without accepting blame by saying, "This situation is unfortunate, and I apologize for it." A genuine apology is often the key to healing wounds. An immediate, sincere apology defuses hostility, no matter how grievous the injury. An apology is not only an expected social politeness, but also a practical step that helps open the door to further communication and possible resolution of the complaint.

Deliver Bad News Positively
There may come a time when you must tell a customer that you will not be able to take a product back, that the item he or she ordered is out of stock, or that he or she must pay in advance. The following list offers some suggestions for delivering unavoidable bad news to a customer.

1. Inform the customer as early in the process as possible. Even though this part of the job is unpleasant, do not put it off.

2. Get to the point quickly. You can warn the customer that bad news is coming in a kind way by saying something like, "You may not like hearing this, but ..." This can sometimes soften the subsequent distress.

3. Treat the customer fairly. Customers remember your courtesy and professionalism long after the actual problem has been forgotten.

Take Ownership and Formulate a Solution

If there is one thing that will frustrate a customer, it is "**ping-ponging**," or being passed from one employee or department to another. Ping-ponging occurs when you come into contact with a customer service rep that either is not given the authority to resolve issues, is not trained properly, or both. If the problem can be fixed on the spot, take care of it. If not, call your supervisor or transfer the customer to the appropriate person who can address the situation. Take ownership of the problem and make sure that it is handled appropriately and immediately. Any solution should conform to your established customer relations policy and take into account contractual and/or warranty obligations, customer expectations, your company's expectations, and your ability to deliver on any decision. Your company may occasionally authorize bending the rules, because doing so will ultimately cost less than it would to lose the customer or potential customers, if the dissatisfied customer leaves and relays a negative story about your company.

Communicate a Solution

When your share your company's response to the complaint, make sure your message is clear and appropriate. Try to avoid technical jargon. A respectful explanation of even an adverse decision can often preserve customer goodwill.

Follow Up

Immediately follow up on any action that has been taken. Contact the customer to ensure that the company has resolved the matter to their satisfaction. For example, appropriate follow-up action could be a letter of apology or a phone call to make sure that the problem has been fixed and that no additional concerns exist. That is also a

CUSTOMER SERVICE TIP

When you are trying to understand a customer's situation, remember that the problem is the enemy, not you.

good time to ask for a second chance by saying, "We hope we will have a chance to serve you again."

Using Scripts

Sometimes tough calls become more manageable when the customer service representative uses a prepared **script**, or predetermined dialogue that states how to respond to common problems. Two advantages of using scripts are that 1) they help CSRs deliver consistent responses to common customer issues and 2) they assist CSRs in developing their own problem-solving responses. Often, when a CSR delivers the right combination of words in a sensitive and sincere tone, the result can be positive in its impact. When a script is not used well, a customer can often tell that a CSR is reading from it and this can be annoying. The response not only sounds programmed, but the customer feels like the CSR does not care about his or her *particular* circumstances.

When implemented well, appropriate scripts include four key elements:

1. *Empathy.* CSRs should begin their responses by focusing on feelings. This means understanding the situation and feelings from the customer's point of view.
2. *Acknowledgment.* This involves recognizing the validity of the customer's complaint, a key step in the process of reaching a solution.
3. *Reassurance.* At this point, CSRs need to restore the customer's confidence in the company.
4. *Action.* Empathizing, acknowledging, and reassuring are not enough. Action is what counts most.

Figure 6.2 on page 94 provides an example of a script that demonstrates the four elements in action.

Figure 6.2

A Sample Customer Service Script

1. "Natasha, you sound pretty upset with the information I have just told you." *(empathy)*

2. "Before we dismiss your request for....." *(acknowledgment)*

3. "Let me make sure there is nothing I am aware of that has changed." *(reassurance)*

4. "I would like to have Mr. Haynes in on this conversation to listen to his ideas about alternatives. I would be interested in hearing them myself. Is that ok with you?" *(action)*

WHAT DO YOU THINK

6.1

Describe the best and the worst complaint-handling experience you have experienced as a customer. Record your descriptions in your journal.

PROBLEM SOLVING

In situations that require handling customer problems on a daily basis, effective problem solving skills are a highly regarded ability. CSRs that are considered especially good problem solvers are analytical and have first-rate interpersonal skills. They not only solve problems but simultaneously handle customers' feelings. Complaining customers will return if a problem is resolved kindheartedly in their best interests. How good a problem solver are you? Take the quiz in Figure 6.3 to find out.

Problem Solving Process

Dealing with customer issues involves more than responding to customer complaints. Records may indicate that a customer is making fewer and fewer purchases, is slow in paying bills, no longer visits your restaurant with regularity and, when they are there, do not seem enthused or even satisfied with their service. There is definitely a problem. The challenge is determining what the problem is and how best to respond to it effectively.

People who are really good at solving problems go about it systematically. They have a way of placing the problem in context. They do not jump to conclusions. They evaluate alternatives. A good way to become a systematic problem solver is to adopt the following five-step *problem-solving process*:

1. *Identify the problem.* This is critical. You must try to solve the *right* problem. Identify the problem by asking the right questions and learning from the responses. What is leading the customer to feel there is a problem? Is it something specific, or is it an intuitive sense on the customer's part that things are not as they should be? Can the customer define the problem?

2. *Analyze the problem.* How often does the problem occur? How severe is it? What might be the causes of the problem? How long has it been going on? Has it gotten worse?

3. *Identify decision criteria.* How will you and the customer make decisions when the time comes? How will you weigh the criteria?

4. *Develop multiple solutions.* Do not stop at the first solution you identify. It may be good, but a much better solution might exist. Evaluate alternative scenarios and as objectively as possible, assess the pros and cons of each one.

5. *Choose the optimal solution.* Develop a base of support that will ensure you can implement the solution. Prepare for contingencies.

When problems are solved methodically, you save time, achieve better solutions, and increase your credibility with the customer and the value of what you have done.

REMEMBER THIS

Figure 6.3 Problem Solving Skills Quiz

YES	NO	QUESTIONS
☐	☐	1. When faced with a new problem, do you start by trying to determine its major cause?
☐	☐	2. Do you compare the problem with other dilemmas you have solved previously to see whether a pattern emerges?
☐	☐	3. Can you set aside trivial details while getting a grasp on the problem's major facets?
☐	☐	4. Can you look at a problem from several different perspectives?
☐	☐	5. Do you feel comfortable asking for input from your supervisor?
☐	☐	6. If a person helps you solve a problem, do you give proper credit to him or her?
☐	☐	7. When you are making limited progress on your own, do you brainstorm with co-workers?
☐	☐	8. Do you know when to stop gathering facts so you can make a decision in a timely fashion?
☐	☐	9. When decisions turn out differently than expected, do you still consider alternatives?
☐	☐	10. When you are still confused despite all your best efforts, do you set the problem aside for a short time to get a fresh perspective?

A total of eight or more "yes" answers suggest that you have excellent problem-solving abilities and the interpersonal skills to make things work for customers and co-workers. Five to seven "yes" answers indicate that you can solve problems but could probably do so more effectively with help from your peers. If you scored lower, reevaluate the process you follow when you are confronted with problems, and use these questions to guide you toward better problem-solving solutions.

Listening and Responding

There are times when we feel that we have solved a customer's problem when, in fact, we have not. Based on our perception of the facts, we came up with a solution to solve the problem that made sense to us. The problem is, we did not listen carefully. We may have focused more on what we were saying than on what the customer was saying. To solve problems effectively, CSRs need to remember to apply their focused listening skills. Effective listening skills are essential to "read a situation" correctly. The ability to solve problems, resolve differences, and capture opportunities involves actively listening. Chances are, a customer will supply you with more information if he or she feels that you are truly committed to understanding what they are saying.

Service-oriented employees deal with problems on the spot. The problem may involve a customer's conflict with another employee, an issue with locating merchandise, difficulty in finding the right department or person to go to with an issue, or just general dissatisfaction or concern about the overall appearance of your establishment. However trivial or even contrived the issues may be, remember that it is real and important to the customer.

Or, the problem may indeed lie with the customer, such as an error in addition when paying a bill, the misperception of items on sale, or the misreading of a menu. The issue may involve an unjust accusation or unfounded comment. The customer may be uninformed, uncooperative, or just bad-tempered. The problem may be delicate, emotional (especially if the person is aged or in some way challenged), and could easily escalate. The benefit of responding to such issues immediately is greater customer satisfaction (even by those observing and not directly involved with the situation), which, ultimately, results in lower customer service costs. The benefits of listening and careful problem-solving analysis helps CSRs to more easily follow these steps:

1. *Determine whether the situation is a disagreement or a real problem.* Ask the customer to state the problem from his or her point of view, and then state the problem from your own perspective. This can help determine where the problem lies.

2. *Analyze your interests and the customer's interests.* Determine ahead of time what concessions management will empower you to make on the customer's behalf and what limitations you have.

3. *Brainstorm creative solutions and generate ideas together.* If the issue is complicated, start with the easy issues and then proceed to the more difficult ones. Always attempt to establish points of agreement early in the listening process.

4. If step 3 does not resolve the situation, make some mutual low-priority concessions. Be patient. You may have to go through steps 3 and 4 more than once.

Figure 6.4 offers five additional suggestions for ways service professionals can work together with customers and be sensitive to their needs.

When problems are passed on to the next level of the organization, the price of service goes up. In other words, service cost is increased because more time to address customer concerns is needed and a more costly manager is now involved in the process. Therefore, successful problem solving early in the process is critical to a company's financial success. Accessibility, ownership, explanation of policies, and follow-through promote effective problem solving in the most efficient manner:

1. *Accessibility.* When customers call your business, they need to know that they will be getting an answer quickly from an employee who is not only willing to help but also very knowledgeable.

2. *Ownership.* When a customer presents a genuine problem that may involve negligence or even incompetence, a CSR should accept responsibility for the situation (even if it is not his or her fault) and apologize without assigning blame.

REMEMBER THIS

Figure 6.4

Problem Solving with Customers

1. Keep your composure.
   - Focus on the real issues.
   - Be creative in your solutions.
   - Know your hot buttons and keep them in check.
   - Break the link between your emotions and the action that needs to occur.

2. Play it "side by side."
   - Put yourself in your customer's shoes by showing respect, not hostility.
   - Express concern for the relationship.
   - Make reasonable requests.
   - Ask questions and invite specific criticism.
   - Use humor, when appropriate.

3. Be firm, but agreeable, to further negotiation.
   - Respond to reason, but not to force or personal attacks.
   - Take sarcasm at face value.

4. Sidestep personal disagreements and keep talking about the customer's issue.
   - Caution, do not threaten. There is a fine line between the two actions. A threat sounds like, "Here is what I will do to you." A caution expresses genuine concern and sounds like, "Here is what the situation will be."

5. Look to the future.
   - Say, "How do we make sure this never happens again?"
   - Suggest a third-party mediator, if all else fails.

3. *Explanation of policies.* When problems occur because of a company policy, a CSR should provide a clear explanation of *what* happened and *why* the company has this policy.

4. *Follow-through.* When commitments are made to customers, CSRs need to be sure they can deliver as quickly as possible on all promises they make.

WHAT DO YOU THINK

6.2

Evaluate your results from taking the problem-solving quiz. What did you learn about yourself? Record your thoughts in your journal.

✓ MAKE IT A HABIT

Resolving Customer Problems

Put your best foot forward and resolve customer problems by routinely making a point to:

- Use customer's names. It shows you are genuinely interested in your customers and helps create rapport.
- Give customers your name and contact information. This action exhibits accountability and communicates an honest desire to help.
- Smile through the phone. When you smile, you sound friendly, interested, and helpful.

NEGOTIATING SKILLS

Though not always needed by CSRs when solving customer problems, it is a good idea to review the basics of negotiating skills, conflict management styles, and conflict resolution strategies that may prove helpful in certain challenging customer situations.

Negotiation is an interpersonal process requiring a give and take between the participants. The following process is recommended to use as a basis in customer situations as well.

1. Describe what we (CSRs) want and feel.
2. Express why we (CSRs) feel as we do and the motives for our desires.
3. Acknowledge the other person's perspective.

4. Look for solutions.
5. Choose one solution.
6. Put the chosen solution into effect.

When using this negotiating process, if a customer's point of view is more logical, recognize that fact and say, "I am glad we explored all avenues, and at this point, I have to agree with you." While such an admission can be difficult, put your ego aside and concede the customer's point gracefully.

There may be times, however, that you may not be able to give in gracefully. When that occurs, take the time to think the problem over objectively. Above all, remember that your priority is to find a feasible solution to the conflict—not to win an argument. Consider using particular conflict management styles in those cases.

Conflict Management Styles

If you have a conflict with a customer, be aware of how you respond. The reaction you give may de-escalate the situation or fan the fires. There are five generally accepted styles for dealing with conflict. Nothing is inherently right or wrong with any of these styles. In fact, each can be appropriate and most effective depending on the customer situation, issues to be resolved, and the personalities involved.

- **Competing** involves an entrenched, almost combative attitude based upon the unshakable conviction that you are right. If you compete, you are assertive in pursuing your own concerns. This style is useful when action is necessary. For example, if there are only a few products left in stock, the customer should be encouraged to place an order quickly, even though he or she hesitates to do so at the time. Care on the part of the service rep must be taken, however, not to come on too strong for fear that the customer backs away.

- **Accommodating** demands complete acquiescence to another's point of view. If you accommodate, you are cooperative, but unassertive. This style is useful when you realize that you are wrong or that the issue is more important to the other person. For example, by replacing a customer's order due to faulty delivery practices, the CSR chooses to accommodate the customer and pay for the re-order costs. Accommodating is a small price to pay to keep a customer's loyalty.

- **Avoiding** might take the form of diplomatically sidestepping an issue, postponing an issue until a better time, or simply withdrawing from a situation that is emotionally, physically, or intellectually threatening. If you avoid, you do not address the conflict. This reaction is useful when the issue is trivial, a confrontation could be damaging, or you need time to cool off or gather information. An avoidance situation, for example, can be the CSR not charging a complaining customer a change-order fee on specialized products ordered because the fee was unintentionally omitted on the original invoice.

- **Collaborating** requires finding creative solutions to a common problem. Rather than avoiding a problem, you attempt to problem solve together with the customer to find a mutually satisfying solution.

- **Compromising** means finding solutions that are mutually satisfactory to both parties. If you compromise, you address rather than avoid an issue. Compromising means splitting the difference or agreeing on a middle ground.[1]

Thoughtful and strategic use of these styles can effectively facilitate conflict resolution. CSRs should utilize one or more of these approaches in the pursuit of a continued and productive business relationship.

Although negotiation involves conferring, discussing, or bargaining to reach agreements, most service reps realize that in practice, resolving conflicts do not always result in the preferred win-win column, but can also produce an undesirable win-lose or lose-lose service encounter.

Conflict Resolution Strategies

When people bargain over positions, they tend to back themselves into corners defending their positions, which results in a number of either win-lose or lose-lose outcomes rather than the ideal win-win result.

The **win-lose strategy** assumes that one side will win by achieving its goals and the other side will lose. Often this approach occurs when the parties start the negotiation process by stating the specific outcomes they want to see.

When the issues involved in a conflict are trivial or when a speedy decision is required, this style may be appropriate. It is also appropriate when unpopular courses of action must be implemented—for instance, when implementing the policies formulated by customer service supervisors or top management.

The outcomes of the **lose-lose strategy** are common when one party attempts to win at the expense of the other. Mutually destructive outcomes can also surface from personal disputes with customers or colleagues and should be avoided. For example, feuding co-workers may destroy their own careers by acquiring a reputation of being difficult to work with or not being team players.

The **win-win strategy** assumes that a reasonable solution can be reached that will satisfy the needs of *all* parties and is the approach that is most desirable for CSRs to use. Instead of looking at their opponent as an adversary to be defeated, win-win participants see customers as allies in the search for a satisfactory solution through collaborative and compromising means.

In most situations, the needs of the negotiating parties are not incompatible; they are just different. The four basic components of a win-win negotiation that CSRs should use are to

1. Focus on interests, not positions.
2. Separate the people from the problem.
3. Generate a variety of possibilities before deciding what to do.
4. Insist that the best solution be based on some mutually acceptable and objective standard.

By focusing on the end result instead of the means of getting there, win-win solutions can frequently be found. You will want to exercise the

[1] Dawn M. Baskerville "How do you manage conflict?" *Black Enterprise,* May, 1993, FindArticles.com http://findarticles.com/p/articles/mi_m1365/is_n10_v23/ai_13707958/?tag=content;col1 accessed January 7, 2011.

win-win style with customers because you have common interests and you desire to maintain a continuing, harmonious relationship. Should these attempts fail, organizations need to have an effective win-back plan and use it.

WHAT DO YOU THINK

6.3

Which conflict management style makes you most uncomfortable in a customer situation? Why? Record your response in your journal.

AN EFFECTIVE WIN-BACK PLAN

As noted, an essential component of any communication with unhappy customers is that you value their business and want it to continue. If it seems that customers have made a decision to withdraw their business, it is important to communicate that you want them back.

The key to success in recovering unhappy customers is having a well-conceived win-back plan. In most businesses, once customers make a decision to terminate the relationship, they do not communicate their intent to the company. A few reasons that most customers would rather walk than complain are listed here:

- They often do not know who to speak to about the problem. Customers think the available sales associates do not have the authority to resolve big problems.

- They think that the complaint will never be acted on so they do not want to pursue it. Customers perceive that dealing with complaints is a low priority for the company.

- They think that the company really does not care about the problem, especially when they hear the phrase "It is company policy."

Increasingly, the task of determining why companies lose clients is made easier because so many organizations collect CRM electronic data pertaining to customers and their buying habits. For example, you can review the customer account history by looking for clues in call reports, replacement orders, and the like. By looking at the pattern of past orders and comparing it with the date of the customer incident, answers might become clear. Whenever possible while implementing a win-back plan, follow up with the most important recovery question, "If we fix that, will you try us again?"

When you are reapproaching any lost customer, your win-back message should include these four points:

1. Acknowledge the customer's past patronage.
2. Point out improvements and changes made since the customer's decision to stop buying.
3. Emphasize the ease with which the customer can re-engage and place another order.
4. Provide a meaningful financial or gift incentive, if possible.

Customer service representatives are a company's frontline of communication, and the quality of their communication greatly affects retention and win-back success with customers. People buy from people, not a company. Upset customers want to be taken seriously. They do not want to hear "You are kidding" or "No way" or "Whatever." They want the CSR to behave professionally and treat them with courtesy and respect.

The secret to successful retention, marketing, and customer fulfillment is to get inside the heads and under the skin of your customers. In other words, think as they think, feel what they feel, and become your own customer. In that mindset, most issues become clear. Always under promise and over deliver. Then, when the product is received and used, ideally it should be better than what the customer expected.

Ethics / *Choices*

In your opinion, is it ever acceptable to stand your ground with a customer and not give in to his or her demands? Explain.

Understand Why Customers Leave

Everyone makes mistakes. Processes and procedures fail from time to time, as illustrated by JetBlue. Customers do not expect companies to be perfect, but they do expect companies to care and make handling customer complaints a priority. Further, they care immensely *why* customers leave.

Today's customers interact with a company using multiple channels, and they often exhibit deeper loyalty than single channel customers. The reason is they expect to get the same consistent service whether visiting a store, logging onto a website, or calling a service center. To gain this loyalty, a firm must internally coordinate sales and service *across* multiple channels so that customer preferences are accessible no matter how the customer chooses to interact. Because of this multi-channel approach, businesses need to know why customers no longer buy from them. In general, four reasons typically surface:

1. *Unhappiness with product delivery, installation, service, or price.* One incident is unlikely to lose a customer, but several incidents of poor service, late delivery, or inaccurate shipment may cause a customer to look elsewhere.

2. *Improper handling of a complaint.* Customers who feel a complaint has not been taken seriously or are displeased with a resolution may search out another competitive product or service—sometimes just for spite.

3. *Disapproval of unanticipated changes.* Whenever companies make changes in the ordering process, price structure, product availability, or sales staff, there is always a risk of offending customers if they were not alerted to these actions in advance.

4. *Feelings of being taken for granted.* New orders and even orders from established customers should not be taken for granted. Every customer should be *resold* on the quality of the business, product, or service in every transaction and thanked for their business each time a purchase is made.

Although customers defect for a number of reasons, Figure 6.5 describes five of the most obvious signs that indicate customers may be thinking about shopping elsewhere.

REMEMBER THIS

Figure 6.5   Indications That a Customer is Defecting

INDICATION	APPROACH RECOMMENDED
1. The squeaky wheel	Companies should track complaints all the way through and make sure that customers emerge from the process happier than when they entered. A customer complaint is a "customer defection alert."
2. The product return	Finding out the reason for returning any product is critical. Is the reason because the product is defective, the customer does not like the product, or it just was not the right size? A string of defective product returns is serious and should be considered a red alert.
3. The quiet customer	Beware of the customers who do not complain because the risk is that they will just leave and never air their grievances. Chances are, however, that they will discuss them with family or friends, other would-be customers.
4. A slow pay	There may be negative issues with your products or services that cause customers to put a company at the bottom of their bill pay list. Find out what those issues are.
5. Falling revenue and reduced sales volume	When customer spending decreases, it is an opportune time to talk to customers. It could be that they have either changed their lifestyle or they have found an alternative product or service. As mentioned in Chapter 4, the business strategy CRM provides an on-track resource to track customer satisfaction.

Figure 6.6   Beneficial Customer Complaints

1. Customer complaints highlight key areas where your product needs improving, your systems need updating or your service needs upgrading.
2. Customer complaints help you identify where your current policies and procedures are inconvenient or unclear or simply not needed.
3. Complaints from customers can point out vital information that is lacking, erroneous or out of date.
4. Customer complaints often elevate important news straight to the top. Leaders and senior management learn quickly about service issues of importance to your customers.
5. Customer complaints give you valuable content and insightful case studies for your service education programs.
6. Sharing customer complaints throughout the organization educates everyone to understand what your customers experience, expect, and insist upon receiving.
7. The things customers complain about may present new business opportunities for increasing revenue.
8. Customer comments and complaints (particularly those along the lines of "company ABC does it this way) can provide you with valuable competitive intelligence, letting you know what others are doing that you are not (yet).
9. When customers complain, you learn which customers are willing to speak up. These customers can (and should) be invited to participate in customer focus groups, surveys, panels, beta-tests, on-site visits and other research activities.
10. Most upset customers simply walk away and then complain about you to their friends, colleagues, acquaintances and family members. Those who complain are giving you another chance!

Ron Kaufman is the author and founder of UP! Your Service. www.UpYourService.com

Benefits Received from Complaints

When things go wrong, customers will exercise their rights and complain. Surprisingly, these complaints can be good for CSRs to hear and beneficial for companies to learn about and act on. On his website, Ron Kaufman details reasons why customer complaints are good news for businesses. These reasons are shown in Figure 6.6.

WHAT DO YOU THINK

6.4

What are two reasons that cause you to stop buying from a store? What could the retailer do to win you back as a customer?

WRAPPING UP

Problem Solving is an effective skill to have on the job as well as to practice in life. Chapter 6 introduced the importance of really listening when customers complain and to always use a systematic approach to handling customer issues and complaints. A service professional's use of conflict management styles and strategies round out the arsenal of tools you can use in solving customer complaints and avoiding the need to implement a win-back plan in the future because customers choose to leave an organization. Unfortunately, that plan is sometimes complicated by extreme customers: quiet customers and vocal customers, the topic of Chapter 7.

FOCUS ON. . .
BEST PRACTICES

First-Call Resolutions

To successfully improve first-call resolutions, companies need to focus on people, process, and product. They also need to determine if they are using the right metrics measurement in call centers to give them the data they need to ensure that first-call resolutions are increased.

In a webcast, Dick Hunter, the former VP of Global Consumer Support Services for Dell, discussed how his company shifted from measuring call time to measuring *how often problems were solved* during the first call. He said: "It's always cheaper to solve a problem in the first call than to try to do it in multiple calls."

The article where Hunter's quote was noted further states that when Dell asked its CSRs to focus on solving customer problems rather than the length of the calls themselves, the average time of a technical support call unsurprisingly increased from 22 minutes to 32 minutes. However, the number of incidents resolved on the first call rose from 44 percent to 65 percent. Although it was some time before this move paid off, it did because total call volume fell. In addition, customer satisfaction scores increased. Instead of cost per call, Dell began measuring cost per resolution.

SOURCES: "Are You Measuring the Right Call Center Metrics?" *IT Business Edge*, September 30, 2009, http://www.itbusinessedge.com/cm/blogs/all/are-you-measuring-the-right-call-center-metrics/;jsessionid=CA5A8982A8FB0507B7792F5E20A9FC5E?cs=36262&decorator=print accessed January 6, 2011.

SUMMARY

- CSRs that are considered especially good problem solvers are methodical, analytical, and have first-rate interpersonal skills.

- A systematic problem-solver uses a five-step method to effectively handle customer complaints. Those steps are: identify the problem, analyze the problem, identify the decision criteria, develop multiple solutions, and choose the optimal solution.

- When used effectively, the following conflict management styles can be a valuable approach to resolving customer complaints: competing, accommodating, avoiding, collaborating, and compromising.

- An effective win-back plan should be in place to recover lost customers because most disenchanted consumers choose to walk rather than complain.

KEY TERMS

accommodating

arbitration

avoiding

Better Business Bureau (BBB)

collaborating

competing

compromising

customer relations policy

first-call resolution (FCR)

lose-lose strategy

mediation

negotiation

ping-ponging

script

win-lose strategy

win-win strategy

CRITICAL THINKING

1. Assume you work in a shoe store and a customer has a complaint about the quality of a pair of shoes she bought last week. What steps would you take in addressing the issue?

2. In your opinion, are the steps necessary to resolve a customer complaint applicable to nearly all service incidents? Explain.

3. Following the four points to include in a win-back message, create a message to a customer of 10 years who wrote to say she would no longer do business with your company because during the past three service encounters, she was treated in a disrespectful manner.

4. Which conflict management styles and strategies are most effective for CSRs to apply in solving customer problems? In your daily interactions, which styles and strategies do you typically use? Why?

WHAT DO YOU THINK NOW?

Project 6.1

Assume you are doing a classroom presentation on *resolving customer complaints*. Reread your responses to the *What Do You Think?* questions that you completed throughout this chapter. What are some service attitudes and practices that promote great resolutions to customer complaints? What service factors advance immediate and careful resolution of customer concerns? Which skills should CSRs have to provide sensitive resolutions to customer complaints? Compile your responses, as directed by your instructor.

ONLINE RESEARCH ACTIVITY

Project 6.2 First-Call Resolution

Assume you are doing a report on the effects of first-call resolution on business profits. As a result of your search on the Internet, list three current items you might use in your report. Include the URLs where you found the information.

COMMUNICATION SKILLS AT WORK

Project 6.3 **CSR Forums—Reacting to Customer Complaints**

A local utility company has recently instituted a roundtable discussion every other Friday at noon, at which CSRs are invited to attend and lunch is provided. The purpose is to allow each CSR to vent and share information about customer issues that might help others react to typical customer complaints. Today, you are discussing the following five CSR reactions.

1. *Apathy:* CSR's attitude of indifference
2. *Passing the buck:* Giving the customer the runaround
3. *Being talked down to:* Treating customers as if they do not understand basic information
4. *Rudeness:* Treating customers in a disrespectful manner
5. *Unresponsiveness:* Not following up on a commitment

Brainstorm with three other students, as directed by your instructor, the severity of each reaction and what a more positive approach might be. Finally, create an appropriate scenario for each reaction and role play a better approach. As an alternative, follow you instructor's directions to join a group and use the instructor-designated discussion board to complete the group project.

DECISION MAKING AT WORK

Project 6.4 **Relocating the Office**

During a recent office relocation, the facilities manager of a local community college consulted with a technical expert on a variety of tools to improve communication among three remote campuses. The tools that the consultant recommended were exactly what were needed, and several of those items were purchased. A few weeks later, the college received a bill from the technical company for time spent consulting on the tools that were purchased. To the community college's buyer, this added cost seemed unfair, since the company received a commission on the items already purchased.

Form groups of four and assume your group is the advisory committee to the facilities manager. As an alternative, follow you instructor's directions to join a group and use the instructor-designated discussion board to complete the group project. With your collective ideas, how might you respond to the following questions?

1. Is there a problem in this scenario? If so, what is it and what caused it?
2. What steps would you recommend the technical company follow to resolve the conflict and preserve the customer relationship?
3. Which conflict resolution styles might be appropriate to use?
4. If directed by your instructor, role play the scenario.

CASE STUDY

Project 6.5   **Resolving Complaints**

Melissa Devlin, the manager of Baby's Little Store, overheard an angry customer yelling at a sales associate. It was obvious that Keanna, her new sales associate, was in a tight spot with a customer.

As the situation revealed itself, this new mother had recently bought a baby mattress for her newborn and was very dissatisfied with the quality of the product after using it only a short time. She felt the mattress was made with unsafe materials and was concerned for her baby's health and safety. When the customer said she wanted her money back, Keanna said nicely, "I will have to check with the store manager to see if we can take back this used mattress for a full refund or not." At that point, the customer lost her temper and said, "What is the issue? Why do you have to check at all?"

1. Evaluate the manner in which Keanna handled the situation. What did she do well in the customer situation and what are some errors she inadvertently made?

_____

_____

_____

2. What suggestions could you make to this problem-solving approach, so that future dilemmas of this type have a more customer-oriented and positive solution?

_____

_____

_____

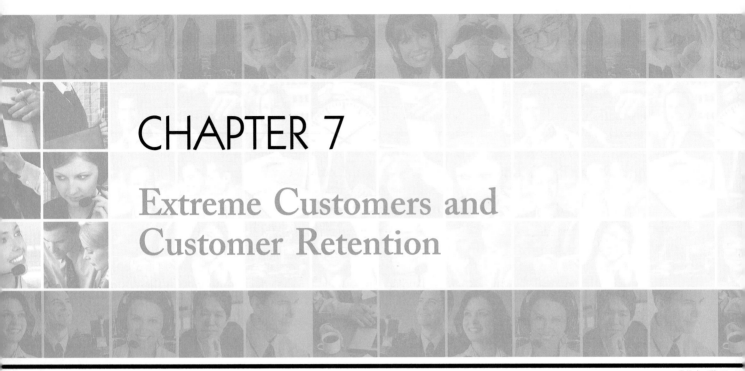

CHAPTER 7

Extreme Customers and Customer Retention

© Kurhan/Shutterstock

Your most unhappy customers are your greatest source of learning.

BILL GATES, CHAIRMAN, MICROSOFT CORPORATION

OBJECTIVES

1. Discuss approaches to use when handling extreme customers, both quiet and vocal.

2. Describe the activities involved in proactive problem solving and customer self-service for extreme customers.

3. Analyze the uses for and types of feedback survey instruments.

4. Identify customer retention strategies and why they are important for quiet and vocal customers.

Hewlett-Packard

Do you dread calling the customer support line to help solve your computer or printer problems? If so, do you then question whether or not you should remain a loyal customer of the company who manufactured the product in the first place? One manufacturer in particular has emerged as a leader in providing exemplary support for their customers. HP® (Hewlett-Packard) has been recognized recently by the Service and Support Professionals Association as a corporation that is committed to service and fully satisfying their customers. HP is aware that disillusioned customers frequently take their computer buying and service needs elsewhere and therefore makes a conscious effort to listen to and learn from their customers.

From an article entitled "Five Tips to Keep Customer Service up When the Economy Is Down," here are two of several strategies that HP uses to retain customers.

1. **Know your customers—and former customers, too**. The article states: "HP's Customer Services Group uses third-party surveys, industry benchmarks and input from customers to get a clear picture of their needs, says Ofelda Gomez, customer innovation and advocacy manager for HP's Personal Systems Group Americas." For example, Gomez says, HP discovered that, when calling for technical support, some of the company's more "tech-savvy customers" considered answering basic questions posed by support personnel to be "a waste of time." Gomez reports that "HP fine-tuned its call-in process so these customers could quickly order the specific part they needed."

2. **Reduce the need for customer service**. The article also observes: "Many times, a few issues generate a large number of requests for customer support. Taking care of these identified issues immediately reduces the need for increased customer support and promotes customer retention." If, for example, the company receives frequent calls about billing issues, it tries to provide ways for customers to find answers to billing questions on their own.

SOURCE: "Five Tips to Keep Customer Service up When the Economy Is Down," http://h71028.www7.hp.com/enterprise/us/en/messaging/feature-ent-customersupport.html accessed March 23, 2011.

EXTREME CUSTOMERS

Everyone has tales of very bad service. Customer service seems so simple—treat customers with dignity and respect, and they will reward you with purchasing your product. Customers indicate that getting a fair resolution during a product or service dispute is a reason for continuing to do business with a company. For example, L.L. Bean built an empire on the simple rule that "no customer should have a product that isn't completely satisfactory." Marshall Field, founder of the Chicago-based department store Marshall Field and Company, said, "Those who come to me with a complaint, teach me. Right or wrong, the customer is always right." Field wasn't saying that the customer is truly *always* right; some customers are very wrong. What Field meant was that, in dealing with complaints, you are dealing with people's perceptions. Although a customer's perception of a problem may be shortsighted or distorted, in his or her eyes it is a legitimate concern.

That challenge is heightened when a CSR has to deal with "extreme customers," that is, either profoundly quiet or vocal customers, whose modes of expressing those perceptions do not resemble those of the average customer. While average customers may get annoyed, they can, in some way, be dealt with fairly easily. When dealing with extreme customers however, CSRs need to apply special skills in order to access and respond to complaints.

Part of the challenge is that, while many CSRs have been annoyed, even angry customers themselves on occasion, they have never been to the silent or vocal extremes peculiar to the customers this chapter will discuss. It is more difficult, therefore, for the CSR to put himself or herself in the customer's shoes, because they have never been to those emotional edges. For that reason, CSRs must approach them and problem solve in a different way. They need specific strategies in dealing with these customers, reaching out to them, and recovering from them.

The Quiet Customer

Should a CSR settle for the old axiom that "no news is good news?" Just because a company isn't hearing complaints, doesn't mean that all of its customers are completely satisfied. While some customers shout, many customers just leave quietly. Silent attrition is deadly, because companies do not have the opportunity to remedy problems and retain customers.

Quiet customers are the ones who don't communicate problems—they let their complaints build up to the point that they think it's easier to simply leave rather than attempt to address the issue. These types of customer complaints are problematic because a company has no tangible suspicion that anything is wrong. According to Andrea Obston, silent customers usually fit into one of these five categories:

1. *The Satisfied Client.* This is what we'd like to assume we have when we don't get complaints—service is fine and customers are happy. There may, however, be fewer people in this category than we think.

2. *The Accumulator.* These customers allow problems to mount up. Then something sets them off and they spout off, listing a string of wrongs that have been building up since their first purchase.

3. *The Thinker.* As Obston describes them, "These customers are the ones who say to themselves, 'They (the business) must know this already so I'm not going to say anything.'"

4. *The Runner.* These customers find conflict so distasteful that they will do anything to avoid it. They would rather run and seek out a new vendor rather than directly communicate their problem.

5. *The Busy Bee.* Obston notes: "These customers use the excuse that pointing out a problem will take up too much of their time and energy. They tell themselves, 'I'm too busy. I'll find the easiest way out.'"[1]

The quiet customer is best characterized as a silent threat because they are dissatisfied customers who don't reach out, and thereby contribute to a picture that everything is fine when in fact it is not. They are at one end of the continuum while the vocal customer is at the other.

The Vocal Customer

Occasionally, every business will encounter a customer who is best described as vocal, angry, even unruly. No matter how carefully you explain your position, this customer will misunderstand and take great offense. Unlike other customers, those who are especially vocal or angry do not respond to reason or goodwill and might become abusive, personal, even threatening. Although these situations are never pleasant, they require self-awareness for the CSR as well as tact and diplomacy. Attempts to understand a customer's emotions and identify what actions and words trigger anger can help a service provider work better under these adverse conditions.

A CSR might encounter these customers online, a forum that might seem to provide escape but

---

[1] Andrea Obston, "Getting Customers to Complain," *Entrepreneur*, October 14, 2004, http://www.entrepreneur.com/sales/customerservice/article72908.html accessed December 29, 2010.

in fact poses a particular challenge. Online customer interactions automatically create a distance between the customer and the CSR because it eliminates the opportunity for any interpersonal, face-to-face exchange. Dealing with an angry customer on the phone or online (chats, e-mails, or online forums) denies you the ability to read nonverbal signals when a customer is upset. It is a big challenge for CSRs to determine customer emotions when they are not interacting face to face. Managing these types of distant interactions will be covered in a later chapter on communication.

Why Customers Get Angry Dale Carnegie said, "The only way to get the best of an argument is to avoid it." Although customers become dissatisfied for a number of various reasons, they generally have one thing in common: The perceived value of a product or service is less than the customer expected. Here are three shortcomings that can cause customers to view products or services negatively:

1. Someone was rude to the customer. Whether the employee realized it or not, this was the customer's perception. Remember that a customer's perception is his or her reality.
2. Someone was indifferent to the customer. An employee projected a "can't-do" attitude and left it at that— with the customer feeling frustrated.
3. No one listened to the customer. This reason is the most troubling. Failing to listen to a customer is a tragic waste of an opportunity for feedback and comes across as insensitive because it hurts a customer's feelings.

Although customers' anger or emotions may not be directed at you personally, you are the one who receives them. To help defuse anger, CSRs must understand why customers get emotional, upset, and angry. While the following five reasons do not constitute a complete list, they are among the most important reasons that explain why angry customers behave the way they do:

1. They have had prior bad experiences.
2. They felt as if they would get the runaround.

3. They resented potential loss of money.
4. They disliked being inconvenienced and having wasted more of their time.
5. They felt a loss of control.

How Customers Get Angry The behaviors of angry customers manifest in various ways. The following are some actions you can expect to see when an angry person lashes out. When customers are angry, they

- blame others,
- can be loud and demanding,
- try to make you angry too,
- have little regard for the rights of others,
- take charge of the conversation by insisting they be heard,
- tend to interrupt the other person,
- refuse to do what you ask,
- threaten to go to your manager or supervisor.

Even the most experienced CSR has dealt with a customer who would only be satisfied by talking to a supervisor. When this occurs, first collect all the information relevant to the problem at hand and present it to the manager. He or she will then have some prior knowledge of the situation and will be able to handle the customer more effectively.

Abusive Behavior If a customer's behavior escalates and is verbally abusive, a suggestion is to move to an office or another enclosure that offers privacy, where the customer can vent without disturbing others. If the customer is particularly problematic, it is advisable to have someone else present as a witness. Once the customer is calm, then decide

CUSTOMER SERVICE TIP

Customer complaints are like medicine. Nobody likes them, but they can make us better.

How can you communicate effectively using empathy and tact with an angry person?

what can be done about the problem. Specialists state: "Keep in mind that in a confrontational interchange, it doesn't hurt to agree a little. When you ease a complainant by saying, 'I understand' or 'What can I do to help?' you are not necessarily agreeing with the customer's position, only with his or her right to be angry."[2]

When working with customers, always focus on determining "how can we?" When a customer is irritated, first discontinue what you are doing and present him or her with your full attention. Actively listen and empathize with the customer, *even if you think he or she is wrong.* It is a natural response to take it personally, but remember: The customer is annoyed about your company's products or services, not with *you.* You can stay in control of your own behavior by staying cool, calm, and collected. Finally, ask as many questions as it takes to understand the full scope of the issue.

When the facts are gathered, tell the consumer what steps you plan to take to solve the problem. Always follow through on your promise to get the problem resolved.

Dealing with Customer Emotions

What CSRs must realize is that an angry customer might not respond to logic. In fact, the more logical

[2] "Resolving Customer Conflicts," *Frontline Learning,* http://www.frontlinelearning .com/Article_Customer_Service_Resolving_Conflicts.html accessed January 14, 2011.

✓ **MAKE IT A HABIT**

Managing Complaints Professionally

You create loyal customers each day when you make every effort to:

- Admit immediately any mistake on your part. It shows you are human and instantly diffuses most emotionally charged situations.
- Look for common ground with the customer. By doing this, you will find solutions that work for all parties involved.
- Stand behind any guarantees and promises you make.
- Handle criticism diplomatically.
- Stress what you *can* do, not what you cannot do.

CUSTOMER SERVICE **TIP**

The best time to deal with a customer's criticism is while the complaint is happening.

you are, the angrier the customer may become. At such times, no matter what you say or how you phrase it, you simply will not be able to penetrate the customer's emotional barrier. Therefore, before you can work on the customer's problem, you must be able to deal with the customer's emotions. To regain the customer's confidence, you need to communicate in a way that renews his or her faith in the relationship. Such communication usually begins with a genuine apology.

Make sure you listen to more than what is being said, because when people are upset, they don't always convey what they mean. Ask questions to gather more information, and use **softening techniques**, which are positive approaches that

REMEMBER THIS

Figure 7.1   Trigger and Calming Phrases

AVOID TRIGGER PHRASES	USE CALMING PHRASES
"It's our policy."	"Here's what we can do ...; Here's how we can handle this ... ." (Quote the policy; don't call it "policy.")
"I can't; we don't"	"I can; we do"
"What seems to be the problem?"	"How can I help?"
"I don't know."	"I can find out."
"You should have. ..."	"Let's do this." (Move to the future, not the past.)
"Why didn't you. ..."	"I can see why. ..."
"The only thing we can do. ..."	"The best option, I think, is. ..."
"I don't handle that; it's not my job."	"Let's find the right person to handle your concern."

help when interacting with customers. Softening techniques include:

- an open posture (no crossed arms),

- kindhearted eye contact (no eye rolling),

- moving the customer to a private area, if needed.

The critical step in calming an angry person is to stay composed yourself. Try to keep your voice relaxed. If you hear your voice sounding rushed or panicked, take a few deep breaths to help you regain your composure. If you notice your jaw clenching, relax your facial muscles. Once *your* emotions are under control, turn your attention to calming the customer. Use calming phrases to describe what you can do for the customer to help solve the problem, and avoid trigger phrases that may further agitate the customer. Examples of trigger and calming phrases are listed in Figure 7.1.

Recovering from the Angry Customer

Most of the time, service mistakes result from situations that are completely out of the control of a CSR. Regardless of whether it is a computer glitch or a mistake that a co-worker has made, it is important to remember that placing blame will not fix a customer's problem. Instead, focus on how you can

help your company to recover from the mistake. Without top-notch service recovery, you will lose customers that were so hard to acquire.

A customer who feels betrayed will be looking for **service recovery**, that is, some gesture of atonement or compensation. To be effective, service recovery should be specific to the situation so it doesn't appear like you are making a concession just to get rid of an angry customer. Typically, when a service failure occurs, a customer can be compensated for the inconvenience in the form of any combination of cash refunds, credits, discounts, or apologies. Two crucial recovery steps that customer service representatives should follow are:

- *Acknowledge the receipt of every complaint immediately.* This shows that you are sufficiently concerned about the problem to contact the customer and that the customer service team is on the job to resolve any issue that concerns customers. Depending how the complaint was presented, either one or a combination of the following actions are appropriate: a verbal acknowledge or a written message (e-mail or letter).

- *Explain in writing exactly how you will remedy the problem.* Tell your customer what will be done to correct the problem and when he or she can expect full resolution.

The Impact of Extreme Customers The following findings from a summary of several studies conducted by Technical Assistance Research Programs, Inc., a company devoted to helping businesses measure and manage the customer experience, should be sobering to any customer service professional. These findings were collected and published by Bruce Temkin, who refers to himself as a *customer experience transformist* and consultant, in his Internet blog.

- About 50 percent of the time, customers who have a problem with a product or service are not likely to tell a company about it.

- Between 50 and 90 percent of these "silent critics" will probably take their future business to a competitor.

- Even when a customer does complain, one out of every two will not be thoroughly satisfied with the company's efforts to solve the problem.

- Dissatisfied customers typically tell eight or more people when they have had an unsatisfactory experience with a company.

- Negative statements have twice the impact as positive information when customers finalize a purchasing decision.

- Word-of-mouth advertising is one of the most important factors influencing a customer's decision to buy from a company.

- It costs between 2 and 20 times as much to win a new customer as it does to retain an existing customer who has a product or service complaint.[3]

WHAT DO YOU THINK

7.1

Have you personally ever complained to a business about its product or service? Was it handled to your satisfaction? Record your recollection of this situation in your journal.

---

[3] Bruce Temkin, "The Hoot Ratings Blog," September 14, 2010, http://hootratings.com/blog/category/statistics/ accessed December 28, 2010.

PROACTIVE PROBLEM SOLVING

If you can put your finger on a customer's problem, you can solve it. Solving problems is one of the primary goals of any customer service professional. When we think of problem solving, however, we generally think of dealing with problems *after* they arise—a sort of crisis-management approach. This is the traditional view of problem solving; however, to exceed customers' expectations and provide exceptional service, successful companies try to anticipate and solve problems *before* they occur. This process is called **proactive problem solving**. To effectively use this process, CSRs are on the lookout for customers who may be dissatisfied. This requires teamwork with and communication among departments and intentionally building a sensitivity to and awareness of both quiet customers and angry customers and how best to serve them.

Customer Self-Service

Being proactive means taking the initiative by *acting* rather than *reacting* to events. When you solve customer problems proactively, you attempt to manage customer expectations and clarify incorrect assumptions the customer may have about the product or service. As you work with your customers, try to anticipate any problems that could arise. For example, at the time of the sale, educate and inform buyers about extra costs and possible delays.

Customer self-service (CSS) is a popular proactive approach in customer service that empowers customers to go to a company's website and initiate most of the queries and functions normally handled by a call center, issues that might include reviewing account transactions, making payments, and investigating various company policies. CSS is not a substitute for person-to-person service options; rather, it offers customers a convenient alternative in response to their demands for responsive and reliable service.

In this way, companies encourage customers to acknowledge and address their own service issues rather than either avoid them or allow them to build to a boiling point. An attractive and informative website that is easy to use and accessible to customers is a critical component of self-service. Used

REMEMBER THIS

Figure 7.2

A Customer-Oriented Website

- **Frequently asked questions (FAQ).** A FAQ page is a place your customer can visit to find answers to the questions most often asked about your products, services, and business. Use FAQs to answer questions about your return or shipping policies or store hours, for example.

- **Your contact information.** Be sure to include either an e-mail address, toll-free telephone number, or mailing address for your business on every page. Make this information effortless to find.

- **A customer feedback form.** Provide an online form that your customers can fill out with specific questions they didn't find in the FAQ. Make sure that you assign a staff member to respond promptly to any queries several times a day.

- **A live chat.** One of chat's great advantages is that reps and customers can literally be on the same page. Customer service chats can give reps the chance to either "push" Web pages (by including links in their chat messages) or actually take over the customer's browser—with his or her permission. Both can be effective ways to give customers targeted information about products and services.

- **An online customer forum.** Online forums provide an environment where customers can quickly respond to each others' questions. The answers customers give each other are often better than answers from company staff. Often, you can learn of problems with your products quickly if you monitor postings.

SOURCE: "How to Provide Customer Service Online" *INC*, http://www.inc.com/guides/cust_self/20909.html accessed December 29, 2010.

properly, a valuable website can act as a resource for customer "self help," because customers like being able to find answers easily that they're looking for, 24/7/365 within a single, accessible source. To ensure user-friendliness, websites should be designed simply and made intuitive for consumers to navigate. Figure 7.2 describes customer service

components that every business should incorporate into their websites, according to an article in *INC* magazine.[4]

One of the most important items self-service systems contain is an accurate and well-written knowledge base. The **knowledge base** is a database created and used by CSRs that contains information on how to resolve common service issues. When a customer submits a question about a service issue, the question goes to a live CSR, who responds to it, subsequently refines the response, and adds it to the computerized knowledge base for the benefit of everyone.

Businesses like self-service because it is a cost-effective way to provide 24/7/365 customer support. Customers similarly like self-service because they can find what they are looking for without delay (call waiting times to speak with an agent, email response lag time). It is an effective win-win proposition for both entities.

WHAT DO YOU THINK

7.2

When you access a company website, which website features do you find helpful and use the most? List those features in your journal.

MEASURING CUSTOMER SATISFACTION

From cost control and customer retention to employee productivity and competitive intelligence, every business has its own unique set of objectives. One thing remains consistent—gaining insight into a customer's needs and expectations is paramount to reaching those objectives. With customer acquisition

---

[4] "How Can We Increase Customer Retention While Reducing Service Costs?", http://www.destinationcrm.com/Articles/Older-Articles/Experts-on-Call/How-Can-We-Increase-Customer-Retention-While-Reducing-Service-Costs-44326.aspx accessed January 20, 2011.

costs high and getting higher, customer defection is a serious burden to a company's bottom line. Measuring customer satisfaction is a useful proactive approach for all customers—especially the quiet and angry ones. **Customer satisfaction** is the mental state that customers have about a company and its products or services when their expectations have been met or exceeded. Most of the time, customer satisfaction leads to customer loyalty and product repurchase.

Many companies believe that, after years of working closely with customers, they know what their customers want. Not until some of these companies face a customer service obstacle do they think about spending the necessary money to solicit customer feedback or to hire someone to monitor customer comments, complaints, and compliments from social media websites. This is a tragic "too little, too late" approach to customer service.

Customer feedback—formal and informal, solicited or voluntary—is one of the major forces in developing quality standards that helps prevent customer dissatisfaction and possible defection. The resulting data from surveys should serve as a compass to guide the development of products and customization of service offerings to meet identified customer issues and needs.

One type of survey strategy employed by confident companies is an internal survey. A customer-oriented internal survey is conducted as a way of "walking in the customer's shoes." Managers and staff complete the same questionnaire as the clientele and answer the questions the way they *predict* customers will answer them. Customers are asked how they would rate the company's performance rather than how satisfied they are with the company.

Survey strategists then measure the gaps and share the results with managers and staff.

Feedback Sources

There are few activities as important as finding out what your customers want for products and what they think of your service performance and current offerings. Fortunately, businesses can use a variety of practical and available resources to get customer feedback.

- *Employees* An organization's frontline employees are those who interact the most with customers. On a regular basis, ask employees and CSRs about products and services that customers are asking for and what issues they complain about the most.

- *Social media feedback* Social media has become a customer-driven feedback platform that is easily accessible to anyone with Internet access. Media websites, such as Facebook, Twitter, and online customer forums, open doors for organizations to increase their brand awareness and facilitate conversations that take account of concerns, complaints, compliments, and suggestions between and among their customers.

- *Comment cards* One of the best ways to find out what customers want is to ask them. Provide brief comment cards on which customers can answer simple questions such as "Were you satisfied with our services?" and "Are there any services you would like to see that don't exist?"

What are some advantages to customers when they provide service feedback to a business?

- *Competition* Ask people who shop at your competitors the simple question, "What is the competition offering that we could offer to serve your needs better?"

- *Documentation and records* Using inventory records and sales receipts, companies can take note of what customers are buying and not buying. If the data are captured on software (CRM, spreadsheet, database), they can be charted and studied to determine buying trends.

- *Mail surveys* Many people are willing to fill out and return feedback forms, especially if they get something of value in return. For example, offer survey respondents a coupon if they complete the survey form (online or via mail) by a certain date.

- *Telephone surveys* Hire summer students or part-time workers for a few days every few months or so to conduct random telephone surveys.

The Mystery Shopper

Although many companies spend significant amounts of money on training their employees, few businesses reinforce the training with a monitoring program. One way that companies can improve the level of customer service is through mystery-shopping programs. A **mystery shopper** is a third-party person who anonymously and objectively evaluates a business for the purpose of analyzing customer service, product quality, store presentation, and other elements of the overall customer experience. Known as "undercover customers," these shoppers visit every type of business

Why are more retail businesses using mystery shoppers?

from restaurants to retail stores, movie theatres, hair salons, banks, and hotels.

Companies use mystery-shopping services for an assortment of reasons. Some managers believe it is a way to resolve potential problem situations *before* they reach higher-level executives. Other companies establish corporate monitoring programs to observe routine operations that ensure consistency. In still other instances, absentee owners monitor the actions of staff members who play an integral part in the success or failure of the business.

These evaluators follow specific instructions during their visits, complete written reports after leaving the store, and work with management to identify the strengths and weaknesses of the business. Usually, the mystery shopper prepares a final onsite visit report that outlines his or her shopping experience.

Mystery shoppers look at the overall task as though through the eyes of the business owner. They perform a variety of activities such as unannounced onsite visits to verify the proper handling of transactions and merchandise. They make random phone calls to a business to report how inquiries are handled, along with evaluations of websites, chats, and e-mail responses. Mystery shoppers are commonly asked to shop a client's competitor so the client can compare its operation to others.

The use of mystery shoppers provides managers and employees with an unbiased evaluation of their operation's quality, service, cleanliness, and value. The general goal of using a mystery shopper is to help in improving productivity, efficiency, and profitability for the company. Specifically, however, smart businesses use the information to reward good employees, identify training deficiencies, and make store improvements in an effort to retain loyal customers.

Feedback Tools

Companies solicit customer opinions through a variety of ways—Web-based surveys, social media websites, mailed surveys, telephone interviews, comment cards, focus groups, and feedback forms enclosed with finished jobs. The obvious goal of most customer feedback is to evaluate how happy customers are with service, product quality, delivery, and overall experience.

Company-developed satisfaction measurement questions typically include items like these:

1. Overall, how satisfied are you with (brand name)?
2. Would you recommend (brand name)?
3. Do you intend to repurchase (brand name)?[5]

People who create survey instruments struggle with the issue of how to measure service quality. Perhaps the most widely used set of measurements is based on five dimensions that are most important regardless of the service industry. These dimensions are as follows:

1. Physical appearance: the attractiveness of physical facilities, website, personnel, and communication materials.
2. Reliability: the ability to perform the promised service dependably and accurately.
3. Responsiveness: the willingness to assist customers and provide prompt efficient service.
4. Assurance: the knowledge and courtesy of employees and their ability to convey trust and confidence.
5. Empathy: the caring, individualized attention a business provides its customers.

The benefits of developing a meaningful survey and using an "ask the customer" approach are to

- *Identify unhappy customers.* The information gathered could signal customer relationships that are in jeopardy. This is important because, unfortunately, most dissatisfied clients ultimately walk away and either never tell companies why, or, in some cases, do so after unpleasant confrontations.

- *Pinpoint the products and services that customers want and need.* Surveying customers is a great way to identify new business opportunities and to assess what customers *think* you offer. In many cases, customers may not be fully aware of all the products and services you offer.

- *Solidify customer relationships.* The act of asking customers their opinions shows that they matter. For example, customers may love your product but be annoyed by minor incidents such as how they are treated by the receptionist or the way a finished product is packaged. Companies may not be aware of these issues; but once brought to the surface they can be addressed and corrected.

When developing customer-satisfaction feedback tools, consider measuring the right issues from the numerous customer-satisfaction attributes listed in Figure 7.3. Remember to refrain from using the word "survey." Few people want to participate in a *survey*; however, many are willing to give *feedback*.

A company-initiated customer response system should include comment cards, post-episodic surveys, and other methods described below.

REMEMBER THIS

Figure 7.3

Measuring Customer Satisfaction

- Ability to meet deadlines and on-time delivery
- Accurate invoice amounts
- Clear and helpful quotes, estimates, and proposals
- Communication of changes in delivery or back-order situations
- Follow-through on commitments
- Overall value, quality, and range of products and services
- Presence of competent employees and helpful CSRs before and after the sale
- Price
- Problem-resolution approach
- Prompt shipments that match orders and specifications

[5] "Customer Surveys," *Pure Survey,* http://www.survey.co.za/customer.asp accessed January 10, 2011.

Comment Cards Hand the card to customers at the closing stage of the transaction. Ask customers to please provide their thoughts, as your company always wants to know how well customer needs are met.

Post-episodic Surveys A **post-episodic survey** gathers information from customers after they have completed a business transaction, such as opening a new account or getting a car serviced at a dealership. Essentially, this is a satisfaction survey dealing with just one service episode. Brief surveys are usually conducted by phone within 24 to 48 hours of the transaction.

Other Methods Electronic surveys, in-store shopper surveys, post CSR call questionnaires, and on-site interviews can also be effective. In addition, create a forum for CSRs to provide anecdotal, subjective feedback from customers about a product's features, functionality, and pricing.

Interpreting Customer Feedback

When customers stop buying from a business, it is important to ask why. Certain responses to this question can help you deal effectively with these likely issues:

- The quality of merchandise
- The quality of service
- An employee's lack of courtesy
- A mishandled complaint
- An invoice or billing problem

These concerns are problematic and compel companies to take action immediately. Further, when customers expand their responses by saying that they informed the company about the problem *before* they stopped purchasing, immediate action is even more important.

Following are four additional issues companies must be aware of prior to interpreting and acting on customer feedback:

1. *Use thorough data-gathering and analysis techniques before acting on complaints.* Often, a company will make a change based on feedback

from only one or two customers. That type of limited feedback is called anecdotal information and does not necessarily represent a trend.

2. *Do not spend a lot of time, energy, and money gathering complaint data and then do nothing with it.* This is perhaps the biggest error organizations can make when handling customer feedback. Use the information to improve the areas that showed customer concern.

3. *Do not take feedback results personally.* The fact is, surveys *invite* customers to criticize. Customers who complain the most and the loudest are really your best customers.

4. *Inform customers about the impact their feedback has had on the way issues will be addressed.* Clients who provide feedback appreciate the same in return. When companies that gather customer data research fail to provide this feedback, they lose credibility with consumers.

Many service-oriented businesses use customer feedback in a different way. In these companies, the object is to uncover everything that is going right. Managers are always on the lookout for "hero stories"—examples of employees going the extra mile to deliver delight and *wow* experiences. Such feedback becomes the basis for ongoing recognition and celebration. Employees see themselves as winners because someone is always being recognized as a result of customer feedback.

Benefits to the Customer

Satisfaction, like quality, is in the eye of the beholder, so the best way to measure customer service satisfaction is to ask your customers. When customers tell you explicitly what you are doing right or wrong, and then follow up with suggestions as to how you can

Ethics / Choices

What would you say to a colleague who wanted to put up in your department a cartoon customers could see that says, "The Complaint Department is in the basement"? Why might this quip be offensive to customers?

improve critical areas of your business, the information is precise and useful. This process benefits everyone—customers, CSRs, and the organization.

Customer feedback can help companies increase service quality, innovation, and most important, customer retention. As noted in a recent online article, surveys should meet the following criteria:

- To find and act on the issues which lead to innovation, employee or customer turnover, or other key operational outcomes.

- To motivate, guide change efforts, and identify the most promising opportunities for improvement.

- To record a baseline from which progress can be measured.

- To create a consensus on priorities or issues to be dealt with.

- To provide a two-way communication with employees or customers.[6]

It is true that you cannot change what you do not measure, understand, hear, and acknowledge. Customer-focused measurements are needed because they explain reasons for lost sales, retention problems, time-consuming and costly complaints, and cost redundancies. Without measurable performance standards, employees are left to guess what good service is. When that happens, customers become disappointed. The following are some common-sense examples of measurable customer service practices that good companies implement:

- Answer telephones by the third ring.

- Serve hot food at a temperature of at least 140 degrees.

- Smile and greet all guests within 10 feet of you.

- Respond to each shopper, so that he or she does not stand in line more than two minutes.

- Offer bellman or concierge service to every hotel guest.

[6] "Employee Surveys, Interviews, and other Data Tools," *Toolpack*, http://www.toolpack.com/surveys.html accessed January 11, 2011.

WHAT DO YOU THINK

7.3

What methods do you prefer using to give companies feedback on service and products? Record these in your journal.

- Speak professionally to clients and avoid the use of slang expressions.

CUSTOMER RETENTION

Why would a company want to turn an angry customer into a loyal supporter? Is it worth the time and general hassle to deal with intense complainers like these customers? One very significant reason is because if you satisfy that extreme customer completely, then he or she may well become your best ally and willingly refer others your way. You have indeed gone that extra mile customers seek.

Customer retention refers to a strategy with the purpose of doing whatever it takes (legally and within reason) to keep a company's current customers on a long-term basis. As noted earlier in this chapter, HP has done an astonishing job at growing its business and keeping customers via smart retention strategies. To be sure, it warrants more than "the customer is always right" rhetoric to satisfy today's savvy customers. Customers are not always right, but they always have feelings—sometimes intense, other times barely perceptible—when they make purchases or engage in business transactions.

Especially in a struggling economy, the enduring value of existing customers is considerable for any organization. When a company loses a customer, it does not lose one sale but a lifetime opportunity of profitability with that individual. The question becomes, "What could that customer have been worth?" To determine the average lifetime value of customers, first estimate how much they will spend with your company on an annual basis and multiply it by the number of years they could potentially use your products and services. For

REMEMBER THIS

Figure 7.4 Customer Retention Strategies

Sell and then sell again	So many businesses do an excellent job of making the initial sale, then drop the ball and get complacent and ignore the customer. On each service encounter, thank customers and remind them again why they've made the right decision to do business with you.
Bring back the "lost sheep"	Reactivating customers who already know you and your product is one of the easiest, quickest ways to increase your revenues. Finding out why they're no longer buying, overcoming their objections, and demonstrating that you still value and respect them will lead to loyal customers.
Frequent Communications Calendar	Use a programmed sequence of communication, such as letters, events, phone calls, thank-you notes, special offers, and cards or notes with a personal touch. This should occur automatically at defined points in the pre-sale, sale, and post-sale process. Communication such as this acknowledges customers and keeps them informed so they want to come back again and again.
Product or service integrity	Long-term success and customer retention belongs to those who do not take ethical shortcuts. Customers will be attracted to you if you are open and honest with them, care for them, take a genuine interest in them, don't let them down, and practice what you preach.

SOURCE: http://marketingwizdom.com/strategies/retention-strategies accessed December 29, 2010.

instance, if an average customer spends $100 a month, 12 months a year, for 10 years, their average lifetime value is $12,000. Now add on the value of all the new customers that your loyal customer will refer to your company. It is easy to see how increasing customer retention and loyalty translates into huge increases in profitability and long life to any company.

Though there are many types of customer retention strategies currently used in business,

Marketing Wizdom's website affirms that the easiest way to grow your customers is not to lose them in the first place. Additional retention strategies they suggest are described in Figure 7.4.

WRAPPING UP

When companies make a serious attempt to resolve conflict as part of their overall commitment to promote customer retention and satisfaction, they make forward-thinking efforts to stay in business and keep customers loyal. Doing this well requires service professionals to listen attentively and adapt service processes to the concerns and needs of extreme customers, that is, profoundly quiet and vocal customers. These efforts also require that CSRs implement deliberate customer retention strategies and continue to measure customer satisfaction through surveys and other feedback mechanisms. These skills require creative training, monitoring, and affirmation, all topics found in Chapter 8: Managing Customer Service.

WHAT DO YOU THINK

7.4

Is there a company that has seriously pursued you to be a long-term customer? As a result, do you buy more products from them and are you loyal to them? Record your experiences in your journal.

FOCUS ON. . .
BEST PRACTICES

USAA

In the insurance industry, few companies are highly regarded by their customers. That is why it is an honor for one company to be singled out as valued and respected by its customers as one that encourages near perfect customer retention. According to an article in *Business Week*, USAA, a private company with $68.3 billion in assets, has unrivaled staying power with its customer base with a client retention rate of 97.8 percent!

Based on a recent Forrester Research customer advocacy rankings survey of more than 4,500 consumers, USAA topped the rankings. In other words, the perception on the part of consumers is that this financial services firm does what is best for its customers, not just the firm's own bottom line.

Forrester Research Vice President and Principal Analyst Bill Doyle commented, "Each year, our data shows that customers who rate their firms high on customer advocacy are more likely to consider their firms for additional products. Customers who rate their firms low on customer advocacy are most likely to say they intend to switch firms in the next year." USAA is a company that has sincerely made retaining its customer base a cornerstone of its success.

SOURCES: http://www.forrester.com/ER/Press/Release/0,1769,1322,00.html and http://www.businessweek.com/magazine/content/10_09/b4168040782858.htm accessed January 20, 2011.

SUMMARY

- CSRs need special skills to deal with extreme customers, customers who are profoundly silent or vocal.

- Proactive problem solving means anticipating and solving problems before they occur.

- Understanding and recognizing customer emotions as well as handling their complaints fairly can help bring the conflict to a satisfactory resolution for both sides.

- The goal of most customer feedback is to evaluate customer satisfaction with service, product quality, delivery, and overall experience.

- Customer retention strategies are intended to keep a company's current customers buying from them on a long-term basis.

KEY TERMS

customer retention

customer satisfaction

customer self-service (CSS)

knowledge base

mystery shopper

post-episodic survey

proactive problem solving

service recovery

softening techniques

CRITICAL THINKING

1. Think of a time when you or someone you know walked away from a business rather than staying to complain about its service or products. Explain why the situation was handled this way.

2. In what ways is it more productive for CSRs to use proactive problem solving when dealing with customers?

3. Think of a time when you observed an angry customer at a grocery store, retail outlet, or bank. Describe the behaviors of the person you observed. How, in your opinion, could this anger have been avoided? Once it occurred, how should it have been handed by a service professional?

4. What companies do you buy from that, like USAA, make it a practice to retain customers? What actions do these companies take to retain you as a loyal customer?

5. If you were designing the best feedback survey for the following businesses, which type would you create and why? For a car repair shop? For a four-star hotel? For a hair and nail salon?

WHAT DO YOU THINK NOW?

Project 7.1

Assume you are doing a classroom presentation on *customer retention strategies*. Reread your responses to the *What Do You Think?* questions that you completed throughout this chapter. What are some service attitudes and practices that promote retaining customers? What service issues must be carefully addressed by CSRs to retain customers over a long period of time? Which skills should CSRs demonstrate that keep customers returning for more products? Compile your responses, as directed by your instructor.

ONLINE RESEARCH ACTIVITY

Project 7.2   Customer Service Survey

Create a 10- to 15-question customer service feedback survey for an industry or a company of your choice. Research several websites and locate sample customer service survey questions you might use as guides in completing this assignment.

COMMUNICATION SKILLS AT WORK

Project 7.3 **Handling Emotions**

Form a group of 3-4 people and pool your ideas to respond to the following four emotionally charged situations. Describe how your group might handle each situation and why each approach is the right one to take. Role play each situation in a professional manner. As an alternative, follow your instructor's directions to join a group and use the instructor-designated discussion board to complete the group project.

1. A customer throws a product on the counter and says, "I want my money back now!"
2. A customer attacks your personal integrity and you can feel your anger ready to erupt.
3. A customer says, "I'll never do business with you again!"
4. A customer says, "You have done this completely wrong. You are incompetent. I want to see your supervisor immediately so I can have you fired."

DECISION MAKING AT WORK

Project 7.4 **CSR Reaction to Customer Complaints**

Cliff, a fellow CSR, is noticeably upset at work this morning. Yesterday, work was incredibly difficult for him because it seemed he had to deal with *the worst of the worst* customer complaints. Today, Cliff has confided in you that, after talking with his wife last night, he is thinking about quitting. According to Cliff, he doesn't think "employees should be expected to take whatever the customer doles out." You are aware that Cliff has other things going on in his life—most notably, his aging mother has recently moved in with Cliff and his family.

1. If you were having a private conversation with Cliff, what would you say to try and calm him down so that he can approach the situation rationally?
2. What do you think is really behind Cliff's desire to quit his job?

CASE STUDY

Project 7.5 **"If There's a Rule, I'll Follow It"**

Carson, a utility company CSR, recently experienced a very frustrating civil brush with the law concerning boundary lines between his and a neighbor's property. As a consequence of this negative legal experience, everyone at work recognizes that Carson is a bit strict when it comes to following rules. However, the situation is beginning to affect his work because his narrow-minded attitude is antagonizing customers.

1. In what ways do situations in someone's personal life spill over and affect service attitudes and behavior on the job? Describe some examples you've experienced.
2. If you were Carson's supervisor, how would you explain to him the best way to interpret which rules he is required to follow to the letter and which ones allow him some flexibility? What steps would you take to help Carson overcome this attitude and get back on track with customers (i.e., simply talk to him, reprimand him, enroll him in training, or…)?

CHAPTER 8
Managing Customer Service

You can't expect your employees to exceed the expectations of your customers if you don't exceed the employees' expectations of management.

HOWARD SCHULTZ, CHAIRMAN, STARBUCKS COFFEE

OBJECTIVES

1. Explain the role of management in setting customer service standards.

2. Describe the working environment and basic duties for most customer service representative positions.

3. Identify reasons companies should train, empower, and reward service professionals.

4. Discuss the qualities that a successful customer service manager should possess.

Enterprise Holdings

Chances are, the last time you rented a car from Enterprise Rent-A-Car, Alamo Rent A Car, or National Car Rentals, the service representative you dealt with was one of 68,000 people employed by Enterprise Holdings. Management teams usually don't bond easily with such a hefty workforce unless top management has intentionally created a special culture. The culture at Enterprise Holdings is illustrated in a statement made by Chairman and Chief Executive Officer Andrew C. Taylor: "Like many other companies, we have fought through difficult economic conditions during the past several years. But thanks to our disciplined management and consistent focus on customer service and costs, we delivered strong results in fiscal 2010."

Taylor further affirmed his organization's commitment to empowerment by describing his employees in this way: "They deliver on our value proposition and work to exceed expectations every day, regardless of whether customers are renting for an hour, a day, a week, or longer. And if things go wrong, our employees are empowered to make it right."

SOURCE: http://www.marketwire.com/press-release/Enterprise-Holdings-Announces-Fiscal-2010-Highlights-1328012.htm, accessed February 14, 2011.

SETTING SERVICE STANDARDS

Thriving companies are made, not born. Setting standards, or benchmarks, in customer service doesn't just happen; they are painstakingly conceived and delivered with care. As noted in Chapter 4, **standards** tell workers what is expected of them, in both the quality and quantity of their work. When organizations have a baseline of service performance standards, they deliver, regardless of *who* the customer is or *how much* he or she spends. Chapter 4 examined how customer service standards need to inform a company's specific strategy for measuring its resources and analyzing its customer base. Standards also need to be the basis for selecting, training, evaluating, rewarding, and retaining CSRs, the key personnel who will reach out to and, hopefully, retain that customer base.

Although every customer service operation is unique, all customer service centers need to measure the same key areas to gauge how well they are doing and to assess the specific areas they can improve

upon. Figure 8.1 explains how companies measure and calculate certain performance standards.

Effective customer service standards reflect an understanding of what customers need, want, and are willing to pay for, as well as what the competition is offering. The best way to evaluate and write standards is by looking at service situations from the customer's point of view. To have meaning, standards must be stated in numbers and be measurable. Words such as *excellent* and *superior* are good motivators, but they need to be translated into specifics of performance. Here are some examples of measurable standards in customer service:

- Ninety-eight percent of online customer inquiries will be answered live within five minutes of their receipt.

- Credits on product returns will be posted to customer accounts within 24 hours of receipt.

- Eighty percent of customer complaints involving $500 or less will achieve first-call resolution status.

REMEMBER THIS

Figure 8.1   Calculating Performance Standards

PERFORMANCE MEASUREMENT	CALCULATION OF STANDARDS
Operations management	Determined by calculating service statistics • Cost per call or cost per minute • Earnings per representative
Service level	Determined by • How well *x* percent of calls are answered in *y* seconds • The percent of calls abandoned
CSR quality and productivity	Determined by • Quality—measured when monitoring calls and checking data accuracy • Productivity—measured by tracking calls per hour and amount of dollars received per sale
Employee satisfaction	Determined by calculating • Employee retention rate • Employee survey results
Customer satisfaction	Determined by calculating • Customer survey results • First-contact resolution rates • Customer retention rates

In flourishing companies with established service standards, the employees appear to be a cut above others because they are courteous and always seem to be smiling. In addition, service professionals in these companies never fail to ask whether they can be of assistance and always seem to be having a great deal of fun doing their jobs. These employees achieve a higher level of productivity for their employers. Were their employers just fortunate to have many happy and enthusiastic people apply for the jobs? Assuming that is not the case, how did it happen?

A customer-oriented business culture starts at the top and is consistently reinforced throughout *all* levels of management. Good managers are responsible for hiring employees with great attitudes and for making decisions that make the best use of human and other key organizational resources.

These managers must work very hard to create a workplace environment where service employees are satisfied. By the same token, to arrive at this core group of enthusiastic employees, companies have hired and fired numerous employees who did not meet their expectations.

Ethics / Choices

Suppose you work with someone who boasts taking 100 customer calls per day when the standard among CSRs on most days is 75. In your opinion, how does quantity of calls taken measure against quality results? Further, what effect does quantity have on repeat customer business?

UNDERSTANDING THE CSR POSITION

HELP WANTED. Individual of high intelligence and personal charm, capable of working under extreme pressure with frequent interruptions, resourceful and flexible, cheerful and even-tempered. The individual selected for this position must be completely trustworthy, as he or she will be entrusted with millions of dollars of the company's business, and must be able to represent customers' best interests with the company while remaining completely loyal to the company. Must be a self-starter with high initiative and an excellent team player. Equal opportunity employer, M/F. Apply Box 3845, Anytown, U.S.A.

As this fictitious, but only slightly exaggerated, classified ad suggests, most companies, as illustrated by Enterprise Holdings, expect a great deal from their frontline service professionals. However, besides the usual benefits packages, many companies don't always give a great deal in return. Formal training is often sketchy, and the general company-wide view of CSRs as clerical workers is compounded by an opinion that they are also troublemakers.

The reason for this perception is that CSRs show up in other departments only when there is a customer service problem that cannot be handled. Mix these elements with the typical pressures of the customer service environment, and it is not hard to understand that problems of morale, stress, burnout, and turnover are common to the customer

service function in businesses. The following sections examine current job information from the *2010-11 Occupational Outlook Handbook (OOH)* about a CSR's working environment, education, certifications and advancement.

Working Environment

CSRs perform a variety of duties that require them to communicate effectively and to work under limited direct supervision, but in cooperation with others. Typically, they work inside offices or cubicles between 35 and 40 hours per week, with occasional overtime, night, and weekend hours. Often, they work under stress from angry or upset customers.

The *OOH 2010-11* notes that, while some CSRs deal with customers face-to-face, others deal with customers exclusively over the phone in call centers, an environment that it describes in this way: "Those who work in call centers generally have their own workstations or cubicle spaces equipped with telephones, headsets, and computers.... Call centers may be crowded and noisy, and work may be repetitive and stressful, with little time between calls. Also, long periods spent sitting, typing, or looking at a computer screen may cause eye and muscle strain, backaches, headaches, and repetitive motion injuries."[1]

The physical job requirements call for CSRs to sit for long periods while using their arms, hands, and fingers. They need to speak, hear, and see well to communicate service information to global customers and produce written correspondence, chats, and e-mail messages.

Education, Certification, and Advancement

How much education is desirable for CSRs? *OOH 2010-2011* points out that "most customer service representative jobs require a high school diploma. However, because employers are demanding a more skilled workforce, some customer service jobs now require associate or bachelor's degrees.

[1] Customer Service Representatives, *Occupational Outlook Handbook, 2010-11 Edition* http://www.bls.gov/oco/ocos280.htm accessed January 27, 2011.

Digital Vision/Getty Images

How can you tell upon meeting and interviewing a person if he or she will be a good CSR?

High school and college level courses in computers, English, or business are helpful in preparing for a job in customer service."[2]

In addition to a formal education, earning a nationally recognized certificate is becoming the mark of professionals in many career fields. **Certification** is an effective way for a CSR to demonstrate commitment to professional development. The National Professional Certification in Customer Service, offered by the National Retail Federation (NRF) Foundation, is a credential that is recognized and valued by the customer service industry. Candidates achieve certification by successfully completing a seventy-five question, online assessment. The candidate may take the assessment either at test sites located around the United States, or a company may arrange for the assessment to be administered provided that there is a proctor trained by the NRF Foundation. Candidates may prepare through courses, handbooks, and other materials provided by NRF.[3]

Questions are based upon skill standards developed by the NRF. These standards define both work-oriented skills and worker-oriented skills. Work-oriented skills are grouped under categories such as Learns About Products and Services, Occupational and Technical Knowledge, Assesses Customers' Needs, and Meets Customers' Needs and Provides Ongoing Support. Worker-oriented skills include Reading, Writing, Speaking, Mathematics, Gathering and Analyzing Information, Making Decisions and Judgments, and many more. Some questions are posed using an audio recording, some through a video recording, and some have more than one correct answer. The candidate must determine the best answer for the problem presented.[4]

The test is administered under strict conduct regulations, and any candidate who does not adhere to those regulations will be ejected from the assessment. Successful completion of the assessment results in certification that is effective for a three-year period. NRF requires that even the successful candidate must remain "in good standing" with their employer, school, or training program. Failure to do so may result in revocation of certification. NRF points out that a candidate who does well on the exam may not necessarily do well as a CSR. However, the test does demonstrate that the candidate who has passed possesses the knowledge and skills deemed by the industry as necessary for the performance of superior customer service.[5]

Promotion opportunities for CSRs tend to be limited, however, this entry-level job is definitely enhanced with a nationally recognized certificate. It is also a good occupation that affords the opportunity to learn solid business skills and often leads to administrative, sales, and other related positions within organizations.

[2] Ibid.

[3] http://www.nrffoundation.com/Training_Certification/Cert_Cust_Service.asp accessed February 17, 2011.

[4] *Certification Handbook*, NRF Foundation, 2008, pp. 16–20. http://www.nrffoundation.com/Training_Certification/Cert_Cust_Service.asp accessed February 18, 2011.

[5] *Certification Handbook*, NRF Foundation, 2008, pp. 10–12. http://www.nrffoundation.com/Training_Certification/Cert_Cust_Service.asp accessed February 18, 2011.

☑ MAKE IT **A HABIT**

Stay Job Current

To be situation-ready and flexible at a moment's notice, make it a practice to:

- understand and adapt quickly to technology upgrades and new products,
- think on your feet in situations that introduce perceived customer emergencies,
- work on your own professional development to keep skills current—especially in using technology and cutting-edge communication devices.

WHAT DO YOU **THINK**

8.2

As a service professional, have you ever participated in any kind of training program? What did you find the most useful about the experience? What did you find the least useful? Record and explain your reactions in your journal.

RETAINING SERVICE PROFESSIONALS

Employees working in customer service areas should be recognized and rewarded for their everyday efforts. Although they are often at the bottom of a company's pay scale, CSRs' contributions to an organization's overall profits are invaluable. Customer service employees know they are valued and appreciated when companies train, empower, and reward them.

Training CSRs

Training begins with the way in which an employer screens job applicants. With today's new generation of workers and exciting new attitudes about the role of customer service, training is taking on greater importance.

Companies that say they can't afford the time or money to give their CSRs regular training sessions end up paying far more than they would have paid for the training itself. When companies make the investment to train their service employees beyond the initial training session, they show that they value them and their work. Usually the initial training session provides an overview of the company and its products, the computer and phone systems in use, and how to respond to typical service questions from customers.

Employees who are not trained to provide good customer service unfortunately find themselves frustrated in their attempts to deal with rude, difficult, and irate customers. If, however, they are trained in ways to defuse complicated situations, there is a much greater chance that good workers will stay, because they are better prepared to handle the job.

Training Curriculum What should a curriculum that teaches good customer service skills look like? In essence, it should emphasize developing phone and interpersonal communication skills that respond effectively to customers and foster a teambuilding environment within the workplace. The curriculum should also include training on the latest customer care technologies, such as live interactive chats, intelligent e-mail response systems, telephone services, and robust self-service search engines. Finally, a critical training goal is to make sure CSRs are knowledgeable about the company's products. When employees are unable to answer a customer's question about a product or service, credibility suffers and this can result in lost sales.

Training Methods People learn at different rates and through a variety of means, including classroom instruction, computerized skills assessment tutorials, on-the-job training, coaching, role–playing, and other instructional methods. The secret to effective learning is to match the delivery to the learner's receptive style, provide enough hands-on training to reinforce the concepts and, if needed, test to *real business* situations. For example, classroom training emphasizes facts that need learning, such as corporate policies and processes. **Coaching**, on the other hand, emphasizes practice, the critical *learn by doing*, that turns information into knowledge and then into practiced experience.

Role-playing, in which participants improvise realistic customer scenarios, is one of the most effective methods for training CSRs. It helps them learn how to interact with customers and make sales. By acting out situations, employees learn how to eliminate on-the-job shyness, prevent intimidation, extract personal information from shoppers, handle irate customers, overcome objections, and share product knowledge. Good topics for role-playing include awkward customer scenarios and handling difficult customers.

Rehearsing in this way helps employees eliminate verbal fillers, those awkward "ums" and "you knows" that can creep into our speech when we are uncertain about what to say. However, role-playing is not the easiest type of training. Some employees are reluctant to participate because the thought of *acting* in front of an audience—even a tiny group—makes them nervous. To be effective, the training technique requires a safe learning environment, a sensitive facilitator, and dedicated time. The benefits gained from role-playing, however, are worth the time and effort, because they boost employee confidence and overall performance.

How comfortable are you in using role-play to learn customer service approaches?

Ethics/*Choices*

Suppose you overheard a co-worker say, "If you need several layers of management to sign off on most customer-related decisions, what's the point of having a customer service center where CSRs are supposedly empowered?" What is your reaction to this statement? Do you agree? Explain your position.

Empowering CSRs

Empowerment is an enormous employee motivational tool that can give a business the competitive edge it needs to survive. As discussed in Chapter 3, empowering employees gives them the authority to provide exceptional customer service. That means bending—sometimes breaking—the rules to achieve customer satisfaction.

Without empowered employees, it is difficult for service to reach the customer level. With little or no service, customers are not likely to return to a business. Management should give CSRs the authority to handle customer complaints and concerns on the spot and allow them to use that authority without fear of repercussion.

When managers do not empower or delegate responsibility for getting the job done, employees tend to react in some fairly predictable ways:

- Often, they become apathetic, developing a "so what?" attitude. Energy declines and productivity slows down.

- When people are unable to exercise their talents, those talents waste away. Without challenges, no new talents are acquired to move the organization forward.

- Employees who are not given responsibility hear the message, "You're not good enough to take control of this job." This leads to the employee being less motivated or less likely to take responsibility at a later date.

- When employees receive only limited responsibility, they tend to break rules, be absent more often, or increasingly show up late for work.

CUSTOMER SERVICE TIP

Happy employees make happy customers.

- Employees feel their hands are tied in the absence of managers, because no one is trained to think independently. This creates problems of succession and poses threats to the longevity of a company.

Rewarding CSRs

Well-trained customer service employees who feel they are valuable members of the corporate team create the magic inside the business that keeps customers coming back. Customer service employees know they are valued when companies use positive reinforcement and public praise. Workers need to know that management notices and appreciates their contributions. When this happens, it encourages similar behavior among other CSRs, and at the same time, it reduces the need for employee turnover expenditures.

Unfortunately, top *sales* performers often earn sizable bonuses or expensive prizes, while top *service* performers are recognized on a much smaller scale, or receive no recognition at all. It is unwise for companies to send the message that service is less important than sales. Even small successes should be celebrated, because they give companies the opportunity to recognize employees on a regular basis.

A recognition event doesn't have to be extravagant, as depicted by Scottrade's recognition Scratch-and-Win Cards program in the Best Practices feature at the end of the chapter. A pizza party, a small gift, a gift certificate, a balloon bouquet, or a special parking spot can make an employee feel recognized and appreciated. Regardless of the appreciation program a company uses, when another employee or manager observes service professionals performing one of the following noteworthy behaviors, a verbal acknowledgement is a must:

- Demonstrating teamwork
- Offering to help someone
- Taking ownership of a problem

- Making a suggestion for cost savings
- Teaching someone something that improves results
- Going above and beyond the call of duty
- Providing excellent customer service
- Making a suggestion that increases productivity
- Finding a potential problem and fixing it

WHAT DO YOU THINK
8.3

What motivates you to stay at a job and do it well? Is it money, pride, recognition among peers and management, or just a natural desire to do your best? Record these motivations in your journal.

MANAGING A CUSTOMER SERVICE DEPARTMENT

Some of the best managers in an organization are promoted up through the ranks. Good customer service managers are comfortable assigning tasks to CSRs because these managers know the job inside and out. They are good at facilitating cooperation between departments as well as with customers because they've "been there, done that." Valuable leaders of customer service departments know how to motivate and monitor CSRs, as well as how to resolve conflicts that inevitably arise in any organization.

Motivating CSRs

It is no surprise that employees are more motivated to provide exceptional support when they know they will be encouraged, recognized, and rewarded, themselves. A strong leader works diligently to understand and motivate workers. Customer service managers must be well organized and capable of helping the department organize itself to accomplish its goals. One of the strengths of a good leader is the ability to see a better future for the department than what currently exists. Managers who create an environment that works for the customers and staff

REMEMBER THIS

Figure 8.2 Motivation Techniques

METHOD	EXAMPLES
1. Managers generate a spirit of service by	• Encouraging laughter, humor, warm greetings, smiles, and compliments. • Demonstrating belief in people through positive words of encouragement. • Casually visiting with staff, seeking their input, and incorporating that information into observable actions.
2. Managers build trust by	• Keeping people informed of change. • Demonstrating flexibility and interest in the personal situations of employees. • Sharing information about the organization. • Defining boundaries and providing reasonable expectations for all workers.
3. Managers develop people by	• Providing timely feedback through effective coaching. • Adapting communication techniques based on the needs of each employee. • Rewarding successes and addressing problems promptly.
4. Managers lead through example by	• Practicing the behaviors and ethics expected of frontline workers. • Giving direction in a respectful manner. • Listening attentively and responding to feedback from staff.
5. Managers stay focused on customer needs by	• Recognizing individuals for giving great customer service. • Implementing employee suggestions that improve service.

set the stage for service excellence. Figure 8.2 describes five effective methods managers can use to motivate CSRs.

Monitoring CSRs

Internally, managers need to watch out for attitudes among CSRs that paint the customer in a negative light. What may start out as harmless talk about customers can wind up becoming a company culture that pits CSRs against customers and can ultimately result in low customer retention. Two ways a manager can determine the quality of service reps' customer relations are:

• *Review e-mail for consistency and core values.* Gather all e-mail and written correspondence from CSRs. Review them for grammar, misspellings, effectiveness of presentation, and politeness. Also, scan the

documents for common words and decide whether those are truly the most fitting words or statements to describe the company and its service culture.

• *Monitor customer service calls.* Listen in unobtrusively to customer service calls. Pay attention to the tone and manner the CSR uses to discuss various situations with customers.

Resolving Conflicts

Managers who never experience conflict on the job are rare. All workplaces suffer from conflict periodically. To be good at resolving work-related conflicts requires a great deal of practice. Interpersonal relationships with people at work may cause tension that you are not aware of. For example, if someone who is normally upbeat and friendly toward you suddenly begins avoiding you, there is probably a reason. If a co-worker is cheerful with everyone except you, chances are a conflict exists. In such instances, use your best communication skills to address the problem through the following nine-step process, based upon a *Human Resource Management* article on resolving conflicts:

1. Make an effort to determine whether there is, in fact, a problem.
2. If there is a problem, set up a private face-to-face meeting to discuss it with the other person.
3. In a "nonconfrontational manner," explain what you think the problem is.
4. Ask for feedback while you are speaking.
5. Listen to the other person with an open mind.
6. Respect others' opinions.
7. Attempt to determine the root cause of the problem.
8. Aim to work out a compromise that pleases both of you.
9. Find a way that both of you can walk away feeling like winners.[6]

The goal of conflict resolution is to reach a compromise that both parties can accept. Regardless of the type of conflict managers may face, there are general guidelines service professionals can follow to bring harmony back into the workplace. To review the rules for disagreeing diplomatically, refer to Figure 8.3.

Handling a difficult person requires skill, but more importantly, it requires courage and time as well. Most of us avoid conflict because we think we don't have the time, energy, or emotional strength to deal effectively with a confrontation. Unfortunately, when difficult people are ignored, they tend to repeat their bad behavior because it works for them. Being firm, assertive, and using the proper techniques will help defuse the situation by coping with it rather than withdrawing from it. Dealing with conflict in an effective, and most especially, a timely manner, is crucial to allowing personnel to have the time and energy to deal with customers.

WHAT DO YOU THINK

8.4

Describe the best manager you ever had. What traits made him or her stand out? Record your impressions in your journal.

REMEMBER THIS

Figure 8.3 Rules for Disagreeing Diplomatically

RULES	WHEN YOU SAY	IT REALLY MEANS
Reflect your understanding of the other's position or opinion.	"I feel, think, want, etc..."	"I am listening to your opinion and take it into account before I state mine."
Let the other person know you value him or her as a person, even though your opinions differ.	"I understand [appreciate, respect, see] how you feel that way."	"I hear you and respect your opinion."
State your position or opinion.	"I feel [think, want]..."	"I don't agree, but I value you—so let's exchange ideas comfortably, not as a contest for superiority."

SOURCE: "How to Resolve Conflicts—Without Offending Anyone," *Human Resource Management* October 2, 2006 http://www.citeman.com/1032-how-to-resolve-conflicts-without-offending-anyone, accessed January 25, 2011.

---

[6] "How to Resolve Conflicts—Without Offending Anyone," *Human Resource Management* October 2, 2006 http://www.citeman.com/1032-how-to-resolve-conflicts-without-offending-anyone accessed January 25, 2011.

FOCUS ON. . .
BEST PRACTICES

Scottrade

When people make a sincere effort to treat everyone with respect and try to *do the right things right*, the pathway to success is sure to have fewer bumps. This approach is Scottrade's founder and CEO Rodger Riney's philosophy, which, according to his bio, "he reiterates throughout the firm by making sure customers receive the best value and associates' dedicated work is rewarded."

An example of a reward system used by this premier stock trading company is the Scratch-and-Win Cards

Scottrade's management team uses to recognize associates for "doing the right things right." These on-the-spot awards are redeemed through the Scottrade online recognition platform and according to Jane Wulf, Executive Director, Human Resources, "The Scratch-and-Wins have been a huge success because they have added an element of excitement and anticipation to the reward program."

SOURCES: http://about.scottrade.com/who-we-are/founder-ceo-bio.html, accessed January 24, 2011 and Louise Anderson, "Turn Best Practices into Common Practices with On-the-Spot Recognition," *Anderson Performance Improvement*, http://www.andersonperformance.com/napmBestPracticesCommon.php accessed January 27, 2011.

WRAPPING UP

Managing Customer Service completes the four-chapter study of Essential Customer Service Skills. Recognizing the importance of setting standards and then using trained (and sometimes certified) CSRs who can apply those standards helps managers direct combined efforts toward achieving successful customer satisfaction. Great managers train, empower, and reward CSRs to preserve their loyalty toward the company, its products, services, and customers. The final part of the textbook requires that the skills learned up to this point support the wide range of Communication Skills needed by CSRs on a daily basis and begins with a discussion of *Communication Essentials*.

SUMMARY

- Setting standards for performance that tell workers what is expected of them, both in quality and quantity of work, is a conscious effort and involves direction from customer service managers.

- Typically, a CSR works inside comfortable offices or cubicles between 35 and 40 hours per week, with some occasional overtime, night, and weekend work.

- Retaining CSRs is greatly enhanced when they experience ongoing training, are empowered to serve customers well, and are publically recognized and rewarded on the job.

- Good customer service managers generate a spirit of service, build trust, develop people, lead by example, and stay focused on customer needs.

KEY TERMS

certification   role-playing
coaching   standards

CRITICAL THINKING

1. Why is it important for managers to use measurable customer service standards? Cite two examples of measurable standards you've followed in previous work experiences.

2. List the pros and cons of a call center work environment for customer service representatives.

3. What is the incentive for companies like Enterprise to train, empower, and reward service professionals?

4. Name two recognition and reward programs you would like to participate in and describe what you think is effective about each one.

5. What skills do you possess that would make you an effective customer service manager? Describe in a short paragraph how you would apply your managerial talents in a customer service setting.

WHAT DO YOU THINK NOW?

Project 8.1

Assume you are doing a classroom presentation on *managing customer service*. Reread your responses to the *What Do You Think?* questions that you completed throughout this chapter. What are some service attitudes and practices that over time prepare you to become an effective customer service manager? What training or retraining can help a service professional to stay effective? What service and CSR issues do you believe are the most challenging to manage? Which communication skills should customer service managers demonstrate? Compile your responses, as directed by your instructor.

ONLINE RESEARCH ACTIVITY

Project 8.2   Customer Service Certification

Obtaining customer service certification testifies that you possess the skills necessary to respond to the challenges of customer service. Locate the National Retail Federation Foundation website and learn the requirements needed to achieve certification. Study the work-oriented skills and the worker-oriented skills and have a class discussion about how these skills relate to your experience as a CSR.

COMMUNICATION SKILLS AT WORK

Project 8.3   Communicating Standards to Customers

You and two other employees have been asked to put together a chart that will be used to train new CSRs in performance standards, accuracy, and production at your company. Using the information from this chapter and other sources you locate relative to this project, agree upon and recommend a standard (method or action) that a CSR can demonstrate to perform each listed characteristic. As an alternative, follow your instructor's directions to join a group and use the instructor-designated discussion board to complete the group project.

1. Attitude
2. Reliability
3. Empathy
4. Exceptional service

DECISION MAKING AT WORK

Project 8.4   Career Advancement or Job Security?

At a recent customer service conference, there was a debate among customer service managers as to whether it is best to hire a CSR who is more concerned with job security or one who is more interested in career advancement. Be prepared to participate on either side of the debate by preparing a defense for the following two statements.

1. **Defend:** When hiring a CSR, it is better to offer stability and longevity on the job over any other factor. Doing so will result in finding a better employee.

2. **Defend:** When hiring a CSR, it is better to offer advancement through a career path and promotion opportunities over any other factor. Doing so will result in finding a better employee.

CASE STUDY

Project 8.5   Cost of Nonservice

A woman was mistreated by a salesperson in a store where she had been shopping once a week for three years. As a result of the poor service, she began shopping elsewhere. Twelve years later she returned to the store and told the owner what had happened. He listened intently, apologized, and thanked her for coming back. Back in his office, he estimated that if the woman had spent only $25 a week in his store, he would have had $15,600 additional revenue over the past 12 years. He had lost her business to nonservice.

1. In your judgment, to what extent does nonservice affect businesses today?

2. What methods can companies use to prevent one incident of poor service from causing substantial revenue loss?

PART 3

Communication Skills

Teresa Laraba, Senior Vice President of Customer Services, Southwest Airlines, Dallas Texas

Responsible for customer service activities, Teresa Laraba joined Southwest Airlines 27 years ago. She started out as a front-line customer service agent at the airport and has always been in a customer service role. Southwest Airlines currently operates six Customer Support and Services Centers located in Albuquerque, Chicago, Houston, Phoenix, Oklahoma City, and San Antonio.

At Southwest Airlines, we take a customer service approach and tone in *everything* we do. We feel it is not only how you treat our external customers, but also how you treat internal customers. A most recent example is that we are scheduling meetings with our pilot groups to talk about what *their role is* as customer service representatives for Southwest Airlines. We attempt to do that with *every* employee group because we believe everyone in our organization serves customers and has an expectation and responsibility to do it well.

1 In your opinion, what are some of Southwest Airlines leading challenges in customer service?

One of the biggest challenges for us is that, as we grow with potential acquisitions, we must make sure there is the desire in *all* 35,000 employees to deliver great customer service. Our large size and geographic spread contribute to that challenge.

A second challenge continues to be to use social media in the best way to validate the Southwest Airlines brand. We are proud to be one of the first airlines with a corporate blog and are very active on Facebook and Twitter as well. We have folks who monitor those communications 24/7. Something we are also very proud of is that we don't have to try hard to get important feedback from our customers. In 2010, we generated 69,374 external commendations.

2 How does Southwest Airlines deal with customer service complaints?

I would say that how we handle them depends on the situation, because customer service is very much about perception. If we have a customer who walks away with a bad taste, we will *always* apologize if we left him or her feeling that way. We are realistic and recognize that every day there is an opportunity for that to happen with 35,000 employees. Somebody is not going to have a good day and may come across as rushed or rude. We never tell our customers that they shouldn't feel offended. We always *thank them* for the feedback, thank them for letting us go back and have a conversation with an employee who may

have said something inappropriate or was perhaps short with the customer.

3 What advice would you offer customer service representatives?

I think it depends on the representative's role with customers and the employees' comfort level. If you have employees who are going to do most of their communication over the phone, as reservations employees for example, we say that we need to hear the "smile in their voice," but we are really looking for employees who *enjoy* those conversations with customers. If, on the other hand, you are looking for employees to serve customers face-to-face, then you want their communication style to use positive and encouraging body language while they use their voice.

Empowerment is another skill we are talking to our new hires about. Today in the airline industry, you are not dealing with just "fun" customer service situations; you may potentially be trying to diffuse a situation on an airplane at 30,000 feet in a metal tube. So, you want a flight attendant, for instance, who knows how to calm people down or to successfully talk through the situation. I guess you could say that our employees need to do a lot of conflict resolution on the fly.

I cannot emphasize enough that we at Southwest do our best to hire the right person up front. We also know that if you do not treat employees or prospective employees with the same level of service as you treat your customers, then you are really missing the mark, because they are also your customers. Prospective employees may not work for you, but they fly on you.

FIRST IMPRESSIONS

What qualities and skills does Teresa Laraba look for in prospective customer service employees? Record your impressions in your journal.

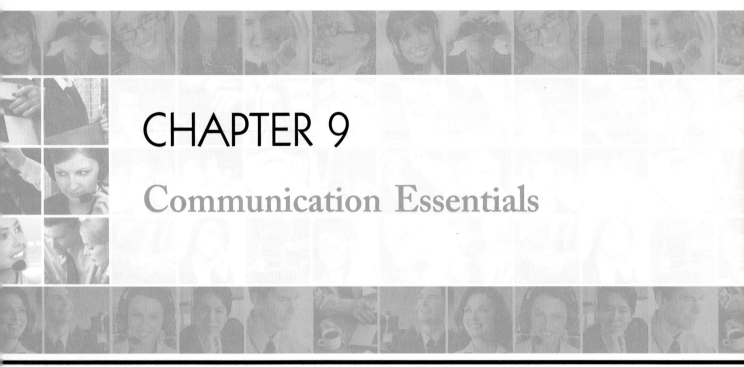

CHAPTER 9

Communication Essentials

*We are what we repeatedly do. Excellence
is not an act but a habit.*

ARISTOTLE, GREEK PHILOSOPHER

OBJECTIVES

1. Explain each of the elements in the communication process.

2. Identify the behaviors of people who communicate using different communication styles.

3. Compose examples of open, probing, closed, alternative choice, leading, and direct questions.

4. Know the fundamentals of business writing.

Avon

If consumers were to think of skin care products they and their friends have used over the years, several brands would come to mind, but Avon would surely be listed among them. Today Avon is global, directly selling to customers in over 100 countries. As a corporation that employs over 5 million independent Avon representatives, the importance the company places on effective communication fundamentals is especially high.

What makes the communication process with customers unique when compared to other cosmetic companies is that Avon representatives contact their customers directly and on an ongoing basis. They use brochures to pre-sell and then follow-up with customers using e-mail, phone, notes, and other methods during the two-week sales campaign.

In describing the uniqueness of Avon's communication approach, its website states that "At Avon, the *direct* part of direct selling also refers to the personal component of this sales channel; it's about building relationships with people and offering them a high level of service and personal attention." This means that all forms and modalities of communication must be used well and with regularity in order to ensure the high level of service and personal attention that Avon customers have enjoyed for over 125 years.

SOURCE: http://www.avoncompany.com/earningsopportunity/directselling.html, accessed January 7, 2011.

THE BASICS OF COMMUNICATION

Communication is important to business. According to Rick Schaefer's article entitled "Effective Communication in the Workplace," "58 percent of effective communication is carried in our body language, 35 percent in our voice inflection and tone, and only 7 percent in our actual words."[1] In every point of contact with customers, service professionals communicate something. As more contact is made with an organization, customers combine their perceptions into an overall impression of the company's customer service.

The truth is, great service requires great communication skills. Think of a time you experienced poor customer service. What made the service poor? Did a failure to communicate contribute to the problem? Were you, as a customer, a part of that failure? For example:

- If you didn't get what you wanted, did you say so?

- If your expectations were not met, did you communicate that to the service provider?

- If you perceived that you were being treated rudely, did you discuss the service provider's behavior toward you?

In general, successful communication is evidenced by a shared understanding between two or more persons. This begins with using the elements in the communication process effectively and responsibly.

The Communication Process

Understanding the communication process can help CSRs become better communicators. The process shows that each communication event, or customer interaction, is unique—that one mind is different

---

[1] Rick Schaefer, "Effective Communication in the Workplace," *Ezine@rticles*, March 29, 2010, http://ezinearticles.com/?Effective-Communication-in-the-Workplace&id=4017537 accessed January 7, 2011.

from another mind. Unless the words or other signals used to send a message have the same meaning or frame of reference, communication differs in some way in the minds of the sender and receiver.

In general, the human communication process follows this pattern: first, a message arrives from a sender, and the senses pick up the message and relay it to the receiver. This is called the **encoding process**. Next, the receiver filters the message and gives it a unique meaning. The meaning triggers a response, and the receiver returns (by voice, writing, or gestures) the shared understanding of the message to the sender. This is the **decoding process**. Finally, a message transmitted back to the original sender is called **feedback**. Refer to the diagram in Figure 9.1. This cycle may continue as long as the people involved want to communicate.

A recent article in *Mind Tools* states that, in order for communication to be successful, "you must understand what your message is, what audience you are sending it to, and how it will be perceived. You must also weigh-in the circumstances surrounding your communications, such as situational and cultural context."[2] To illustrate that process, the **communication model** contains six elements: sender, receiver, message, channel, shared understanding, and feedback. The model, an expansion of David Berlo's 1960 Sender-Message-Channel-Receiver model, endeavors to explain what happens when we communicate successfully.

1. *Sender* The sender has an idea to share with another person. That idea is in the sender's mind and the goal is to get it into the receiver's mind.

2. *Receiver* The receiver is the person or persons with whom the sender is trying to communicate. After the receiver hears the message, feedback is sent to the sender.

3. *Message* The message contains more than words. It also encompasses a combination of feelings, attitudes, facial and body gestures, and other unique personality traits.

4. *Channel* This refers to the medium through which a message is transmitted to its intended audience. Broadly speaking, for customer service, two effective channels include print media (letters, e-mails, web pages) and broadcast media (phone, personal conversations, chats, meetings).

5. *Shared understanding* The degree to which a receiver understands what a sender is trying to communicate depends on human and personality factors involving similarities and differences between the communicators and any previous perceptions each may have relative the topic of discussion.

6. *Feedback* As previously mentioned, feedback is the receiver's reaction sent back to the sender. Each of us has experienced from time to time the feeling, "He doesn't have a clue what I'm talking about." In most cases, we reach this conclusion by interpreting the verbal or nonverbal feedback the receiver is generating.

REMEMBER THIS

Figure 9.1

The Communication Process

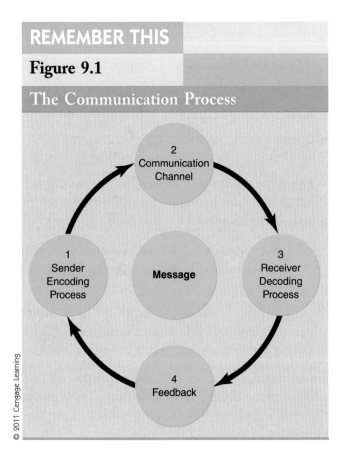

© 2011 Cengage Learning

---

[2] Mind Tools, Introduction to Communication Skills: Why Communications Skills Are So Important, http://www.mindtools.com/CommSkll/CommunicationIntro.htm accessed January 25, 2011.

Mixed Messages

Even though people sincerely want to clearly communicate with each other, a mixed message may result. A **mixed message** is a single communication that contains two meanings. One part of the message—usually the verbal part—is positive, while the other part of the message—usually the nonverbal component—contradicts the verbal portion and is negative. For example, a salesperson says, "Thank you" to a customer as she rings up the purchase, but does so in a hurried tone and with no eye contact. When the verbal portion and the nonverbal portion of a message contradict one another, the nonverbal portion is almost always believed. This is because nonverbal communication is perceived as less conscious, more honest, and harder for people to fake.

Organizations unintentionally send hundreds of mixed messages to customers every day. One example is company policies that claim to be intended for the convenience and protection of the customer, messages that some customers feel are actually designed to make life easier for managers and their employees. Procedures that require customers to move from one workstation to another to get "taken care of" may provide assembly-line efficiency for the company, but what they communicate to the customer is quite different. When one person sees to our needs, it feels warm and caring. When we interact with many different people, we don't feel nurtured and "taken care of"; instead, we feel processed.

Prodakszyn/Shutterstock.com

In what ways can people communicate mixed messages?

WHAT DO YOU **THINK**

9.1

Describe a recent experience you've had with another person where a mixed message muddled clear understanding and became frustrating to one or both of you. Record your experience in your journal.

COMMUNICATION STYLES

Good communication skills—both verbal and written—require a high level of self-awareness and an ability to adapt to the situation. This means that you can make another person more comfortable with you by selecting and emphasizing certain behaviors that fit your personality. The selection you make should help you respond naturally to another person's communication style.[3] In business and in our personal lives, we encounter and practice three basic communication styles: aggressive, passive, and assertive. CSRs should make every effort

---

[3] Tarun Paten, "Listen," January 1, 2006, http://comwell.blogspot.com/ accessed January 5, 2011.

to become assertive communicators, but still acknowledge that customers will use all three styles.

Aggressive Communication

A person who has an **aggressive communication style** is closed-minded, listens poorly, has difficulty seeing another person's point of view, interrupts other people while they are talking, and tends to monopolize the conversation. Typically, an aggressive communicator feels he or she must win arguments at any cost.

Unfortunately, this communication style fosters resistance, defiance, and retaliation. It exacts a high price in personal and business relationships, especially when it comes to satisfying customers. Aggressive communicators express their thoughts and feelings in ways that violate or disregard the rights of others. They tend to:

• humiliate and dominate others,

• make choices for others,

• show a lack of respect for others' rights,

• use sarcasm, insult others, and make unfair demands.[4]

Passive Communication

People who communicate using a **passive communication style** tend to be indirect and hesitant to say what is really on their minds. By avoiding or ignoring problems, passive communicators are likely to agree externally, while disagreeing internally. They often feel powerless in confrontational situations because they don't like to make waves or upset anyone.

Passive communicators fail to express their feelings, thoughts, and beliefs, and so, typically give in to others. As a result, they allow others to make choices for them. In general, passive communicators:

• believe that other people are more important or more correct than they are,

• are concerned that they will anger someone if they express their true feelings,

In this room, which participants are using aggressive, passive, or assertive communication styles?

• beat around the bush when trying to make a point,

• say nothing is wrong and then become resentful about the situation later.[5]

Assertive Communication

A person who practices an **assertive communication style** tends to be an effective, active listener who states limits and expectations and does not label or judge people or events. By confronting problems at the time they happen, assertive communicators leave themselves open to negotiating, bargaining, and compromising in such a way that everyone involved wins.

The greatest advantage assertive communicators have is the ability to exercise their rights without denying the rights of others. Moreover, they express feelings honestly and directly, while practicing mutual respect for others. Assertive communicators state their message without being blunt or rude and consciously practice good eye contact, while using appropriate hand gestures and other suitable body language to make their point.

The assertive communication style is the one to strive for when serving customers. However, the reality is that very few people use only one communication style. For example, the aggressive style can be essential when a decision has to be made quickly or during an emergency or you know you

[4] http://www.au.af.mil/au/awc/awcgate/sba/comm_style.htm accessed January 25, 2011.

[5] Ibid.

REMEMBER THIS

Figure 9.2   Communication Styles

STYLE	BEHAVIORS	NONVERBAL CUES	VERBAL CUES
Aggressive	• Puts others down • Has a know-it-all attitude • Doesn't show appreciation • Is bossy	• Frowns • Squints eyes critically • Is critical • Uses a loud tone of voice	• "You must (should, ought, or better)…" • "Don't ask why. Just do it."
Passive	• Sighs a lot • Clams up when feeling badly treated • Asks permission unnecessarily • Complains instead of taking action	• Fidgets • Smiles and nods in agreement • Has slumped posture • Speaks in a low volume	• "You have more experience than I do." • "I don't think I can…" • "This is probably wrong, but…" • "I'll try."
Assertive	• Operates from choice • Is action-oriented • Is realistic in expectations • Behaves in a fair, consistent manner	• Has open, natural gestures • Uses direct eye contact • Has a confident, relaxed posture • Uses a varied rate of speech	• "I choose to…" • "What are my options?" • "What alternatives do we have?"

SOURCE: Joni Rose, "Communication Styles," January 21, 2007, http://www.suite101.com/content/communication-styles-a12116 accessed January 18, 2011.

are right and that fact is crucial to the outcome for both parties. The passive style also has its critical applications, such as when an issue arises that is much more important to the customer's happiness than to the business's. In this case, passive communication on the CSR's part may be the best option to keep the customer happy. The passive style may also be useful when emotions are running high, and it makes sense to take a break to calm down and regain perspective about the situation.[6]

WHAT DO YOU THINK

9.2

In what circumstances do you become an aggressive communicator? A passive communicator? Record these reflections in your journal.

Refer to Figure 9.2 for more information about behavior and nonverbal and verbal cues of each communication style.

COMMUNICATING WITH CUSTOMERS

The Internet and self-service have reduced person-to-person communication to minutes and sometimes seconds. For CSRs to provide superior customer service in this fast-paced, competitive business world, they must be able to gather information appropriately by asking and answering questions. When working with global and diverse customers, *how* CSRs pose a question is often as important as *what* they ask.

Asking Questions

Time and again, customers call with questions. To answer customers' questions and address their needs, you should ask questions also. Typically, questioning others continues a discussion or pinpoints and clarifies issues when gathering pertinent information.

[6]Ibid.

Asking a question skillfully increases the likelihood of quickly getting a solid understanding of the issues. In general, the person doing the questioning is in control of the discussion. Therefore, all questions should be asked in a positive way. A *positive question* is one that the customer is not afraid to answer. By rewording a "you" statement into an "I" statement, you can steer clear of questions that use sarcastic language or a threatening tone.

For example, avoid, "What exactly are *you* getting at?" or "Could *you* get to the point a little quicker?" Say instead, "*I* don't understand what you are trying to tell me," or "Could you please try to explain it in a different way so *I* can understand better?"

Relative to questioning techniques, avoid bombarding the customer with questions or using a multiple-question approach when serving customers.

- *Bombardment approach* asks too many questions in a short period of time and puts customers on the defensive. This tactic controls the conversation but may limit the information gained. "Why" questions, if improperly asked, often cause individuals to become defensive.

- *Multiple-question approach* asks many questions wrapped up as one. When a question actually contains several questions, clients may get confused about which one to answer. Also, various global customers do not receive rapid-fire questions favorably as this creates distrust.

To get the response you want, you need to know how to choose the appropriate type of question to ask. During the course of a normal conversation, you use all types of questions to gather a lot of data into information you can use. Depending on the situation, use an assortment of open, probing, closed, alternative choice, leading, and direct questions.

1. **Open questions** request information in a way that requires a more complete answer than a simple "yes" or "no." They encourage an individual to talk, and they elicit maximum information to identify causes so you can work more quickly and effectively toward solutions. Open questions usually begin with action verbs

or "How," "What," or "Why." As a result of asking open questions, CSRs are able to gain more information, and that, in turn, makes offering solutions or suggestions to customer problems much easier. Examples are, "Describe the kind of engine noise you are hearing," "How may I assist you?" and "What information were you given when you spoke with the CSR yesterday?"

2. **Probing questions** use information already established to clarify points and ask for more details. Often, these questions promptly follow up a previous question and response. For example, "Who did you speak with yesterday?" "When did you purchase the product?" "Can you always be reached at this telephone number?" and "Tell me more about how you are feeling."

3. **Closed questions** usually elicit a *yes* or *no* answer. Closed questions can be useful in the concluding minutes of a customer conversation to confirm small details and to make sure that you have covered all the topics concerning the customer's query. These questions elicit specific information and usually begin with "Where," "Are," or "Do." Examples are, "Do you want these items delivered?" and "Are there other questions you have for me at this time?"

4. **Alternative choice questions** provide alternatives for the customer to choose from. These questions can be particularly useful when dealing with difficult customers. The approach is to ask customers what they would like you to do for them, but then limit their responses by providing them with two or three alternatives that also suit you. Examples are, "I could find this information for you and call you with an answer by the end of the morning, or would you prefer me to fax the information later in the day?" and "Would you like me to get our supervisor, or would you like to give me an opportunity to try to help first?"

5. **Leading questions** help speed up interactions with people who find it difficult to make a final decision. They also help the customer confirm information in an easy way. Some examples

are, "You would like to receive the catalog updates on a monthly basis, then?" and "So, you would agree on a delivery this coming Thursday, if I can get you a discount?"

6. **Direct questions** can be open or closed. However, all direct questions have two characteristics in common: the name of the other person is always used, and the question is posed as an instruction. Examples are, "Tell me, Mrs. Epperson… ," "Explain to me, Mr. Siskowski… ," and "Describe to me, Ms. Frederick…" Using the other person's name puts you in a better position to get his or her immediate attention. In phrasing the question as an instruction ("Tell me…"), you are giving a subconscious order.

Answering Questions

Answering customer questions effectively is equally important as asking the right questions. Here are several tips to consider before answering customer questions:

- *Understand the question.* Pay attention to every word the customer uses when asking a question. Once you understand the question, then respond.

- *Decide whether you know the answer.* If you are not sure that your response is accurate, do not answer. Although quick responses are preferred, providing correct information is always the first priority.

- *Remember, you are an expert.* As a CSR, you know your job better than anyone else. If you are certain you are right and you can back up your answer

with facts, politely assert the truth of what you say. Again, do not promise something you cannot deliver.

- *Take enough time.* If a customer needs assistance, don't refuse to help because you are too busy. Also, do not pass the client from person to person.

- *Smile.* If you've got a cranky customer or one who insists you are not right, bend over backwards to make him or her happy. Be pleasant and smile when answering the customer's questions.

- *Avoid responding to a question with a question.* Questions should be asked only to clarify the original question; beyond that—answer, don't ask.

- *Be careful with your power.* Never belittle a customer or criticize a question you receive. For example, don't say, "Can't you see the sign over the door that says…?" or "You mean you don't know?"

- *When you don't know, admit it.* If you are sure you don't know the answer to a question, say so. Admit you don't know, but make an effort to find someone who does.

Using Positive Language

Language impacts whether a message is received positively or negatively and is a great tool that must be used carefully. For example, the impact of unpleasant news can be softened by the use of positive language. **Positive language** projects a helpful, encouraging feeling rather than a destructive, negative one.

No doubt you are familiar with cynics, people who often criticize ideas or provide reasons why something won't work. The cynic's constant challenging creates a negative service environment and increases

Ethics/ **Choices**

Assume you started a new customer service job and after a short time, determined that it was a standard procedure to promise customers products that can't be guaranteed a reasonable delivery. Would you express your concerns or start thinking about finding another job? Explain.

confrontational situations. For example, a cynical CSR might respond to a new customer service proposal with, "I don't know why you are suggesting that! We've tried it in the past and it didn't work, so why do you think it will work now?"

People who are cynical don't always have negative attitudes. Perhaps, they have not learned to phrase their comments in more constructive, positive ways. **Negative language** conveys a poor image to customers and may cause conflict and confrontation where none is necessary or desired. Its use should be avoided. The following message, taken from Robert Bacal's article on "Using Positive Language," could take place at a business service counter or in a letter:

"We regret to inform you that we cannot process your application to register your business name because you have neglected to provide sufficient information for us to do our job. Please complete *all* sections of the attached form and return it to us promptly."

The message has a tone that suggests that the recipient is to blame for the problem. Contrast this example with the following rewritten, more positive approach that Mr. Bacal suggests:

"Congratulations on your new business. To register your business name, we need some additional information. Please return the attached form, completing the highlighted areas, so we can send your business registration certificate within one week. We wish you success in your new endeavor."

Bacal aptly points out that "the negative example tells the person what he or she has done wrong but doesn't stress the positive actions that can be taken to remedy the problem. The positive example sounds completely different and has a more upbeat and helpful tone." Bacal goes on to describe the following characteristics for negative language:

- It tells the recipient what cannot be done.

- It has a subtle tone of blame.

REMEMBER THIS

Figure 9.3 Common Negative Language

Expressions that suggest carelessness	• "You neglected to specify…" • "You failed to include… • "You overlooked enclosing…"
Phrases that suggest the person is lying	• "You claim that…" • "You say that…" • "You state that…"
Expressions that imply that the recipient is not too bright	• "We cannot see how you…" • "We fail to understand…" • "We are at a loss to know…"
Demanding phrases that imply coercion and pressure	• "You should…" • "We must ask you to…" • "We must insist that you…"
Phrases that might be interpreted as sarcastic or patronizing	• "No doubt…" • "We will thank you to…" • "You understand, of course…"

SOURCE: Robert Bacal, "Using Positive Language," *Conflict911.com*, October 2000, http://conflict911.com/conflictarticles/poslan.htm accessed January 6, 2011.

REMEMBER THIS

Figure 9.4

Examples of Positive Phrasing

- "If you can send us your bill of sale, we will be happy to complete the process for you."
- "The information we have suggests that you have a different viewpoint on this issue. Let me explain our perspective."
- "Might we suggest that you... [suggestion]."
- "One option open to you is... [option]."

SOURCE: Robert Bacal, "Using Positive Language," *Conflict911.com*, October 2000, http://conflict911.com/conflictarticles/poslan.htm accessed January 6, 2011.

- It includes words such as *can't*, *won't*, and *unable to*, which tell the recipient what the sender cannot do.

- It does not stress positive actions that would be appropriate.

On the other hand, positive language displays these qualities:

- It tells the recipient what can be done.

- It suggests alternatives and choices available to the recipient.

- It sounds helpful and encouraging rather than bureaucratic.

- It stresses positive actions and consequences that can be anticipated.[7]

To move toward more positive communication, identify and eliminate universal negative language. Bacal lists some familiar expressions that should be avoided whenever possible in communicating with customers. These are shown in Figure 9.3 on page 146, while Figure 9.4 offers his examples of conveying the same information with positive phrasing.

Handling Customer Requests

When handling customer requests, special service skills are sometimes required. The best response to a service request is "yes," but sometimes "I'm not sure" cannot be avoided, or "no" is even required. Here are some suggestions as to how to handle each circumstance:

Saying "Yes"   Use a friendly voice tone, combined with positive, cheerful words. Clearly tell the customer what you can do for him or her.

Saying "No"   Empathize with the customer and help if you can. Explain why you cannot complete the request. Choose words that are calming and soothing. When customers are distracted or emotionally upset, they may not hear what you intended to say, so make every effort to use positive, clear, effective phrases.

Saying "I'm Not Sure"   Use this phrase when you are not sure if the request can be completed, what options you can offer, or if you don't have the authority to address the request. Always follow this statement with, "But I'll be happy to find out."

Sensitive Issues

While most of the previous discussion has dealt with typical business situations involving products and services, it is important for CSRs to be aware that customer responses may be influenced by factors beyond the "typical" concerns of billing, deliveries, or faulty merchandise. Mike Johnson, in an article written for Clement Communications, Inc, reminds readers that

We are in the business of serving people who have real lives and experiences. When individuals approach us for assistance, we see only a snippet of their existence. We have no way of knowing what challenges or crises they are

CUSTOMER SERVICE TIP

Use creative ways to say "no" to a customer. If you must use the word policy, do so only for matters of legal compliance, ethics, or absolute performance standards, such as employee or customer safety.

[7] Robert Bacal, "Using Positive Language," *Conflict911.com*, October 2000, http://conflict911.com/conflictarticles/poslan.htm accessed January 6, 2011.

quietly coping with as they approach us. Providing rude or apathetic service is always bad business, but to provide it to a person who is suffering mental or physical pain is simply bad human behavior.

When serving others, it is safe to assume that some of the customers you encounter on most days are undergoing personal distress. Who these people are or what crises they face will likely never be revealed, but rest assured, your actions will make a positive or negative impact on their outlook for the day. The following are some sobering thoughts about various crises people (customers) in America face every day. For each situation, reflect and then ask yourself how you will treat these people when they come to you for service.

Johnson provides the following list of situations that may impact a customer's interaction with a CSR:

- *Death of a loved one* Each day around the world, many customers are dealing with shocking news about the death of a loved one.

- *Suicide* Unfortunately, people today will either take their lives or will attempt suicide. This means that sometime today, many CSRs unknowingly have the opportunity to convince these people they are valuable human beings.

- *Divorce* Today, thousands of spouses will be served with papers for divorce. For many of them, this will be a surprise causing absolute devastation.

- *Missing children* Today, innocent children will be listed as missing. How you treat their parents when they come to you for service will make a difference.

Ethics / Choices

How would you act in response to a customer who was talking to you about exchanging a faulty product for an account credit, and suddenly her eyes filled with tears and she was unable to continue?

- *Loss of job* Today, thousands of people will be laid off, fired, or otherwise removed from their jobs. How will you treat these people when they come to you for service?[8]

WHAT DO YOU **THINK**
9.3
What types of questions and negative/positive phrasing do you use less often than others? Record in your journal how you might use these new communication tools in the workplace.

FUNDAMENTALS OF BUSINESS WRITING

In addition to face-to-face communication with customers, CSRs are also required to communicate effectively in writing. From simple e-mails and chats to formal customer letters, CSRs will need to compose documents that educate, persuade, inform, or enlighten the customer. Writing is an essential element of business communication. The ability to write effectively is a skill you learn; it comes naturally to only a few gifted individuals.

Business writing experts say that the most important strategy behind good written communication is to be *clear*. Striving for clarity is important, even if the subject is difficult. It is much better to be as honest as you can be with customers, within whatever limits are set by your work, rather than to write around the problem. After clarity, the next most important writing strategy is the skillful and professional presentation of the written communication. Presentation reflects your company's professionalism, quality, and reputation. The costs of sloppy and poorly written documents with spelling or grammatical errors can be staggering to organizations.

[8] Mike Johnson, "You Never Know What Crisis Your Customer is Facing," Clement Communications, Inc., October 2000, http://www.mikeleejohnson.com/CustomerCrisis.html accessed January 6, 2011.

Should it matter if you organize your writing using a digital computer device or pen and paper?

Identify the Audience

Clear writing is essential if you want your message to be understood by the recipient; what makes writing clear will vary and is ultimately dependent on your target audience. Before you write, it is critical to understand whom you are addressing.

When conveying written or spoken information, walking in your customers' shoes is good advice. Who are they and what are their needs? What is important to them and do they know your products? How can you make sure that what you have to say becomes important to them? What is your current relationship with the person—a current, new, or lapsed customer? Answering these questions requires an awareness of your audience. Moreover, the vocabulary you use and clear organizational structure you give the piece of writing depend on who you are addressing and what the purpose of your message is.

Write Clearly with a Purpose in Mind

Before writing the first sentence, decide what the message should be. Are you conveying information to an upset customer? Are you following up with a customer to clarify issues from a recent phone conversation? Do you want your reader to *do* something when he or she finishes reading your message? If you aren't sure what your purpose is, your reader won't be either. If you want your reader to take some type of action, clearly state the benefits he or she will receive by doing what you ask in terms that are meaningful to this person.

Effective writing requires the ability to identify your objective and organize a series of thoughts. You then prioritize the key points you want to make that support that purpose. For some, an outline works best, because it allows writers to visualize their thought processes on paper and in some detail. For others, the best ideas come from using the creative approach of simply jotting down ideas as they brainstorm the major elements of the message they want to convey.

Get to the point by presenting your primary message or call to action as quickly as possible. Few busy people have the time or patience to wade through long introductory paragraphs before coming to the point of a document. Provide just enough information to capture readers' attention and let them know what is being asked of them.

Use the Proper Tone

Tone is present in all communication activities— spoken or written. The overall tone of any written message affects the reader, just as one's tone of voice in oral exchanges affects the listener. **Tone** refers

CUSTOMER SERVICE **TIP**

When writing to customers, some important books to have on hand are a dictionary, a thesaurus, and one or two office handbooks. These reference tools are also available online, as apps to be downloaded on an electronic device, or as part of a word-processing software package, such as Microsoft® Word.

to the writer's attitude toward the reader and the subject of the message. When creating proper communication tone, remember to:

Be Confident Careful preparation and knowledge about the ideas you wish to express instill confidence. Use words that are respectful and positive showing a confident attitude of helpfulness.

Be Courteous And Sincere A writer builds goodwill by using a tone that is always polite and sincere. When you are respectful and honest, readers are more disposed to accept your message, even if it is negative.

Use Nondiscriminatory Language Nondiscriminatory language addresses all people equally and expresses respect for all individuals because it avoids discriminatory words and inappropriate remarks. It is particularly crucial, when communicating with

a global audience, not to appear patronizing or dismissive.

Stress The Benefits For The Reader A reader will want to know, "What's in it for me?" Your job is to write from the reader's perspective, or with a "you" attitude. It's better to say, "Your order will be available in two weeks" than "I am processing your order tomorrow."

WHAT DO YOU THINK

9.4

What are your strengths as a writer? As a result of studying this section, in what ways can you improve your professional writing skills? Record your thoughts in your journal.

FOCUS ON. . .
BEST PRACTICES

Communication Seminars for CSRs

Whether on-site workshops or online webinars, one-day seminars that cost between $100 and $200 per participant are increasingly popular for businesses that want a very directed push toward improving customer communication. Specifically geared to a particular audience, these short-term training opportunities can be "canned" or tailor-made to a business's employees, which include CSRs, sales professionals, marketing managers, and front-line workers.

To locate an assortment of seminar offerings available across the country, use a phrase such as *customer service communication seminars* in your favorite search engine and thousands of choices will be displayed.

There are a variety of topics and types of seminars available. For example, the Fred Pryor Seminars/CareerTrack website, in promoting their workshops, states, "We've drawn from what is working in companies all across America." One of their popular seminars is entitled *Smart Techniques for Better Communication* and covers the following topics:

- How to prevent misunderstandings
- Ways to make a winning first impression
- The secrets to good rapport with customers and associates
- Easy techniques for crystal-clear, positive communications

SOURCE: http://www.pryor.com/mkt_info/seminars/desc/KC.asp#Communication, accessed January 7, 2011.

WRAPPING UP

Though business communication modalities are varied and may span many miles with customers from other cultures or within the United States, the importance of service professionals consistently applying first-rate communication essentials cannot be overstated. From understanding and successfully applying the elements in the communication process and model to recognizing communication styles in yourself and others, these basics are central to serving customers well. Add in the need to be sensitive to customers when asking or answering questions and as a result of your study, you are better prepared to learn one of the most important communication skills, *Customer-Focused Listening*, the topic of Chapter 10.

SUMMARY

- The major elements in the communication model are the sender, the receiver, a message, channel, shared understanding, and feedback.

- When communicating with customers use the assertive style, but also be alert to the business use of passive and aggressive styles.

- When clarifying issues with customers, consider the information you want to get and choose from among the six types of questions: open, probing, closed, alternative choice, leading, or direct.

- In written communication, understand who you are addressing, what you want your message to accomplish, and how to incorporate the right tone for the message.

KEY TERMS

aggressive communication style
alternative choice questions
assertive communication style
closed questions
communication model
decoding process

direct questions
encoding process
feedback
leading questions
mixed message
negative language

open questions
passive communication style
positive language
probing questions
tone

CRITICAL THINKING

1. Have you or anyone you know attended a communications seminar provided by an employer? If so, in what ways was it more or less effective than training that used other approaches?

2. Recount a situation you participated in or observed recently in which all elements of the communication model were successfully implemented and resulted in a shared message. Was the communication successful? What, if anything, might have improved communication between the sender and receiver?

3. Describe the behaviors of a person you know who predominately uses a passive communication style, one who uses an aggressive

communication style, and one who uses an assertive communication style. How did each of those styles impact upon their dealings with customers and colleagues?

4. Assume that a customer returns an article of clothing or a household item for a refund or credit. Develop six queries a CSR might use in this situation that make use of each type of question: open, probing, closed, alternative choice, leading, and direct.

5. Describe your reaction to a business letter or e-mail message you've received recently that you perceived as having an inappropriate tone. In what ways was it insensitive? How did it make you feel?

 WHAT DO YOU THINK **NOW?**

Project 9.1

Assume you are doing a classroom presentation on *communicating with customers*. Reread your responses to the *What Do You Think?* questions that you completed throughout this chapter. What are some service attitudes and practices that advance clear customer communication techniques? What service issues must CSRs recognize and work around when communicating with customers? Which fundamental communication skills should CSRs use, in both spoken and written communication, to minimize any form of mixed or vaguely communicated messages? Compile your responses, as directed by your instructor.

ONLINE RESEARCH ACTIVITY

Project 9.2 **Digital Writing Tools**

Research a number of websites and locate several articles on current digital or computer equipment and software that businesses use to communicate in writing with customers.

As a result of your research, develop a poster showing the writing tools, prices, features, benefits, and so on of at least four products businesses should consider. Share your poster with the class in either a panel discussion or an oral report, as directed by your instructor.

COMMUNICATION SKILLS AT WORK

Project 9.3 Language That Makes a Difference

Brainstorm with other students to provide more appropriate responses to each of the negative language statements shown here. As an alternative, follow your instructor's directions to join a group and use the instructor-designated discussion board to complete the group project. *Hint:* Use "I" statements rather than "you" statements.

1. "You didn't do this right."

_____

_____

2. "You are wrong."

_____

_____

3. "Wait here."

_____

_____

4. "What's your problem?"

_____

_____

5. "You aren't making any sense."

_____

_____

6. "Why are you so upset?"

_____

_____

DECISION MAKING AT WORK

Project 9.4 The New CSR—Temporary Hire

A temporary, six-month CSR position has just been filled at Dallas Distribution Center. The new hire is Abhey Patel, a very nice and bright person, who everyone agrees works extremely hard. Abhey has recently established citizenship in America from his homeland, India. Realizing the need to write to customers using proper English and grammar, the other CSRs have been covering for Abhey, proofreading his letters and e-mail messages for him. He is currently enrolled in an ESL (English as a Second Language) night class, but he hasn't mastered all the fine points yet.

Respond to these questions regarding Abhey's situation:

1. What are some ways that Abhey can complete his duties on his own more easily?

_____

_____

2. Do you feel that the supervisor should be informed that Abhey has not yet developed his business writing skills and that others are helping him with his work? Is this practice of helping Abhey hurting his co-workers or the company?

_____

_____

CASE STUDY

Project 9.5 "I'll Take That Customer!"

Neal Erwin has a reputation he has always been proud of in the Haskin's Bookstore customer service department. He takes calls from customers that others don't want to deal with. Sometimes, when he is on the phone with a customer, he asks co-workers to come near his desk to hear his side of the argument. In the past, he has gotten loud and belligerent with customers and later has even boasted of "winning."

Things have changed, however, and Neal is now in trouble with management because of a recent incident. A loyal 20-year customer, who spoke to Neal on the phone last week, contacted owner Mr. Charles Haskins and told him in no uncertain terms that she was taking her business elsewhere.

1. In your opinion, should Neal have been allowed to get away with his behavior to customers? Explain.

2. As a co-worker of Neal's, would you have any responsibility to report his aggressive communication style to his supervisor?

CHAPTER 10

Customer-Focused Listening

Kurhan/Shutterstock

The most important thing in communication
is to hear what isn't being said.

PETER F. DRUCKER, MANAGEMENT CONSULTANT

OBJECTIVES

1. Distinguish among the three levels of listening.

2. Explain the consequences of ineffective listening.

3. Develop techniques for becoming an effective listener.

4. Describe obstacles that impact customer-focused listening.

Whirlpool

The best way to understand customer needs is to listen to customers. After Whirlpool merged with Maytag in 2006, it developed a new and comprehensive service strategy where listening to customers was among the top training programs it instituted.

In an article by Mila D'Antonio, Whirlpool's national Director of Customer Care Lynn Holmgren explains that the integrated contact center's mission of *No customer will be lost because of me* is the basis for a new training initiative. As D'Antonio notes, "Called Customer Boot Camp, these immersion tours allow employees who work outside the call center to hear the voice of the customer directly by listening in on calls and also interact with call consultants." Connecting with customers in this way has served to broaden the understanding of the Whirlpool customer experience for over 400 employees each year.

SOURCE: Mila D'Antonio, "Whirlpool Puts a New Spin on Loyalty," *1to1 Media*, February 23, 2009, http://www.1to1media.com/View.aspx?DocID=31400&m=n accessed January 15, 2011.

LEVELS OF LISTENING

Customers have needs beyond completing a simple business transaction; they have emotional needs as well. There is no better way to meet these needs than by listening with attentiveness and understanding as Whirlpool employees do. Successful service representatives understand the benefits of customer-focused listening, and they continually fine-tune their listening skills whether face to face with the customer, on the phone, in written messages, or via an online chat.

As stated in an article by Madelyn Burley-Allen in *HR Magazine*, people listen at different levels of efficiency throughout the day, depending on the circumstances, their attitudes about the speaker, and their past experiences. Most people have difficulty listening effectively

- when dealing with conflict or emotionally charged people,
- when criticism is being directed at them, or
- when they're feeling anxious, fearful, or angry.

Because listening is a learned skill, practicing intentional awareness of your listening behavior will go a long way toward helping you become an effective listener. By dividing listening into three levels, it is easier to characterize certain behaviors that affect listening efficiency. These levels are not sharply distinct. Rather, they are general categories into which modes of listening fall. They often overlap, depending on the situation.

Burley-Allen reminds us that, as a person moves from the least effective level to the most effective level, "the potential for understanding and retaining what is said and for effective communication increases."[1] The following descriptions of the three levels, as proffered by Ms. Burley-Allen, will help you understand the distinctions in how each level is expressed by listeners.

CUSTOMER SERVICE TIP

More is learned by listening than by talking.

[1] Madelyn Burley-Allen, "Listen up: Listening is a learned skill and supervisors need it to improve their employee relationships-Management Tools\Supervisor Resources," HR Magazine, November 2001, http://findarticles.com/p/articles/mi_m3495/is_11_46/ai_80327074/, accessed January 11, 2011.

Level 3 Listening

A level 3 listener may be daydreaming, forming a premature reply, or faking attention while thinking about unrelated matters. In general, this type of listener is more interested in talking than in listening. Unfortunately, this reaction can result in either the speaker or the listener moving away from the conversation.[2]

Have you ever attempted to return a purchase, make an inquiry, or make a payment to a sales person who was engaged in a conversation with another sales person? Perhaps the conversation involved gossip, complaining about a supervisor, or even flirtation, but whatever it was, it had the sales person's attention. When you found you had to keep repeating what you needed, and the sales person made it obvious that you were an annoyance and an interruption, it was clear that the sales person was not listening attentively. When service interactions occur with either the customer or CSR listening at level 3, nothing constructive occurs. More often than not, the listening exchange can evolve into responses that cross annoyance with defensiveness, causing serious communication breakdowns. It is easy but inexcusable to be distracted. Only the customer should be the focus of your attention.

Level 2 Listening

Level 2 listeners focus on words, but many times they miss the intent—what is being expressed nonverbally through tone of voice, body posture, gestures, facial expression, and eye movement. As a result, level 2 listeners hear what the speaker says, but they make little effort to understand the speaker's intent. This can often lead to misunderstandings, incorrect actions, and loss of time.[3]

You may have had the experience where you approached a CSR with an urgent (perhaps repeated) inquiry about lost items at a dry cleaner or a promised delivery that never happened. The CSR *seemed* to be listening to you. He nodded his head periodically, but when he phoned a supervisor and related the situation, he left out key details regarding what you needed. In this case, there's a good chance that level 2 listening was occurring. Without both parties using previously described feedback and questioning tools throughout the communication exchange, *appearing to listen* may result.

Level 1 Listening

Level 1 listeners view listening as an opportunity to gather new and useful information. They suspend judgment, are empathetic to the other person's feelings, and can see issues from the other person's point of view. These listeners take extra time to mentally summarize the stated message, question or evaluate what was said, and consciously notice nonverbal cues.[4]

CSRs who listen at this level serve customers best. They *work* at listening completely because it helps them understand the customer and respectfully serve his or her needs by means of a professional and composed approach.

Blend Images/Jupiter Images

What actions are needed to listen as though the other person is the only one in the room?

[2] Ibid.

[3] Ibid.

[4] Ibid.

WHAT DO YOU THINK

10.1

Reflect on previous conversations or group meetings you've participated in and describe the circumstances in which you listen at each of the three levels. Record your listening tendencies in your journal.

INEFFECTIVE LISTENING

Most people have the ability to be good listeners if their minds aren't cluttered, if they agree with what is being said, or if they like the person they are conversing with. However, when any of these conditions are not met, it is difficult to listen attentively. For example, suppose a sales associate at a popular department store was abruptly told that corporate requires an immediate inventory of stock in her department over Saturday night. Unfortunately, she has already made plans with her friends for the weekend. Because of this conflict, she could likely become an ineffective listener with the next customer. Although unintentional, it still happens.

A speaker may be an excellent communicator, but if, as a listener, he or she is distracted by outside interference or pays attention only to expected responses, selective listening may occur. **Selective listening** is hearing only what you want to hear—sorting out what's not important or of no interest to you. A selective listener is one who finds concentration difficult, has a cluttered mind, or may be tense with emotion. Effective listening under these circumstances is difficult.

Reasons for selective listening abound. One may be as simple as the kind of day you are having and how you are reacting to it. It's important to recognize that when you feel anger, joy, excitement, or boredom, as each of these conditions influences your listening habits. Another reason for selective listening might be that you tune out someone who strikes you the wrong way due to appearance, ethnic background, or manner. When

this happens, notice how little you hear of what this person says.

As soon as people say things we don't want to hear, many of us slip into a selective-listening mode. We either tune these speakers out or we become so busy planning our responses to their ideas that we don't hear what they are saying. Instead, we should hear them out. It is through attentive listening, not selective listening, that we discover important information that may alter our opinions and subsequent actions during customer service exchanges.

WHAT DO YOU THINK

10.2

Do you listen selectively? Cite some examples from your work or school experiences that show you either are or are not a selective listener. Record your examples in your journal.

EFFECTIVE LISTENING

Effective listening has many benefits. It saves time, money, and emotional drama, because people who listen well make fewer mistakes and create fewer interpersonal misunderstandings. For business, good listening skills result in happier customers and less worker turnover. When companies listen to their employees, workers feel more valued and display higher morale. For employees who are good listeners, they see tangible rewards in the forms of company recognition and promotions.

Focused listening earns respect because good listeners are perceived by others to be patient, open-minded, sincere, and considerate. Employers, teachers, and friends attach importance to them because they assist speakers in making their points and conveying ideas efficiently. Improving listening skills is never a waste of time; the benefits are vital to success and self-worth in the world of customer service. The benefits of effective listening to the global customer will be covered later in the chapter.

Fully understanding the meaning of what someone says requires energy and discipline, both of which contribute to what is known as active listening. **Active listening** is listening with your whole mind and body—not just your ears. It requires putting your own feelings aside while trying to understand what the other person is saying. Don't assume you know what a customer wants after he or she speaks the first few sentences. When CSRs fail to listen actively, it results in not fully understanding the customer's needs. Listening is not a passive activity.

Two positive things happen when you practice active listening: the customer senses you care, and you gain a more comprehensive picture of the service situation. This is especially true with global customers who feel particularly gratified that a CSR makes an extra effort to listen, especially when listening could be hampered by a heavy accent or a poor phone connection. Greater understanding allows you to respond more effectively and to meet a customer's biggest need—to be heard.

Below are five strategies that will help improve your active listening skills:

1. *Be ready to listen.* Do this with your eyes, head, and heart as well as your ears. Have paper and a pen or pencil handy, or clear your computer screen and be ready for the next customer contact. Eliminate all distractions that are not conducive to an effective listening environment. Be aware of any internal, physical distractions that you feel, such as hunger, fatigue, headache, or emotional stress. These disruptions can affect your ability to listen carefully.

2. *Be ready to take notes.* If you are speaking to the customer on the phone, let him or her know you are taking notes. Say, "I'm concerned about this, so I'm writing it down." When customers know you are taking notes, they are less likely to repeat themselves. This may also help them organize their thoughts so they state their messages more clearly.

3. *Demonstrate that you are listening.* While the speaker is talking, nod in agreement or ask

questions if something is unclear. Use your body language, stance, posture, and eye contact to show attentive silence. When talking on the phone, use caring words, such as "okay" and "I understand," to provide verbal reinforcement. These prompts let the customer know you are actively listening.

4. *Ask questions.* The goal here is to get the customer talking. Ask appropriate and thoughtful questions in order to clarify the speaker's words and determine the true nature of the problem.

5. *Restate the customer's points.* Don't just repeat what the customer said, but put the message in your own words and emphasize the main points as you understand them to be. This way, you will know when you are on the right course, because the customer can correct you, if necessary.

Take the quiz in Figure 10.1 on page 160 to determine how your listening skills rate.

Service representatives who are skilled listeners communicate more effectively and make better decisions than those who are not. People tend to filter the information they hear. **Filtering** is the process of interpreting messages through our own biases. All too often, what we think we hear is not the correct understanding of what was said. This is important to recognize because for CSRs who serve diverse customers from around the world, using personal filters can result in deflecting or stopping the listening process. A way to counteract filtering is to participate fully in the conversation and look for the underlying feelings in each message. Feelings are often more important than the words themselves.

Here are some winning strategies for developing valuable listening skills:

- *Realize that listening is hard work.* To listen well, prepare yourself mentally. Don't allow yourself to do other things as you listen, such as answering the phone, doing paperwork, playing solitaire on the computer, or checking your e-mail.

- *Make good use of the thought–speech ratio.* People can think much faster than a speaker can talk. As a result, it can be difficult to concentrate on what

Figure 10.1 Listening Skills Quiz

TRUE	FALSE	
☐	☐	1. During a conversation, I ask questions to clarify details.
☐	☐	2. I don't let distractions pull my attention from the conversation.
☐	☐	3. I don't use expressions such as "really" and "uh-huh" to mask my inattentiveness.
☐	☐	4. I don't allow myself to think about other topics while listening to others.
☐	☐	5. I maintain eye contact while talking to others.
☐	☐	6. I don't fidget or do other tasks while another person is speaking.
☐	☐	7. When someone asks me for advice, I make sure my facts are correct.
☐	☐	8. If I can't ignore a distraction, such as a ringing telephone, I make plans to continue the conversation at a later time.
☐	☐	9. I don't rush the other person to make his or her point in a conversation.
☐	☐	10. I follow up with the person from time to time to see what progress has been made since our initial conversation.

How did you do? Each "True" response puts you one step closer to giving customers the great service and attention they deserve. Consider "False" responses as opportunities for improvement.

another person is saying if we let our minds wander or start thinking ahead to fill in the gap.

- *Seek to listen in more than one way.* Listen with your eyes as well as your ears. Look for nonverbal clues to see whether they reinforce or contradict what the person is saying.

- *Don't begin speaking the moment the person stops talking.* Pause a moment before responding to demonstrate that you are not rushing through the conversation and are trying to understand what was said. As a result, the speaker will feel comfortable in sharing more information with you.

- *Develop an open posture that encourages the other person to talk.* Use these techniques: lean toward the speaker while maintaining a comfortable distance, gesture toward the person as you listen and respond, and use the speaker's name in the conversation.

Effective listening involves more than just *hearing* (the physical act of processing sounds) what the other person is saying. It requires finding the real meaning of the words as well as the unspoken message behind those words. Refer to Figure 10.2 to review specific behaviors that are a part of focused and effective listening.

Feedback

Feedback is a significant element in the communication process. After receiving a message, the receiver typically responds in some observable way. This feedback response can be in the form of a follow-up comment or question or possibly facial and body gestures. Lacking feedback, neither the sender nor receiver can confirm that the message was correctly understood.

A key advantage to receiving customer feedback is that it can indicate communication obstacles, such as how each person interprets words and gestures. Feedback not only regulates the listening process but can reinforce and stimulate it as well. To show understanding of the message, a listener can draw on two types of feedback—responsive and reactive. **Responsive feedback** characterizes the listener's feelings: "When you [action], I feel [reaction]." **Reactive feedback** affirms the speaker's message: "I had a similar experience. It was: …" (Be careful not to use this technique to achieve one-upmanship over the speaker.)

REMEMBER THIS

Figure 10.2   Listening Techniques

1. Stay present	Don't let your mind wander. Many are composing a response before the speaker has a chance to completely finish his/her thought.
2. Make eye contact	Let the speaker see your interest by regularly making eye contact.
3. Ask questions for clarification	This is not your time to respond. Get really clear about what is being said. If you don't understand, ask questions in an open non-charged manner.
4. Acknowledge feelings	If the speaker is telling you something about his/her feelings, acknowledge them. You don't have to agree to show that you see the speaker is upset or happy about something.
5. Restate or paraphrase	Make sure you are getting the information the speaker is presenting by periodically repeating what you hear in different words the speakers. "Let me see if I've got it so far."
6. Seek first to understand and then be understood	Before you state your thoughts and ideas make sure you totally understand and acknowledge the speaker's thoughts.
7. Give nonverbal feedback	While the speaker is speaking, be sure to smile, nod, frown, shrug your shoulders, or raise your eyebrows—whatever is appropriate.
8. Silence	Don't be afraid of this. Periods of total quiet will allow you and the speaker to think about what was said. When you are sure the speaker has completed his/her thoughts on the subject, it will be time for you to comment.
9. Take in all the information both verbal and nonverbal	Focus on the meaning of what is being said and also what is not being said.
10. Get permission	Sometimes people just want to be heard. At other times they are seeking advice. Give advice only when requested and only after the person has had a chance to give you the whole story. If you are not sure, ask if the person is looking for your input.

SOURCE: Alvah Parker, "Top Ten Listening Techniques" http://www.evancarmichael.com/Business-Coach/107/Top-Ten-Listening-Techniques.html, accessed February 8, 2011.

Empathetic Listening

When customer concerns have emotional overtones, empathize before giving an answer or advice. Customers can bring a wide range of emotions to the discussion, from frustration to out and out rejection. **Empathy** is seeking to understand the other person's position without personally getting emotionally involved. Good listeners know that when you put yourself in the customer's place, you are in the position to better analyze the message from his or her perspective.

Empathy not only bolsters understanding but also is a powerful tool for customer loyalty. As an effective listener, you set in motion a positive, mutually rewarding process by demonstrating interest in the customer and what he or she is saying. Empathetic listening encourages honesty, mutual respect, understanding, and a feeling of security in the customer. When you listen empathetically, you seek to understand the beliefs, emotions, and goals of other people.

According to Reginald Adkins, who puts forward five tips for empathetic listening, the foundation of the technique is summarized in the following simple steps:

1. *Provide the speaker with your undivided attention.* This is an instance where "multitasking" or "rapid refocus" will get you in trouble.

☑ MAKE IT A HABIT

Be a Helping Agent

Use these helping skills with customers who just need someone to listen to them while they talk through problems:

- Listen passively with accompanying non-verbal behaviors (eye contact, nodding of the head, etc.) that communicates your interest and concern.
- Use what the customer says to formulate good questions to better understand what the problem is.
- Encourage the person to continue talking toward an eventual solution with understanding, acceptance, and empathy, by saying, for example, "Oh, I see" and "Mm-hmm."
- Encourage the speaker to expand on thoughts and feelings by saying, "Would you like to talk about it?"

2. *Be non-judgmental.* Don't minimize or trivialize the speaker's issue.
3. *Read the speaker.* Observe the emotions behind the words. Is the speaker angry, afraid, frustrated, or resentful? Respond to the emotion as well as the words.
4. *Be Quiet.* Don't feel you must have an immediate reply. Often if you allow for some quiet after the speaker has vented, they themselves will break the silence and offer a solution.
5. *Assure your understanding.* Ask clarifying questions and restate what you perceive the speaker to be saying.[5]

CUSTOMER SERVICE **TIP**

Be aware that people listen, process, and react to messages in a variety of ways, depending on their behavior, cultural background, and relationship to the speaker.

Cultural Listening Cues

Serving a variety of customers and knowing how to provide responsive service that effectively communicates with diverse customers is vital for successful customer relations. As more businesses compete in global markets, the chances are great that you will be listening to speakers for whom English is a second language. As such, communicating presents unique challenges for both listener and speaker.

One particular challenge facing international customers is learning the inflection and sentence patterns of the English language. It is not easy when those patterns conflict with those of the speaker's native tongue. What can CSRs do to become better listeners while non-native customers are speaking?

- *Avoid making judgments about incorrectly accented speech.* Many multilingual speakers use an insightful but complex variety of English expressions. Although their speech may retain remnants of their native languages, don't assume that their struggle with pronunciation means that they are unintelligent.

Ethics/Choices

Suppose you work with a person who, after serving certain ethnic customers, makes comments about how slow to understand he feels this ethnic group is. Would this bother you enough to let your co-worker know how you feel about his service attitude?

---

[5] "Five Tips for Empathetic Listening," August 9, 2006, *Stepcase Lifehack,* http://www.lifehack.org/articles/communication/5-tips-for-empathetic-listening.html accessed January 14, 2011.

- *Be a patient listener.* Strive to overcome the urge to hurry the conversation along. Give non-native speakers time to express their thoughts fully.

- *Don't finish the speaker's sentences.* Allow non-native speakers to choose their words and complete their sentences without volunteering your help. By practicing patience, you may find that customers end up saying something quite different from what you had at first expected.

- *Don't correct grammar and pronunciation errors.* Although you might be trying to help, it is better to focus on what's being expressed and to refrain from teaching English.

- *Don't pretend to understand.* It's all right to tell a non-native speaker that you are having difficulty understanding him or her and ask the person to please repeat the thought.

WHAT DO YOU THINK

10.3

Evaluate your results from taking the listening skills quiz. What did you find out about yourself? Describe your personal evaluation in your journal.

ROADBLOCKS TO LISTENING

Spoken messages delivered by truly great communicators are clear, consistent, direct, human, and personal. However, even the best communicators can occasionally, create obstacles when responding to another person. The good news is that you can remove these communication roadblocks by becoming better at listening. A recent blog on the United Wellbeing website notes twelve roadblocks to effective communication. Six are adapted here.

1. *Judging or criticizing.* Although we are often taught that criticism helps people improve, it is not always the best response when trying to help a person with a problem. An example of this is if you are told by a CSR colleague, "You aren't being a very good team player." Even if the intention is to be supportive, by judging or criticizing, we may inadvertently demean a person who is already struggling.

2. *Naming or labeling.* For example, telling someone "Your response sounds conservative (or liberal)" could stop the listening process. Responding to a person in this way makes him or her feel inadequate by attaching a stigma to the person, problem, or behavior.

3. *Commanding or ordering.* Sometimes we think we have the best, most obvious solution to a person's problem, but responding with a command or an order about what someone should do implies that the person is not competent to judge or act independently.

4. *Moralizing.* When a listener responds by telling someone what to do and then backs up the solution with a moral or theological authority, it is known as moralizing. Moralizing implies that the speaker lacks the moral compass to come up with a responsible solution on his or her own.

5. *Diverting.* Diverting happens when listeners attempt to throw aside a speaker's problems by switching to a more comfortable topic. By doing this, the listener loses the opportunity to truly understand the speaker's concerns and therefore loses the chance to strengthen the relationship.

6. *Advising.* Advising is premature problem solving that tells the other person how to solve a problem. We tend to do this when we see our solution as the only one. Saying, for example, "I told you to do it this way," should be avoided. It implies that the speaker is not able to see a solution to the problem.[6]

Figure 10.3 on page 164 provides examples of each of these roadblocks, as well as an alternative that describes an improved approach to listening.

---

[6] http://unitedwellbeing.wordpress.com/2010/04/02/effective-communication/ accessed January 30, 2011.

REMEMBER THIS

Figure 10.3　Communication Roadblocks

ROADBLOCK	WHAT IT SOUNDS LIKE	AN ALTERNATIVE
Judging or Criticizing	"You're wrong," "I disagree," "You're not thinking clearly."	Step back from your own situation and try to see the problem from the perspective of the speaker.
Naming or Labeling	"That's a silly idea," "You are just being shy," "Why are you so careless?"	Try to see through your immediate responses and truly listen to the speaker.
Commanding or Ordering	"You must …," "You have to: …"	Try to work together to develop a solution.
Moralizing	"It's the right thing to do," "You should know that what you are doing is wrong."	Recognize that everyone has a personal choice and set of values and that the speaker does not necessarily share yours.
Diverting	"Just forget about it," "Something similar happened to me; let me tell you about it."	Try to put the speaker's issues ahead of your own. Before you move on, ask the speaker whether he or she has finished speaking.
Advising	"Why don't you … ," "It would seem to me that you should: …"	Try to let the speaker talk through a problem. Often the solution will emerge with little more than a few nods or words of encouragement from you.

WHAT DO YOU THINK

10.4

Of the six roadblocks to listening covered in the chapter, which three are you most aware of and tend to use as a communicator? How might you improve these roadblocks in a customer service situation? Record your self-evaluation in your journal.

WRAPPING UP

Customer-Focused Listening is a skill that refines innate abilities through self-reflection and constant practice. The best of the best service providers throughout the world work hard to develop and integrate effective listening skills in their daily practice of global customer service. Skilled practitioners avoid selective listening when confronted with tedious or annoying customers. Rather, they focus empathetically on the *total* customer message. Effective listeners learn to practice their skills in both face-to-face situations and long-distance phone or digital modes of communication. An attentive and responsive listener will stand out as a top performer in any organization— large or small, corporate or government, profit or nonprofit.

When combined with visual cues that are reflected by *Nonverbal Communication, Dress, and Manners,* covered next, a total professional emerges, a CSR who is likely to become the recipient of customer, managerial, and peer recognition. These positive responses can, in turn, lead to promotions, awards, and many other exciting opportunities.

FOCUS ON. . .
BEST PRACTICES

Multiple Listening Posts

What great companies do as a matter of practice often defines who they are and why they are recognized nationally. Marketing Professor Mary Jo Bitner at Arizona State University's W. P Carey School of Business, describes how great service organizations like Harrah's, Mayo Clinic, and Ritz-Carlton utilize multiple listening posts to capture the voice of the customer.

She poses these suggestions to organizations: "Listen and respond. Customer feedback is valuable and rare. Set up 'listening posts' throughout your organization and act on what you hear. These posts can be as informal as having a one-on-one conversation with a client at least once a week or as formal as a customer satisfaction study. Listen sincerely and thoughtfully and then base decisions on accumulated input."

Reprinted in part with permission of Professor Mary Jo Bitner, as published on www.leader-values.com.
SOURCE: Mary Jo Bitner, "Eye of the Beholder" Leader Values, 2005, http://www.leader-values.com/Content/detail.asp?ContentDetailID=968 accessed January 15, 2011.

SUMMARY

- The levels of efficiency at which people listen throughout the day are influenced by circumstances, people's attitudes, and their past experiences.

- One result of ineffective listening is selective listening which is hearing only what you want to hear.

- Active listening means listening with your whole mind and body—not just your ears.

- To understand better what speakers are saying, listeners can use feedback that is responsive and reactive.

- Six roadblocks to communicating and listening are judging or criticizing, naming or labeling, commanding or ordering, moralizing, diverting, and advising.

KEY TERMS

active listening   filtering   responsive feedback
empathy   reactive feedback   selective listening

CRITICAL THINKING

1. How effective do you think Bitner's suggestion for companies to set up "listening posts" throughout your organization might be? Cite examples.

2. Which of the three levels of listening is most commonly in use as you interact with others in customer service situations? Cite examples and explain.

3. Describe two communication incidents you have experienced recently in which active listening and empathetic listening took place. Compare the listening outcome for each occasion.

4. Of the six communication and listening road-blocks, which three do you think CSRs should most avoid using when serving customers? Explain.

WHAT DO YOU THINK NOW?

Project 10.1

Assume you are doing a classroom presentation on *customer-focused listening*. Reread your responses to the *What Do You Think?* questions that you completed throughout this chapter. What are some service attitudes and practices that promote the sincere desire to pay attention to what customers say? Which service situations promote effective listening and feedback? Which skills should CSRs practice that complement customer-focused listening? Compile your responses, as directed by your instructor.

ONLINE RESEARCH ACTIVITY

Project 10.2   Planning a Listening Workshop

Research a number of training websites that conduct listening seminars or workshops. As a result of your research, write a one-page training plan describing the topics you would include in a customer-focused listening workshop for service professionals. Submit to your instructor, as directed.

COMMUNICATION SKILLS AT WORK

Project 10.3   Words That Smile

Note your reactions as you hear a classmate recite the three statements below. For the speaker: frown while making the statement the first time, and then repeat the same message with a smile. Assume that you are speaking with a real customer. How different are the messages communicated to and understood by the customer when you frown compared to when you smile?

1. "Our commitment is to top-quality service."

   _____

   _____

   _____

2. "I'm glad you chose to do business with us today."

   _____

   _____

   _____

3. "What can I do to help you?"

   _____

   _____

   _____

DECISION MAKING AT WORK

Project 10.4   The International Traveler

Assume you are working in the hotel industry and an international traveler is asking directions to a local landmark or popular restaurant in the area. Although you have repeated the instructions several times, the traveler doesn't seem to understand your directions. You are wondering what you should do next.

What are two creative steps you might suggest that you or your hotel can take to prevent this frustrating situation from happening in the future?

CASE STUDY

Project 10.5   "I Know You Believe..."

Everyone in the company lunchroom was laughing as each person cited a real-case scenario that fit with the meaning of a well-known quotation. The anonymous quotation that caused the laughter and subsequent discussion was, "I know you believe you understand what you think I just said, but I'm not sure you realize that what you heard is not what I meant."

1. How does this statement relate to the topics covered in this chapter?

   _____

   _____

2. To what extent do you think this statement is true and applicable to service encounters?

   _____

   _____

3. Relate a personal situation you've experienced recently when the outcome was illustrative of this quote, and share it with your class members.

   _____

   _____

Kurhan/Shutterstock

CHAPTER 11

Nonverbal Communication, Dress, and Manners

Etiquette is the science of living.
It embraces everything.

EMILY POST, AMERICAN WRITER AND SOCIALITE

OBJECTIVES

1. Identify the elements and interpretations of body language.

2. Discuss the importance of having a dress code in the workplace.

3. Cite examples of business etiquette and manners.

Service Uniforms

When you go to a store or restaurant, do service employees who wear a uniform seem more professional and committed to service? Does it seem that you are served more completely when service professionals wear name tags on their service uniform? Every day service professionals in fast-food restaurants, hotels, and major retail stores, wear uniforms, such as aprons, shirts, or vests. UniFirst, a company that sells uniforms, touts that "Some symbols are world famous, others are less well known. That is also true for the 'image uniform.' When it comes to a positive corporate identity, employees in distinctive uniforms can be a surprisingly powerful symbol."

Another article in *Entrepreneur* points out that, "More than 32 million U.S. workers go to work each day wearing uniforms. Uniforms can project a consistent and unified image for companies that regularly interact with the public... For employees, uniform programs help them avoid having to buy, clean, and repair their work clothes."

SOURCES: "Custom Image Programs," *UniFirst* Online at http://www.unifirst.ca/products/products_custom_image.html accessed January 20, 2011 and "Making Uniform Decisions" and *Entrepreneur*, March 2002 http://www.entrepreneur.com/humanresources/managingemployees/article50160.html accessed January 19, 2011.

CUSTOMER-FRIENDLY BODY LANGUAGE

"Stop slouching and sit up straight. Stand with your back flat, your shoulders back, your head held high, and your feet planted firmly on the floor." How many times have you heard this from someone—most likely your mother—over the years? Showcasing our intelligence and professional abilities is as much about presentation, including body language, dress, and manners, as it is about verbal communication.

The Importance of Body Language

As a CSR, remember that, as you communicate, you not only receive body language signals, you send them as well. **Body language** is a type of non-spoken communication that includes tone of voice, eye movement, posture, hand gestures, facial expressions, and more. To really understand the full meaning of a message, pay special attention to a person's body language, because nonverbal cues are more immediate, instinctive, and uncontrolled than verbal expressions. As such, they bring attitudes and feelings out into the open.

According to Tanya Reiman, a body language expert, "during our conversations, especially the first minute, only 7% of the first impression we give is via words. The remaining 93% will be based upon paralanguage; pitch, amplitude, rate, and voice quality of speech as well as body language."[1]

Body language communicates our attitudes to customers, and it can either reinforce or contradict our words. We react more to what we *think* someone meant than we do to the words he or she actually said. For example, you may tell a customer that you are happy to help her, but if you frown, slump, or refuse to make eye contact, in most cases, the customer will not believe you. This is because people

[1] http://www.tonyareiman.com/articles/body_language accessed January 20, 2011.

REMEMBER THIS

Figure 11.1 Body Language

NONVERBAL BEHAVIOR	INTERPRETATION
Brisk, erect walk	Confidence
Standing with hands on hips	Readiness, aggression
Arms crossed over chest	Defensiveness
Walking with hands in pockets, shoulders hunched	Dejection
Putting hand to cheek	Evaluation, thinking
Clasping hands behind back	Anger, frustration, apprehension
Resting head in hand, eyes downcast	Boredom
Rubbing hands	Anticipation
Gesturing with open palm	Sincerity, openness, innocence
Pinching bridge of nose, eyes closed	Negative evaluation
Tapping or drumming fingers	Impatience
Tilting head	Interest
Stroking chin	Trying to make a decision
Looking down, face turned away	Disbelief
Biting nails	Insecurity, nervousness

SOURCE: Used with permission of SPARC/DeltaBravo.net http://deltabravo.net/ accessed January 19, 2011

are more likely to believe nonverbal signals, such as a frown or a lazy posture, than words.

Body language is a crucial communication tool for delivering great customer service. Figure 11.1 describes several body language signs and their possible meanings. Understanding body language in the workplace isn't trivial—it is a career necessity, because interpreting it well will give you a big advantage when serving diverse customers.

Interpreting Body Signs

Positive body language, besides communicating an attitude of caring and cooperation, conveys professional stature and self-confidence. For example, listeners consider those who speak with conviction in a calm voice to be competent and trustworthy. Learning the major elements of body language that follow and how to interpret them during service exchanges will give you more confidence when communicating on the job.

Eye Contact The eyes communicate more than any other part of the human anatomy. For example, staring or gazing at others can create pressure and tension. What is more, fixing one's gaze at someone without any other gesture, such as nodding or saying "I see" can make someone nervous. Rolling your eyes sends the message that you aren't taking the other person's ideas seriously. Shifty eyes and too much blinking can suggest deception; whereas, people with eye movements that show they are relaxed and

Can you "hear" a smile on the phone?

comfortable, yet attentive to the person they are conversing with, are seen as more sincere and honest. Because of increasing diversity in the marketplace, you may encounter customers from other cultures in which direct eye contact is considered offensive. Be sensitive and take your cue from the customer.

Voice You may have noticed that you can "hear" a smile on the phone. Your tone of voice can sound either interested and caring, or aggressive. Interested and caring works best for most customer situations. Notice the tone of voice others use and what feelings that tone evoke in you. Tone of voice is especially important on the phone, when visual cues are missing from the conversation.

Smiling Show customers you enjoy helping them by smiling at appropriate times. If you smile even when you are not feeling your best, your own brain does not distinguish the difference and sends signals that you are feeling upbeat and positive. The result can be that you cheer up yourself—and the customer. However, avoid smiling when a customer is expressing anger. If you do, you may upset the customer even more by making the customer feel that you are not taking his or her issues seriously.

Posture Slouching and leaning postures send the message, "I'm tired, bored, or uninterested in your concerns." A military stance is unnecessary, but an alert posture reinforces the customer's feeling that you are interested in helping. Remember also not to crowd a customer and to provide enough personal space between the two of you. **Personal space** refers to the distance between people as they interact and communicate.

Gestures Gesturing, especially during tense conversations, can mean the difference between sending a message of trust and cooperation and one of suspicion. For example, placing your hands on your hips typically conveys aggression. Crossing your arms over your chest suggests defensiveness. Slamming something down abruptly indicates you are angry. Become aware of your hand movements as they are the punctuation marks to the words you use.

Author Joy Davidson notes that "By paying careful attention to body language, and noticing when someone makes a sudden transition from one attitude to another, you'll have a good idea of what the other person is thinking—whether or not that's what he or she is saying."[2] As you communicate with customers, be mindful of these four typical interpretations of notable body language cues:

1. *Openness and warmth:* open-lipped smiling, open hands with palms visible
2. *Confidence:* leaning forward in the chair, keeping the chin up, putting the tips of the fingers of one hand against the tips of the fingers of the other hand in a "praying," or "steepling," position
3. *Nervousness:* smoking, whistling, fidgeting, jiggling pocket contents, clearing the throat, running fingers through the hair, wringing hands, biting on pens or other objects, twiddling thumbs
4. *Untrustworthiness or defensiveness:* frowning, squinting, tight-lipped grinning, crossing arms in front of the chest, darting eyes, looking down when speaking, clenching hands, pointing with the fingers, rubbing the back of the neck

Understanding other people's body language is not enough for effective communication. CSRs must understand their own body language as well, because controlling nonverbal signals can improve their image and increase their success with customers. Joy Davidson suggests practicing the following gestures in front of a mirror. Doing so, she suggests, will help the practitioner become "confident, open and in control":

- Walk with a brisk, easy stride and with eyes looking forward.

- Stand evenly on both feet. Keep your arms relaxed and casual. For example, keep one hand in your pocket and use the other one for gesturing as you speak.

---

[2] Joy Davidson, "Office Tics—Understanding Body Language," *Men's Fitness,* July 1998. http://findarticles.com/p/articles/mi_m1608/is_n7_v14/ai_20946890/?tag=-content;col1 accessed January 20, 2011.

- Move slightly closer to others if you want to warm up the relationship. Avoid hostile postures, such as hands on your hips or clasped behind your head. Also avoid defensive gestures, such as turning your body away from the listener.

- Look at others straight on. Meet their eyes and then occasionally let your gaze drift elsewhere to keep from staring.

- Keep your gestures loose, yet controlled. If those around you seem reserved or nervous, avoid excessively exuberant or frantic movements.[3]

WHAT DO YOU THINK

11.1

Do you agree with the statement "Actions speak louder than words"? In what ways does this thought apply to your service experiences? Does it support or refute them? Record your opinion in your journal.

DRESSING TO MAKE A GOOD IMPRESSION

As noted throughout this text, as a CSR, you must have technical skills, communication skills, and interpersonal skills. To showcase these abilities, you also need image skills. The importance of image and attire in the business world is very real. Whether you wear a uniform as discussed in our opening feature or your own clothes, your image is like the weather—people notice when it is extremely good or extremely bad. Your *image* is your reputation and a reflection of how others perceive you, both through your conversation and appearance.

When people look at you and see the way you act, as well as the way you dress, they draw impressions concerning your ability, your credibility, and,

most importantly, whether you are sincere and should be taken seriously. The bottom line, however, is that people want to be taken seriously, and attire can help or hurt in that effort.

Workers today do not dress as formally as they once did, yet the concept of dressing for success is just as relevant, given the competitiveness of today's workplace. Knowledge and skills are instrumental, but image and appearance still continue to be key factors in moving into better jobs. To achieve success, you must look successful by presenting an image of competence, self-confidence, and professionalism.

Most of us have heard the expressions, "You never get a second chance to make a first impression," and "First impressions are lasting ones." Whether interacting with fellow employees on the job or meeting with customers, your attire, behavior, and attitude say a lot about you. Those who wish to move ahead in their careers must think carefully about what they wear. Clothing choices can help or hinder those goals.

Dress Code

While employees must decide what to wear to work every day, employers must decide what parameters to put on that decision and how to enforce those guidelines. A generation ago, most professional workers were expected to dress up for work, wearing business suits that demonstrated their conformity with corporate America. Today, most workplaces allow *business casual dress*, a more relaxed look. This allows workers to express their individuality— and therein lies the problem.

What happens when a worker's choices do not conform to the image that the employer wants to project *to customers*? Company dress codes are protected by law, and employers in the United States have a legal right to ask you to adhere to them. In an article entitled "Dress for Work Success: A Business Casual Dress Code," Susan M. Heathfield notes: "A work **dress code** is a set of standards that companies develop to help provide their employees with guidance about what is appropriate to wear to work." Heathfield rightly observes that some dress codes

---

[3] Ibid.

may require formal attire, while others may permit business casual and even casual style clothing. The degree of formality required in a company dress code is usually contingent upon the frequency of face-to-face interaction between employees and customers.[4]

On the other hand, a *casual dress code* is usually allowed if customers do not visit that business location. However, not all casual clothing is suitable for the office. Heathfield suggests these guidelines to help you avoid what is inappropriate to wear to work.

- Clothing that reveals too much cleavage, your back, your chest, your stomach, or your underwear is not appropriate for a place of business.

- Any clothing that has words, terms, or pictures that may be offensive to other employees is unacceptable.[5]

When deciding on an appropriate dress code, most organizations take into consideration the following three factors:

1. The business's public image
2. The nature of the work performed by the employees affected by the dress code
3. Safety standards

Some employers oppose casual dress because, in their opinion, too many workers push the boundaries of what is acceptable. They contend that absenteeism, tardiness, and flirtatious behavior have increased since dress-down policies were adopted.

Regardless of what critics say, employees generally enjoy casual dress policies. Supporters argue that comfortable clothes and a more relaxed working environment lift employee morale, increase employee creativity, and improve internal communication. Employees also appreciate reduced clothing-related expenses. Regardless of how informal the outfit, clothes should always be clean and pressed, stain- and odor-free, and not ripped, torn, or frayed.

For an organization, providing a reasonable dress code is important for a number of reasons.

- Employees need to exhibit the look that confirms professionalism for customers and co-workers.

- Managers need specific guidance on what is appropriate for their staff to wear to work.

- Different managers, in different departments, have different standards for what is fitting work attire. Employees, sometimes rightly, ask *why* certain clothing is acceptable in one department and not in another.

- Employees complain to their supervisors and the human resource department when they feel other employees are dressed inappropriately. Without a dress code in place, there is no standard to assess whether this is true.

For a description of a typical business casual dress code for employees who regularly interact with customers in person, see Figure 11.2.

Ideally, each company has developed a written description of the types of clothing that are acceptable.

What attitude does each worker project in his choice of dress?

[4] Susan M. Heathfield, "Work Dress Code," *about.com Human Resources,* http://humanresources.about.com/od/glossaryd/g/work_dress_code.htm accessed January 19, 2011.

[5] Susan M. Heathfield, "Dress for Work Success: A Business Casual Dress Code," *About.com Human Resources,* http://humanresources.about.com/od/workrelationships/a/dress_code.htm accessed January 19, 2011.

REMEMBER THIS

Figure 11.2 Business Casual Dress Code

CLOTHING	SUGGESTED	NOT RECOMMENDED
Slacks, Pants, and Suit Pants	Slacks and other cotton or synthetic material pants, wool pants, flannel pants, dressy capris, and nice looking dress synthetic pants are acceptable.	Inappropriate slacks or pants include jeans, sweatpants, exercise pants, Bermuda shorts, short shorts, shorts, bib overalls, leggings, and any spandex or other form-fitting pants such as people wear for biking.
Skirts, Dresses, and Skirted Suits	Casual dresses and skirts, and skirts that are split at or below the knee are acceptable. Dress and skirt length should be at a length at which you can sit comfortably in public.	Short, tight skirts that ride halfway up the thigh are inappropriate for work. Mini-skirts, skorts, sun dresses, beach dresses, and spaghetti-strap dresses are not acceptable.
Shirts, Tops, Blouses, and Jackets	Casual shirts, dress shirts, sweaters, tops, golf-type shirts, and turtlenecks are acceptable attire for work. Most suit jackets or sport jackets are also acceptable attire.	Inappropriate attire for work includes tank tops; midriff tops; shirts with potentially offensive words, terms, logos, pictures, cartoons, or slogans; halter-tops; tops with bare shoulders; sweatshirts; and t-shirts unless worn under another blouse, shirt, jacket, or dress.
Shoes and Footwear	Conservative athletic or walking shoes, loafers, sneakers, boots, flats, dress heels, and leather deck-type shoes are acceptable for work.	Flashy athletic shoes, thongs, flip-flops, slippers, and any shoe with an open toe are not acceptable in the office.
Hats and Head Covering	Head covers that are required for religious purposes or to honor cultural tradition are allowed.	Hats are not appropriate attire in the office.

SOURCE: Susan M. Heathfield, "A Relaxed, Casual Dress Code," *About.com Human Resources*, http://humanresources.about.com/od/workrelationships/a/dress_code.htm accessed January 19, 2011.

Some companies seek legal counsel to ensure that their policies do not discriminate against men or women and that the wording is explicit. By using common sense and exercising good judgment, dressing to make a good impression is easy. Following is a list of suggested *non-clothing* guidelines covering hair, nails, and makeup, in business today from an article that appeared in *Ebony* entitled "Dressing for Success in Corporate America":

- *Hair* Today, facial hair is commonplace and hair length runs from the shaven head to a neatly tied ponytail. Your hairstyle should be neat, and your hair color should be natural looking and complementary to your complexion.

- *Nails* Long, elaborately decorated nails may be frowned upon in many companies. Short, clean

nails in a French manicure or one-tone polish (light pink or earth tones) are always stylish. For men and women, clean and cared-for nails send a positive message to customers.

- *Makeup* Your makeup should be subtle and paired to your overall look. Choose shades that are natural and flattering to your complexion. The natural look with polish is the hallmark of good grooming.[6]

- *Jewelry* For both men and women, jewelry worn in an office environment should be in good taste and not flamboyant or distracting. Investing in jewelry

---

[6] "Dressing for Success in Corporate America," *Ebony*, January 2001, http://findarticles.com/p/articles/mi_m1077/is_3_56/ai_68504377/ accessed January 20, 2011.

and accessories that showcase your distinctiveness is a good idea. For example, colorful silk scarves, pins, and bracelets can add a touch of individuality and interest to your wardrobe.

- *Perfume and cologne* Use discretion and taste in choosing office scents. Fragrances can linger in a closed office and seem stronger to others than you believe they are. Also, be aware some people are chemically sensitive to perfume and cologne and increasingly places of business are discouraging their use.

Facial Piercings and Body Tattoos

We make hundreds of judgments about people every day, many of them based on personal preferences. Personal prejudices don't stop at the office door, and this can pose a particularly compromising situation for employers relative to piercings and tattoos.

In 2010, Sara Dobosh reported that the Food and Drug Administration estimated that more than 45 million Americans have at least one tattoo, and a 2010 Pew Research report revealed that 38 percent of 18–29 year olds sport a tattoo, while 32 percent of the 30–45 demographic have body art.[7]

Employees often feel the employer has no right to restrict the display of piercings and tattoos. That is not true. In an article entitled, "Body Art in the Workplace," the author notes that "companies can limit employees' personal expressions on the job as long as they don't infringe on employees' civil liberties. According to the Equal Employment Opportunity Commission (EEOC), employers are allowed to impose dress codes and appearance policies as long as they do not discriminate or hinder a person's race, color, religion, age, national origin, or gender."[8]

As noted by Ira S. Wolfe, the reason behind policies forbidding piercings and body art always comes back to the impression made upon, and reaction elicited from, the customer: "Companies faced

with inked and pierced applicants can demand eyebrow rings or tongue rings be removed and tattoos covered to help project the proper image to customers. That is because some customers, particularly older ones who dislike tattoos, could be turned off and they may be less likely to do business with it. Loss of business is a justifiable reason to restrict the display of body art in whatever form it takes."[9]

WHAT DO YOU THINK

11.2

In a particular work position you've held over the past few years, what was the acceptable dress code you followed? Was there a written dress code, or did you tend to dress like others in that work environment? Evaluate the appropriateness of your dress to that business setting and record your thoughts in your journal.

PRACTICING ETIQUETTE AND MANNERS

In light of our shrinking world, as well as the expanded media coverage throughout that world, good business etiquette is crucial, as behaviors are

---

[7] Sara Dobosh, "Piercing the Workplace Stereotype," *FOXBusiness*, July 22, 2010, http://www.foxbusiness.com/personal-finance/2010/07/22/piercing-workplace-stereotype/ accessed January 19, 2011.

[8] Regina M. Robo, "Body Art in the Workplace," mysalary.com, http://www.salary.com/Articles/ArticleDetail.asp?part=par228 accessed January 18, 2011.

[9] Ira S. Wolfe, "Tattoos and Body Piercings Get Under Manager's Skin," http://ezinearticles.com/?Tattoos-and-Body-Piercings-Get-Under-Managers-Skin&id=4416050 accessed January 18, 2011.

more closely scrutinized than ever in the past. Proper business etiquette goes beyond using the right fork at a lunch meeting, to include developing effective people skills and practicing politeness. In general, **business etiquette** dictates the rules of acceptable behavior that identify the application of correct or polite manners in a typical business situation.

Etiquette is about presenting yourself with the kind of polish that shows you can be taken seriously. Many potentially worthwhile and profitable alliances have been lost because of an *unintentional* breach of manners. Most behavior that is perceived as disrespectful, discourteous, or abrasive is unintentional and could have been avoided by practicing good manners or etiquette. Basic knowledge and practice of etiquette is a valuable advantage, because, in a lot of situations, a second chance may not be possible or practical.

Any time you make contact with a customer, you are making a mini-presentation of yourself, ultimately representing your company, service, and products. In today's stress-filled world, coupled with the ups and downs inherent in everyday life, experiencing day-to-day pleasantries is very nice. Good manners are said to be two-thirds common sense and one-third kindness. Experiencing a moment of pleasant kindness can be uplifting. Respecting others is truly empowering as well.

No matter how tired you might be, or how abrasive a customer might become, service professionals must practice good manners. An environment in which people treat each other with kindness and consideration is certainly one in which a client enjoys doing business. Learning the rules of business etiquette is not hard to do, nor is it costly. In fact, practicing etiquette skills is one of the best professional development tools workers can use to increase their chances of success.

Employers value well-mannered employees because they are a reflection of the company itself. Do people really notice good manners? Even though lifestyles are more informal and relaxed in today's society, good manners are appreciated. Using polite language, turning off cell phones out of courtesy, holding the door, sending a thank you note, offering

CUSTOMER SERVICE **TIP**

Behaviors that go against kindness, logic, and efficiency get in the way of good business. In fact, they lead to bad business.

a smile—these are just a few favors people appreciate. Saying "please" and "thank you," warmly greeting customers and co-workers, and showing patience are essential skills for anyone's success.

The rules of etiquette can be compared to a common language that all successful professionals must learn to speak. People make choices in the business arena, and they choose to do business with people they like and respect. Etiquette skills can help establish productive relationships with colleagues and customers. Successful relationships begin when you exhibit courtesy, respect, and concern for the comfort of others. In the end, of course, better relationships mean better business.

Soft Skills

Etiquette at work includes all aspects of the work environment—completing work as promised, getting to work on time, being courteous to others, being an active member of the work team, practicing good human relations, listening, following through on commitments made, and solving problems in a timely and effective manner. In the workplace, these are referred to as soft skills or *people skills*.

Some may ask whether **soft skills** like punctuality, positive attitude, and cooperation are more important than knowing how to perform a job. These soft skills are just as important because they help service professionals become successful. For example, a dependable worker will most likely be given more responsibility, advancements, and pay increases over an undependable co-worker. People who display refinement make better impressions, and others want to be around them. Customers do business with people they like; it is that simple.

People with good attitudes usually respect their co-workers, accept responsibility, and accomplish more each day. Your attitude is evident in your body language, the way you complete tasks, your attention to detail, your consideration of those around you, the way you take care of yourself, and your general approach to life. Given the ubiquitous usage of today's handheld technology devices, a few words are in order concerning their presence in today's office environment. A good cue to adhere to is: We should conduct ourselves differently with them in the workplace than in our home or dorm room. For example, texting personal messages, placing private phone calls within earshot of others, surfing the Internet, or e-mailing friends from a smartphone are inappropriate actions to take while working. Good manners, a dedicated attitude, respect for others, and self-discipline work together to make good things happen for customer service representatives.

Unfortunately, the importance of these soft skills is often undervalued, and there is far less training provided for them than hard skills (i.e., document creation or telephone techniques). For some reason, organizations seem to expect that people know how to behave on the job. They tend to assume that everyone knows and understands the importance of being on time, taking initiative, being

CUSTOMER SERVICE **TIP**

Respect is at the heart of good manners. All good manners are based on thoughtfulness for others and respect for them as individuals of equal value.

friendly, and producing high-quality work. It's just not enough to be highly trained in technical skills, without developing the softer, interpersonal and relationship-building skills that help people to communicate kindheartedly and collaborate effectively.

Cultural Politeness

As businesses become increasingly more global and bring people of diverse cultures and backgrounds closer, learning the skills of proper etiquette on a global level is one of the most important elements for service success and customer growth. The ability to appreciate and respect cultural differences can be very helpful in understanding *why* people act in certain ways and gives you a better understanding on *how* you should act while conducting business with them.

What needs to be said here about different cultures is just that—they are different. No one

MAKE IT **A HABIT**

Minding Your Manners

Endeavor to avoid business etiquette blunders with customers by remembering to:

- Use a firm handshake when you are introduced to a customer because it demonstrates professionalism and self-confidence.
- Never interrupt when someone is speaking; speak only when the other person has stopped talking.
- Smile and make eye contact with customers because it makes them feel instantly recognized.

Why is showing politeness to others especially important in today's global service industry?

can expect to know every nuance. Mistakes will be made and unintentional blunders committed, but some of these errors can be avoided by suppressing one's own cultural biases. Most mistakes come in the form of spoken and body language or omitting something that should have been taken care of.

We all carry our own culture with us, so everything we see, hear, or feel is filtered through our cultural biases. Americans are often noticeable because they tend to be unreserved in their behavior and informal and casual right from the start in both business and social relations. For example, many people are more apt to use an acquaintance's first name after meeting him or her. This is a tradition unheard of in some cultures. Using an acquaintance's first name can be somewhat offensive to some, especially in countries where it is very important to build relationships *before* business takes place. The *Etiquette International* website provides information to help people become more poised, polished, and professional when interacting with persons of another culture and offers the following suggestions relative to time, greetings and names, and personal space and touch. Here are some examples:

- *Time* The website notes that "Differing attitudes toward time are the major source of annoyance in international interactions, yet few people give it much thought. How far in advance appointments and bookings must be scheduled, and to what extent punctuality is stressed or ignored are all important considerations." Americans, who believe that time is something to be watched, organized, and managed carefully may experience conflict when dealing with a customer or colleague from a culture that is more relationship-oriented, and who "considers time as flowing and flexible, beyond human control, and to be accepted whatever happens." As the website advises, "It pays to develop some flexibility to avoid angry outbursts."

- *Greetings and Names* It is important to remember that, greetings indicate respect for the status of the recipient, and introductions must likewise be aware of considerations of rank and custom. "Who acknowledges whom, how deeply one bows, and how long speaks volumes." It is also important to be aware of which cultures invert the arrangement of first name and surname. Otherwise, one may commit the unintentional but still potentially offensive familiarity of addressing someone by his or her first name. As the website advises, "Never call someone by the first name unless you are specifically asked to do so; virtually nowhere else are people as informal in the manner of address as in the United States. Don't forget the honorifics or titles that go with the name. They are usually a point of pride."

- *Personal Space and Touch* The differences in space and touch among cultures reflect each society's attitudes and values. Understanding and appreciating these differences is vital to successful intercultural communication. "Infringing upon another's personal space or inadvertently backing away when they enter your bubble can send unintended negative messages. Touching someone—a hand on the forearm, an arm around the shoulder, a pat on the back—is one of the easiest ways to violate personal space."[10]

Attention to detail is not only a polite practice; but in today's economy, it is a very smart business practice. Sensitive and professional interactions always promote successful cultural exchanges.

WHAT DO YOU THINK

11.3

Describe two encounters you've recently experienced with a person who demonstrated a) poor etiquette or manners and b) good etiquette or manners. Contrast the impressions you were left with in both situations and record them in your journal.

---

[10] "First Get Good," Etiquette International, http://www.etiquetteinternational. com/Articles/FirstGetGood.aspx accessed January 20, 2011.

FOCUS ON. . . BEST PRACTICES

Job Interview Reminders

Do you get nervous before going out on a job interview? For example, how do you prepare yourself for a customer service job interview prior to leaving the house in terms of dress and general readiness to present yourself in the best way? Because you might not know prior to the interview what the organization's dress code is, it is always a good idea to err on the side of dressing conservatively.

The *Economic Times* reported in 2009 about a survey conducted by the jobsite CareerBuilder, that asked over 2,700 hiring managers about common mistakes made by job candidates that affected the outcome of their job candidacy. According to the survey, 57 percent reported that dressing inappropriately is the most common mistake committed by a job seeker during the interview. The survey noted the second most common mistake was "appearing disinterested" during an interview. Other common mistakes included speaking about previous jobs in a negative mode (52 percent), appearing to be arrogant (51 percent), and using a mobile phone (46 percent) during the interview.

SOURCE: "Dress Smart for Job Interview: Survey," February 20, 2010, http://economictimes.indiatimes.com/news/news-by-industry/jobs/Dress-smart-for-job-interview-Survey/articleshow/5627240.cms accessed January 18, 2011.

WRAPPING UP

To say service professionals should make a determined effort to do the right thing and treat customers as *they* would like to be treated sounds like common sense. It takes a determined awareness to understand and use *Nonverbal Communication, Dress, and Manners* in the best way during interactions with customers. Whether individuals are face-to-face or at a distance from each other, how either party respects and makes the other person *feel* can manifest in an exciting beginning or an unfortunate ending to a service relationship. Apply your knowledge of manners as you study the last chapter in the text, *Telephone and Digital Communication.*

SUMMARY

- Using appropriate body language is critical when dealing with customers and includes tone of voice, eye movement, posture, hand gestures, and facial expressions.

- Dressing appropriately and being well groomed make a statement about you and your employer.

- Good manners contribute to a positive first and lasting impression in social and business situations, as well as give you a favorable reputation, especially with customers from other cultures.

KEY TERMS

body language   dress code   soft skills
personal space   business etiquette

CRITICAL THINKING

1. Have you ever left a job interview thinking that you did not make a very good impression? In hindsight, can you analyze why you had that feeling and describe it? Might you have committed one of the job interview mistakes noted in the Best Practices feature?

2. Of all the elements that constitute body language, which three would you describe as the most important when serving customers? Explain.

3. If one customer expressed confidence and another expressed nervousness, what types of body language signals would you look for in each instance? How good are you at interpreting body language during customer service exchanges? Discuss.

4. In your opinion, what societal factors make it difficult for organizations to establish a proper dress code in today's workplace?

5. When shopping in a retail store or online, how important is it to you for service professionals in person or through virtual chats to practice good business etiquette and manners? Explain.

WHAT DO YOU THINK NOW?

Project 11.1

Assume you are doing a classroom presentation on *A CSRs Image in the Workplace*. Reread your responses to the *What Do You Think?* questions that you completed throughout this chapter. What are some service attitudes that have an effect on projecting a successful workplace image? What service environments may diminish a CSR's work appearance and behavior? What manners are needed to be a top service provider? Compile your responses, as directed by your instructor.

ONLINE RESEARCH ACTIVITY

Project 11.2   Soft Skills

With two classmates, research a career exploration website or a number of websites for large corporations, and locate several job descriptions for customer service representative positions posted within the last 30 days in a major city near you. Pay particular attention to the descriptions that request soft skills, such as punctuality, positive attitude, willingness to learn, and cooperation.

As a result of your group's research, prepare a simple poster of the printouts of job descriptions you were able to locate, and highlight the soft skills that are mentioned. Present your poster and discuss noteworthy findings to the class, as directed by your instructor. As an alternative, follow your instructor's directions to join a group and use the instructor-designated discussion board to complete the group project.

COMMUNICATION SKILLS AT WORK

Project 11.3 Good Manners Strategies

Manners are being taught less and less. Supporters of this statement believe that knowing and practicing good manners is not a matter of vanity, snobbery, or trying to impress, but simply a matter of being kind and sensitive to the needs of others. The use of good manners creates a considerate, gracious, and respectful atmosphere in which to live and work.

Form a group and discuss some strategies for dealing and communicating with persons who do *not* use good manners when interacting with others in the workplace. Report back to the class on the top three strategies your group developed. As an alternative, follow your instructor's directions to join a group and use the instructor-designated discussion board to complete the group project.

DECISION MAKING AT WORK

Project 11.4 Manners and Business Etiquette

While eating lunch at the food court in the mall, Simon, a CSR at a retail store within the mall, witnessed a customer service incident in action. A woman approached the counter with a crushed Styrofoam cup and said, "This cup fell off our table and broke. I need another drink and I need someone to come clean up our table and the floor." The tone of her voice suggested that somehow the restaurant was responsible for her broken cup. At that point, Simon noticed that the staff quickly gave her a new drink. Then the manager appeared with a smile and said, "I would be glad to clean that up for you." The staff who served the woman was exemplary in their manners and etiquette throughout the service exchange. When Simon went back to work at the department store, he relayed his observations to his colleagues.

1. What do you think the likelihood is of this type of customer service practice in most businesses today? Can you name any businesses that provide exemplary etiquette and manners similar to that shown at the restaurant?

_____

_____

2. In your opinion, what do you think contributes most to staff with manners and etiquette? Were they hired with these qualities or were they trained in these behaviors, in this case, by the restaurant?

_____

_____

CASE STUDY

Project 11.5 Enforcing a Dress Code

Cecilia recently went to work for a telecommunications firm in San Francisco as the receptionist. In the first week, several other employees went out of their way to go through the lobby just to see her. She is very attractive, and everyone soon learned she was a former model at local trade shows.

Cecilia's image started to create problems within the company. Though Cecilia was a nice person and didn't appear conceited, her appearance was a distraction to the organization. The office manager discovered that work had slowed down since Cecilia was hired. For instance, male sales reps were stopping by and spending time chatting with her; female workers were making catty remarks behind her back and seemed to be spending more time having negative conversations. Three comments overheard were, "She's too perfect," "Cecilia wears way too much makeup," and "She dresses too nice for this place."

Make notes regarding what is happening here. Include the roles in this situation of the receptionist, visitors to the front lobby, other employees, and the office manager. Each person or group is playing a role. Using the questions below as a guide, be prepared to discuss how you would resolve this situation.

1. Do you think the office manager should view this problem as one that will work itself out with time? Why or why not?

_____

_____

_____

2. What steps should be taken to get work back on track? What should the manager say to the other workers? Is Cecilia to blame at all in this situation?

_____

_____

_____

CHAPTER 12

Telephone and Digital Communication

*Regardless of the changes in technology,
the market for well-crafted messages will
always have an audience.*

STEVE BURNETT, OWNER, THE BURNETT GROUP
(MARKETING CONSULTANTS)

OBJECTIVES

1. Detail the essential customer service skills needed when communicating over the phone.

2. Describe the purpose and extent of business use of voice and virtual technologies.

3. Evaluate the quality and delivery of your service voice when speaking on the phone.

4. Distinguish between inbound and outbound telemarketing activities.

5. Identify and describe Web-driven service technologies.

BUSINESS IN *ACTION*

SKYPE

It's hard to believe that you can place an overseas or cross-country call for free, but that is exactly what you can do with Skype. This software application allows users to make voice and video calls over the Internet 24/7/365.

Its incredible usage around the world is phenomenal, and there appears to be no stopping its popularity and growth. According to Courtney Boyd Myers, there were over 27 million Skype users online as of January 10, 2011, with Skype reporting an average of 124 million users per month. *Newsweek* reports that "Skype may find that the ocean of money once available to telephone companies will become just a pond as more and more calls are routed over the Internet."

Whatever Skype becomes in the next ten or so years, today it is serving a vacant niche that consumers and businesses alike appreciate and use.

SOURCES: Courtney Boyd Myers, "Skype Signs On Over 27 Million Users In One Day," January 1, 2011, http://thenextweb.com/apps/2011/01/10/skype-signs-up-over-1-million-users-in-one-day/ accessed February 1, 2011 and "The Future of Skype," http://www.newsweek.com/2010/08/10/the-future-of-skype.html accessed January 31, 2011.

ANSWERING THE PHONE

Despite the increased popularity of using the Internet to conduct business, the phone continues to be a vital link between businesses and customers. Whether a caller is asking a question about office hours or ordering merchandise, the politeness and helpfulness of the person at the other end of the phone are paramount for building relationships, instilling trust, creating a positive experience, and, ultimately, driving repeat business for an organization.

Phone greetings are critical because they help form first impressions. From a new customer deciding whether to do business with you to an irate customer judging your competence, how you answer the phone makes a difference. When companies choose employees who will give that first greeting to customers, it is important to select individuals who sincerely care about the business and can convey that sentiment to customers who call. How many times have you called a company at its main number, only to be put on hold immediately by the receptionist, without even getting a chance to say anything? Or worse, gotten trapped in an automated phone system intentionally designed to deprive you of contact with a live person?

When developing that all-important opening message, remember that there is power in simplicity. For best results, incorporate three fundamental rules into your first message: be pleasant, brief, and sincere. The key elements of a phone greeting are the department or company name, your name, and an offer of assistance. An example from someone in the customer service department might sound like this: "Customer service, this is Stacey. How may I help you?" It may sound simplistic, but practice saying your standard phone greeting until you can hear

CUSTOMER SERVICE **TIP**

Make your voice friendly and approachable when speaking to a customer on the telephone.

Figure 12.1 Telephone Tips

Use welcoming words.	Answering callers' requests with, "I'll be glad to help you" makes customers feel more confident in your ability.
Use the caller's name often.	A caller's name is the most personal possession he or she has. By recognizing and using it frequently, you make the caller feel better about the service.
Maintain an enthusiastic and personable tone.	Your voice is an all-important delivery system for your words. Speak distinctly and clearly, while matching your talking speed and volume to that of the other party.
Be flexible.	Callers want to know what you can do, not what you cannot do. First-call resolution is the goal.
Avoid negative and controlling words.	"Problem," "complaint," and "You should have..." are words and phrases that can illicit negative responses.
Avoid using abbreviations and technical language.	The caller may not understand industry jargon, which prevents sharing effective and clear information.
Give verbal clues to show you are actively listening.	Phrases such as "I see" and "Please tell me more" are welcome words to the caller.
Promise to call back on unresolved issues and then follow through.	If a call involves some research of the facts, assure the person that you will call back before the end of the day, if only to say, "I don't have the answer yet, but I'm still researching it."

each word clearly. Keep in mind that even though you have spoken the same greeting all day long, this is the first time your caller has heard it.

A pleasant greeting sets the stage emotionally, and listeners tend to mirror the emotional state of a speaker. It is typical for people to respond in kind to what they are getting. For example, if you answer the phone gruffly, chances are the caller may become defensive, but if you answer the phone pleasantly, the caller will be more agreeable. Figure 12.1 provides additional phone tips.

The Basic Process

The manner in which CSRs handle themselves on the phone is critical, and the following steps provide the basic process service-type communications should follow:

1. *Stay close to the phone.* Answer the phone by the third ring. When customers call, their hope is not to leave a message, but to speak with a live person, conduct business, and move on to their next activity.
2. *Be courteous and polite with each caller.* Customers deserve to be treated with respect, no matter what message you are delivering to them.
3. *Use a computer or have paper and pencil handy to take notes.* This will allow you to focus on solving the problem rather than remembering a myriad of significant details.
4. *Bring closure to the call.* Customers need to know what to expect next and when their concerns will be resolved.

Transferring Calls

To provide the best service for customers, sometimes you will have to transfer callers to another person or department. Unfortunately, this is something that often irritates customers. If you are receiving a large number of transferred calls, perhaps other team members should have information in response to common customer inquiries in advance, so they won't have to transfer calls as often. However, when calls must be transferred, keep it simple and positive. Transfer with care, and apply these strategies:

1. *State what you can do, not what you cannot do.* Turn a negative into a positive by letting customers know you are acting for their benefit. For example, you might say something like: "I can help you by letting you talk to Nate in Accounts Receivable. Should we get disconnected, his extension is 530. May I connect you now?"

2. *Avoid using the word "transfer."* Customers don't like this word. Instead, say: "Let me connect you to..." or "I'll let you talk with..."

3. *When transferring a call to someone else, pass along the customer's name and any facts you have obtained so far.* This will make customers feel that they are making progress, because they don't have to repeat their information. You can pass along customer information in two ways:

   • If you have conference call or video chat capability, send the caller directly to the desired party while you are still on the line. You will be able to tell the receiving CSR the essence of the concern or issue while the customer is listening.

   • Convey the message to the receiving person while the caller is on hold, so the caller does not have to repeat the information again.

4. *Stay on the line.* Attempt to become familiar with the general responsibilities of each department and person, so you transfer the caller only once. Also, before transferring a customer's call, it is good practice to ask for his or her phone number. If you accidentally disconnect the call, you are prepared to call the customer back.

5. *Do not transfer the customer, if that is his or her preference.* Customers will likely tell you if they have already spoken to multiple people. If you are not the correct person to address a particular problem, find out as much as you can

about the situation and agree on a time to call the customer back. Do the research yourself and try to resolve the issue without passing the customer off again.

Placing Callers on Hold

If customers don't like the idea of being transferred, they certainly won't like the idea of being put on hold. Pushing your hold button a little too quickly or a little too often can easily damage customer relationships and should be avoided. The best alternative is not to put a customer on hold at all, but that option is not always reasonable. Ask the caller whether he or she can be put on hold, and then wait for a response before doing so.

When putting a caller on hold cannot be avoided, follow these basic phone courtesies:

• *Tell the caller why you would like to put him or her on hold, and ask for permission to do so.* Bear in mind that the caller might not have time to wait and may prefer either to call back or have you return the call later.

• *Keep callers on hold no longer than 30 seconds.* Time seems to move more slowly when you are waiting on the phone. Thirty seconds seems like much longer to people on hold, and they may become angry and simply hang up.

• *Thank the customer for holding.* Always say, "Thank you for holding" rather than "I'm sorry you had to hold." Emphasize the positive by thanking the customer, not the negative by apologizing.

• *Offer to call the customer back instead of putting him or her on hold.* If you know the process will take a little extra time, offer to call back within a certain time frame, and then make sure you follow through.

- *Check back frequently.* If resolving the problem is taking longer than you thought it would, return to the caller at least every 30 seconds to explain what's happening and to ask whether he or she can continue to hold.

Most customers who call businesses understand that it could be a while before they speak with a service representative. That doesn't mean they appreciate waiting in silence. Many companies use a **messaging on-hold** system, a pre-recorded program for callers to listen to while they are on hold. Companies can choose the system to play music, a voice message, or a combination of both. The advantage of using this phone system is that it lets callers know they are still on the line and waiting for the next available person to speak with them. It can also let them know where they are in the call order (queue) and the average wait before they will get a live person on the phone. Many callers find it helpful to have this information so they can determine whether they want to hold or call back at a later time.

☑ MAKE IT **A HABIT**

Handling Irate Callers

With phone technology expanding, irritated customers can be more sensitive, so make it a point to:

- Tell the customer the issue is important to you—for example, by saying, "Thank you for bringing this matter to our attention."
- Express a sense of urgency and ownership regarding the customer's concern by saying, "I'll take care of this right away."
- Apologize at least twice—once on hearing the problem and again after finding a solution.
- Always remember to thank customers sincerely for doing business with your company.

WHAT DO YOU **THINK**

12.1

How many times in the past few weeks have you been put through *voicemail jail* and were never connected to a live person? Did the experience influence your decision to buy from this business in the future? Record your reflections in your journal.

VOICE TECHNOLOGIES

Communicating in the global marketplace is easier for people and businesses because of ground-breaking voice technologies. These technologies include Internet Voicemail Services, Voice over Internet Protocol, and the popular Voice Response systems.

Internet Voicemail Services

To manage voicemail better, online voicemail service providers offer an array of options for businesses that want the convenience of handling voice messages online and a professional sounding "virtual office" presence for callers. Google Voice is an example of a popular Internet-based voicemail service provider.

A virtual voicemail service provides you with a phone number that you can distribute on business cards, flyers, and letterhead. Some virtual voicemail providers allow you to forward your existing home, office, or mobile phone number to the service as well.

Voice over Internet Protocol (VoIP)

If you've never used or heard of VoIP, get ready to change the way you think about long-distance global phone calls. **Voice over Internet Protocol (VoIP)** is a method for taking audio phone signals and turning them into digital data that can be transmitted over the Internet. Skype is one of the most used examples of VoIP. In addition to voice transmission, Skype also allows users to combine video and audio modes through what are called *video chats*. This visual approach is a more personal way for those involved to feel included in conversations. In addition, it enhances understanding by allowing for the nonverbal forms of communication discussed in Chapter 11. VoIP is also known as Internet telephony, broadband telephony, and other names.

Voice Response Systems

Any contact with an organization contributes to a customer's perception about that organization, whether it is with an employee in a phone conversation or through voicemail. *Voicemail*, which functions much as an answering machine does, allows callers to leave a voice message for the called party.

Although voicemail remains popular, do not assume that customers are satisfied with leaving a message. Instead, understand voicemail from the caller's perspective. Customers want to feel that their phone calls are important to a company. What drives customers to frustration about some phone systems is not the fact that they are automated, but that they think no one is paying attention to their needs.

A well-designed phone system is fast, easy to use, cost effective, and, most important, caller-friendly. Whether you are planning a simple voice-mail system to take messages or a sophisticated voice-processing system that lets people choose from a menu of recorded options, the key is keeping callers in mind and making the process easy for them to use.

Some companies approach voicemail as a way to reduce head count, and that can be a practical benefit. However, if designed correctly, a greater benefit of using voicemail is providing access to customer service personnel for customers. A well-phrased message can provide a kind of mini-introduction of the company or person to the caller, giving a hint at personality and details about availability. If the person being called listens attentively to voicemail messages, he or she can learn a great deal by paying attention to tone and delivery, An efficiently designed system can be an effective tool for quality customer service. Some tips on maximizing the positive and avoiding the potential negative aspects of voicemail systems are shown in Figure 12.2.

REMEMBER THIS

Figure 12.2 Customer-Friendly Voicemail Systems

Stay on top of it.	Update your voicemail greeting frequently, stating the date, which lets callers know you actually use the system. Inform callers your messages are checked frequently, so they have confidence their call will be heard and returned.
Avoid "voicemail jail."	When callers bounce from message to message and can't reach a live person, they begin to feel uncomfortable and captive to the event. Early on, give callers an easy way to transfer directly at any time to a receptionist by pressing one or two digits on their phones' keypad.
Keep greetings and instructions short.	Strive for a 5-second voicemail greeting and 15 seconds for instructions. Callers get impatient; they want action.
Attempt to give instructions the same way every time.	Always state the action first, then the correct key to press—for example, "To speak with our receptionist, press zero."
Don't make technology a villain.	Voicemail should not be used to *avoid* phone calls. People expect that you will regularly answer your own phone.

Recording an Outgoing Greeting It is important that CSRs answer their phones whenever possible so customers don't get the impression the company is avoiding them and does not want to take care of their needs. The truth is, however, that at times, businesses must use voicemail because CSRs do take lunch breaks and assist other customers, for example.

Follow these suggestions when creating an outgoing voicemail greeting:

- State your name, title, and reason you cannot answer the phone at this time. Indicate how often you check your voicemail. CSRs should return calls at least every two hours.

- Ask the caller for key information—name, company's name, phone number, why the customer is calling, and when the caller can be reached.

- Always return calls promptly. Customers realize that you may not always have the information when you promised, but calling customers with straightforward updates shows concern and promotes the company's reputation in a first-rate way.

Leaving a Voicemail Message When making a call, savvy communicators know they might have to leave a recorded message, so they plan before dialing a number. Be clear and brief in any voicemail message you leave. To deliver a message effectively, move through it quickly, and be straightforward so the receiver understands what is expected by the end of the message.

Here is a plan that works well when leaving voicemail messages:

1. State your name, the date and time, your company name, and why you are calling.
2. Say what you would like the receiver to do in the form of a statement or request, giving a reason if you are prepared to do so.
3. Say, "Thank you."
4. Finish with, "Feel free to call me back at the following number," and then state the number slowly and clearly so it can be written down. Repeat the number again for clarity.

Remember that voicemail messages can easily be forwarded, so don't leave a message unless you are comfortable having it heard by other people.

Photodisc/Getty Images

Is your service voice pleasant, courteous, and helpful when others hear you speak?

WHAT DO YOU THINK

12.2

If you were to advise a company you do business with on how to use voicemail more effectively, what two suggestions would you make? Record these in your journal.

EVALUATING YOUR VOICE DELIVERY

A person's voice can reveal many emotions: happiness, sadness, anger, or even ambivalence. When you speak, customers listen to your tone of voice, words, and overall delivery techniques. Are you sincere? Do you sound helpful in your approach with others? Do you show empathy and concern for their needs? A positive and caring tone in challenging customer situations says, "I understand how you feel and I'd be frustrated, too, if that happened to me."

The following list offers general guidelines for using your voice effectively, especially while on the phone:

1. *Use a steady, moderate rate of speech.* Speaking too fast can suggest to the customer that you are nervous or in a hurry. Additionally, listeners may have a hard time understanding a fast talker. Speaking too slowly can signal that you are bored or lack confidence. Find your balance.
2. *Never allow your voice to become overly loud or shrill.* If a customer is yelling at you, you may be tempted to respond in kind, but resist that impulse. Maintaining a moderate volume and rate of speech can help calm an upset customer.
3. *Increase the energy in your voice.* The phone can rob your voice of some of its natural expressiveness and energy, so be sure to compensate adequately with more enthusiasm.

Phone conversations tend to be rather informal in both business and personal situations. Figure 12.3 shows some noteworthy suggestions to keep in mind when speaking on the phone.

Showing courtesy to others and incorporating good phone etiquette can help businesses gain a competitive edge for one basic reason—people are more likely to return to a company and to buy more products and services when they are treated well.

REMEMBER THIS

Figure 12.3 Acceptable Phone Language

ACTION	ACCEPTABLE STATEMENTS
Introducing yourself	"This is Ken." "Good morning, Ken speaking."
Asking who is on the phone	"May I ask who is calling, please?" "Excuse me, who is calling, please?"
Asking for someone	"May I have extension 321?" "Is Charlie available?"
Connecting someone	"I'll put your call through." "Please hold while I connect you."
Taking a message	"May I tell him who is calling?" "Would you like to leave a message?"
Replying when someone is not available	"I'm afraid Tom is not available at the moment." "I'm sorry, but Tom's line is busy."

Ethics / Choices

Sometimes a boss or another employee is on the phone when you wish to speak to him or her, so you must wait. What do you do? Do you stand far enough away so that you do not hear the conversation or go back to your desk and return later? Discuss the best way to handle this situation.

WHAT DO YOU THINK

12.3

What techniques do you use to establish a personal connection with customers over the phone? Do you modify those techniques when communicating with angry or difficult customers? If so, how? Record your responses in your journal.

Digital Vision/Getty Images

What skills and service attitude do CSRs need in order to speak with hundreds of customers each day?

TELEMARKETING ACTIVITIES

Technology has changed the way companies do business. Forget what you think telemarketing is and embrace the reality that it is used by the smallest to the largest companies in the world to introduce new products, gauge customer satisfaction, and schedule qualified sales appointments. Telemarketing is a form of direct marketing. Whether organizations outsource inbound or outbound telemarketing customer service, time and money are saved because businesses do not provide office space for these telemarketers, paying only for the specific services needed.

Most people think of inbound telemarketing as customer support. **Inbound telemarketing** programs are used mainly by companies to take orders, generate leads, and provide service to customers with questions or concerns. In contrast, **outbound telemarketing** involves the telemarketer cold calling prospects who are not expecting a call. The two steps needed for businesses to launch an outbound telemarketing campaign are to first define the

targeted market and then develop a script and a telemarketing list for the outbound telemarketer's use.

At some point, each of us has received calls from telemarketers, and, chances are, we have responded to them in various ways. Whether a customer's response is of interest or an annoyance, part of a telemarketer's job is dealing with every range of emotion he or she encounters. It takes special *people skills* when CSRs become telemarketers.

In January 2005, telemarketers and sellers were required to begin searching the National Do Not Call Registry at least once every 31 days and to drop from their call lists the phone numbers of consumers who had registered. As a result, the National Do Not Call Registry puts consumers in charge of the telemarketing calls they receive at home.

WEB-DRIVEN SERVICE TECHNOLOGIES

A 2010 survey by the U.S. Department of Commerce reported that "During the first decade of the 21st Century, U.S. broadband Internet connectivity by households has grown dramatically as its importance to our economy and way of life has grown. In October 2009, according to the Census Current Population Survey data, 63.5 percent (75.8 million) of U.S. households used a high-speed Internet service (*i.e.*, technologies that are faster than dial-up, such as DSL, cable modem, fiber optics, satellite, and wireless). This represented a 25 percent increase from just two years earlier (50.8 percent in October 2007)."[1]

On a global usage basis, Internet World Stats reveal there were an estimated two billion Internet users worldwide in June 2010, a figure which represented about 29 percent of the population worldwide.[2]

Widespread users from around the world rely on the Internet for many reasons—product research, daily purchases, bill payments, social networking, and communication with CSRs. In doing so, they transact business using popular online service technologies at a level not even dreamed of a few years ago.

Chats

With the greater number of online businesses and international customers, companies are turning to customer support chats to expedite resolution of customer issues. A chat program permits interaction with a service representative in a moment's time and has the potential for increased sales due to immediate response.

Chats allow agents or specialists to *approach* customers while they are online and offer assistance, usually through a pop-up request. Once contacted, the website visitor may decline or accept the invitation to chat. If the visitor accepts the invitation, he or she interacts in a manner similar to that used in instant messaging, in a private, secure, one-on-one chat. Though some businesses use chats, most are cautious and take a conservative approach toward this technology because some customers consider being invited to chat as intrusive.

Online Forums

Online forums allow users to share information and post responses to one another in online discussion groups. These discussions are not in real time the way chats and instant messages are. Instead, they are referred to as threaded discussions and may span a few days, as the need exists.

A message forum should be seen by organizations as an opportunity to have a discussion with a number of interested individuals who may be looking to make purchases or communicate with someone with a compliment, concern, or suggestion for improvement.

Blogs

Web logs, or blogs, are a growing electronic communications method that consists of millions of online journals linked together in a vast network. Not only do individuals on the Internet set up rapid-response blogs, but businesses do as well.

As Gavin's Blog asserts, "Blogs are different. They evolve with every posting, each one tied to a moment. So if a company can track millions of blogs simultaneously, it gets a heat map of what a growing part of the world is thinking about, minute by minute…. Most blogs are open to the world. As the bloggers read each other, comment, and link from one page to the next, they create a global conversation."[3]

Cloud Apps

Short for cloud application, a *cloud app* is the phrase used to describe a software application that is accessed via the Internet and is not physically installed on a personal or business computer system. Michael Learmonth, in an article for *Advertising Age*, says that "These "cloud" computing services—generally free applications that exist on the web such as Gmail, Twitter, Facebook, Skype …. are now woven into the lives of just about everyone on the web."[4] Thought as tools

[1] "Digital Nation: 21st Century America's Progress toward Universal Broadband Internet Access," U.S. Department of Commerce, p. 4, February 2010 http://www.ntia.doc.gov/reports/2010/NTIA_internet_use_report_Feb2010.pdf accessed January 30, 2011.

[2] Internet Usage Statistics: World Internet Users and Population Stats, Internet World Stats, June 30, 2010, http://www.internetworldstats.com/stats.htm accessed February 1, 2011.

[3] Gavin's Blog, http://www.gavinsblog.com/2005/04/24/business-week-and-blogging/ accessed February 1, 2011.

[4] Michael Learmonth, "Spotty Customer Service Haunts Free, 'Cloud' Services," September 7, 2009, *Advertising Age*, http://adage.com/digital/article?article_id=138846 accessed February 1, 2011.

for individuals, companies and organizations around the world now use these free applications to track critical communication and feedback from customers.

E-Mail

E-mail, an ongoing service technology, is used extensively to communicate with customers because it is easy for businesses and consumers to use. It allows for contact in a familiar fashion and avoids the need for waiting on hold for a customer service representative.

Unfortunately, because e-mail is part of the virtual world of communication, many people exchange business messages the same way they do in virtual chat rooms—with much less formality and, at times, too much anger and aggression. Therefore, before clicking the send button on your e-mail, know who will be receiving the message. Doing so encourages you to think about the *tone* of your writing. E-mails sent to external customers will probably be more formal and brief, whereas e-mails to an internal customer or colleague might be less formal.

E-mail abuse in organizations is problematic. Three ways companies can minimize the rise of e-mail abuse and safeguard its best and highest use are to enact strict policies, educate employees and managers about those policies, and then enforce them. When using a business e-mail system, all employees should bear in mind these reminders:

- *E-mails are public documents.* Therefore, include only statements that you can openly defend, should your e-mail message be circulated or shown to parties not intended to see it.

- *The employer owns the e-mail.* All messages that are created, sent, or received using a company system remain the property of the employer, not the employee.

- *The e-mail system is for business communications only.* Taking care of personal business while working is unauthorized and should be carried out at home.

- *Offensive and inflammatory messages are strictly prohibited.* These actions can be grounds for termination in most organizations.

Ethics / Choices

What if you worked in a Customer Service Department with someone who sent instant messages to her friends while serving customers and who also speckled her e-mails to customers with smileys. Would you say anything to her or your supervisor?

WHAT DO YOU THINK

12.5

Which technologies do you prefer using in your interactions with businesses? List these and state why in your journal.

- *The use of passwords does not indicate that messages are confidential.* Even with a password, the company will be able to intercept and read e-mails.

WRAPPING UP ... FUTURE CHALLENGES FOR CUSTOMER SERVICE

The 3rd edition of *The World of Customer Service* has distinguished itself by stressing the importance of serving well the global customer in today's fluid business environment. The book especially emphasizes two distinct but inter-related components of customer service. First, service professionals these days need to be personally empowered to deal with complex situations in a manner never before thought about. CSRs need to be continuously sensitive to the customer-centered approach when dealing with unique cultural feelings, customs, and norms relating to wide-ranging diversity issues. Second, when service providers use technology to gather information, they need to use the information as *tools* that are proactive in *learning about* customers and *reaching out* to them in a more personal and informed way. Remember that essential customer service skills will

FOCUS ON. . .
BEST PRACTICES

Virtual Assistants

The explosion of the Internet and its relation to the global economy has produced a new business opportunity known as the *virtual assistant*. Because businesses use e-mail systems, answering services, automated phone messages, and Cloud apps to service customer issues, someone like an *outsourced* virtual assistant is tasked to virtually manage them at a distance.

The International Virtual Assistants Association defines a *virtual assistant (VA)* as "an independent entrepreneur who provides administrative, creative, or technical services by using advanced technological modes of communication and data delivery." To be successful, the virtual assistant must have excellent communication, technology, and customer service skills. Working from his or her own office space, VAs solve customer problems by:

- Addressing customer complaints (calls, e-mails, instant messages),
- Handling product issues between business clients and their customers,
- Answering customer questions,
- Sending out e-mails, catalogs, and newsletters to subscription customers.

With a high number of consumers becoming angry or frustrated at using an automated phone system, a virtual assistant is not only an economical solution, but is a practical one for many organizations.

SOURCES: International Virtual Assistants Association, http://www.ivaa.org/ accessed February 1, 2011, and Chaov, "The Virtual Assistant Customer Service Expert," July 22, 2009 http://www.bukisa.com/articles/125886_the-virtual-assistant-customer-service-expert accessed February 1, 2011.

always include striving for first-call resolution. It will always require special service skills when serving extreme customers who may be adversely affected in part due to these new communication methods and digital devices that irritate an already upsetting customer situation.

In light of personal empowerment and rapidly growing technology, customer service finds ever more creative ways to move forward as illustrated by some of the ideas mentioned by the service professionals featured in this text. Al Smith, for example, in his Lexus interview spoke about the social media team that searches for creative, proactive ways to reach out to customers. Teresa Laraba, of Southwest Airlines, spoke about empowering flight attendants because, as we recognize today, flying is a more challenging business than it used to be. Enthusiastic applied skills; more sensitivity to cultural diversity; an awareness when serving customers' needs, informed by the strategic use of CRM have given the world a newly defined service environment. This environment is challenging; it is unknown and budding because, as the economy and world change, so do the service needs of customers around the world.

SUMMARY

- During phone conversations with customers, always be professional and courteous throughout the entire interaction.

- Treat voice technologies as an extension of yourself and use them as tools to help serve the customer.

- When speaking with customers over the phone, pay attention to your tone of voice, choice of words, and overall delivery technique.

- Telemarketing is the use of the phone to sell directly to consumers; it consists of calls that are inbound, outbound, or a combination of both.

- Examples of popular Web-based service technologies are chats, blogs, Cloud apps and e-mails.

KEY TERMS

messaging on-hold

Voice over Internet Protocol
(VoIP)

inbound telemarketing
outbound telemarketing

CRITICAL THINKING

1. Think of someone you know who has outstanding customer-friendly phone skills. Describe why you have this opinion of that person.

2. If you were hiring a receptionist, CSR, virtual assistant, or telemarketer, what essential phone service skills would you look for in your top candidates? List and describe.

3. Describe a voicemail system you have used that you consider being customer-friendly. Describe one that you consider not to be user-friendly.

4. Do you think Cloud applications, like Skype, Twitter, Facebook, and the like, will continue to increase in usage among customer service providers and their organizations? Discuss your reasons.

5. In your opinion, which Web-based technology best serves the greater good with today's diverse global customers? Why?

 ## WHAT DO YOU THINK **NOW?**

Project 12.1

Assume you are doing a classroom presentation on *customer service digital technologies.* Reread your responses to the *What Do You Think?* questions that you completed throughout this chapter. What are some service practices that require the professional use of digital technologies? What service issues might conflict with the use of these technologies? What are some ways CSRs can stay informed about new developments in digital technology products? What traits or skills should a CSR possess to use communication technology effectively? Compile your responses, as directed by your instructor.

ONLINE RESEARCH ACTIVITY

Project 12.2   Voicemail Update

Research a number of websites and locate several articles about recent developments in the installation and use of business voicemail systems. As a result of your research, write a simple paper recommending additional features or upgrades to the voicemail system at your school or at work.

COMMUNICATION SKILLS AT WORK

Project 12.3   Answering Phone Calls

Form a small group with at least two other students and write the messages you would use to respond to the three phone-answering situations below. As an alternative, follow your instructor's directions to join a group and use the instructor-designated discussion board to complete the group project.

1. Assume you are working for First City Bank. When calls come in, they go directly to your phone; there is no receptionist. How should you answer each call?
2. Assume you are an employee in the registration office of a local career school. All calls are first answered by a receptionist and then transferred to your desk. How should you answer each call?
3. When your boss is not available, you answer her phone. What should you say when she is in a meeting? What should you say when she is on a coffee break?

DECISION MAKING AT WORK

Project 12.4   Calls at Work

Assume a good friend calls you on your direct line at work with the intent to chat. After you've done some catch-up on personal news, she suggests that the other reps can handle your calls for a little longer. You are starting to feel uncomfortable with what is happening. Decide how you would handle this situation with your friend and describe the specific reasons for your actions. Would your behavior in this situation be different if your supervisor's office was nearby?

CASE STUDY

Project 12.5   The Phone Order Fiascos

Rick Francis is a CSR who receives a call from a new customer wishing to place an order. Rick has a basketball game broadcasting very softly on the radio, and he thinks the customer cannot hear it. The customer begins to give the order, but Rick interrupts and puts her on hold because he cannot find anything to write with. Because the customer has a heavy accent, Rick has a hard time understanding and says, "Huh?" quite frequently during the phone conversation. Rick concludes the transaction by saying, "Thanks for placing the order."

Form a small group and discuss what should Rick have done differently during this customer dialogue. As an alternative, follow your instructor's directions to join a group and use the instructor-designated discussion board to complete the group project.

GLOSSARY

A

accommodating A style of conflict management that demands complete acquiescence to another's point of view.

active listening Fully understanding the meaning of what someone says by listening with your whole mind and body—not just your ears.

aggressive communication style A style of communication in which the person is closed-minded, listens poorly, has difficulty seeing another person's point of view, interrupts other people while they are talking, and tends to monopolize conversations.

alternative choice question A question that provides specific choices for the customer to select from.

amiable personality The personality type that wants to build relationships, give others support and attention, values suggestions from others, and fears disagreement.

analytical personality The personality type that is systematic, well organized, deliberate, values numbers and statistics, loves details, and tends to be introverted.

anger management A process of learning to recognize signs that you are becoming angry, and taking action to calm down and deal with the situation in a positive way.

Angie's List A review service of companies that hire out contractors that provides live call center support and help.

arbitration A legally binding process that begins when both parties sign an agreement permitting the arbitrator to conduct a fact-finding hearing and make a final decision.

assertive communication style A style of communication in which the person uses active listening, states limits and expectations, and does not label or judge people or events.

authority The power or right to give commands, enforce obedience, take action, or make final decisions.

avoiding A style of conflict management where one diplomatically sidesteps an issue, postpones an issue until a better time, or withdraws from a situation that is emotionally, physically, or intellectually threatening.

B

Baby Boomer Generation Born between 1946 and 1964, this generation has a significant influence on society; they make up the majority of the political, cultural, industrial, and academic leadership roles in the United States.

baseline standard The minimum level of service it takes to satisfy customers under ordinary circumstances.

Better Business Bureau (BBB) A recognized third-party complaint handling mechanism in the United States that has dedicated itself to playing a leadership role in the resolution of consumer-business disputes.

blog Also referred to as web logs. A website where entries are made in journal style and displayed in reverse chronological order. They contain text, images, and links to other blogs or web pages, and are part of a wider network of information.

body language Nonverbal messages that include tone of voice, eye movement, posture, hand gestures, facial expressions, and more.

burnout The state in which a person feels psychological exhaustion and decreased efficiency resulting from overwork and prolonged exposure to stress.

business etiquette The rules of acceptable behavior that identify the application of correct or polite manners in a typical business situation.

C

certification A nationally recognized certificate that indicates a proficiency in a professional skill or career.

closed question A question that usually elicits a "yes" or "no" answer.

coaching A training method that emphasizes learning by doing and turns information into knowledge and experience.

collaborating A style of conflict management that requires attempting to solve the problem together with the customer to find a mutually satisfying solution.

communication model An illustration of the communication process, consisting of six elements: sender, receiver, message, channel, shared understanding, and feedback.

competing A style of conflict management that involves an entrenched, almost combative attitude based upon the unshakeable conviction that you are right.

compromising A style of conflict management where solutions are found that are mutually satisfactory to both parties.

contact point The method that a customer uses to communicate with a company.

cross selling The act of promoting products related to the one ordered, thus selling an extra product in the process.

culture A system of shared values, beliefs, and rituals that are learned and passed on through generations of families and social groups.

customer expectations The ideas and beliefs that a customer has before a transaction occurs.

customer loyalty The practice of finding, attracting, and retaining customers who regularly purchase from you.

customer perceptions The opinions that are formed by the customer during and after a business transaction.

customer profile Demographic information that is collected about customers, explaining who the customers are and what they want in terms of service.

customer relations policy A company policy that is the foundation for maintaining customer goodwill and that lays out the foundation for communicating with customers and for handling customer complaints.

customer relationship management (CRM) A business strategy used by companies that integrates the functions of sales, marketing, and customer service, and uses technology and wide-ranging databases of information to improve service to customers in a more personal way.

customer retention A strategy with the purpose of doing whatever it takes (legally and within reason) to keep a company's current customers on a long-term basis.

customer satisfaction The state of mind that customers have about a company and its products or services when their expectations have been met or exceeded.

customer self-service (CSS) A proactive approach in customer service that empowers customers to go to a company's website and find answers to most of the queries that normally go through a call center.

customer service The process of satisfying the customer, relative to a product or service, in whatever way the customer defines his or her need.

customer service life cycle (CSLC) A concept that encourages companies to think in terms of differentiated involvement with the customer during distinct stages of use of a product.

customer service representative (CSR) The frontline service provider who deals with customers on a day-to-day basis.

customer-centric service A service strategy that puts the customer first, demonstrating a service-oriented commitment.

D

data mining The process of extracting patterns from data located in the data warehouse.

data warehouse Provides a common location for all crucial business data regardless of the data's source.

decoding process A step in the communication process that occurs when the receiver's brain filters the message and gives it a unique meaning.

direct question Open or closed questions that are posed as instructions and use the name of the person being addressed.

disability A condition caused by an accident, trauma, genetics, or disease, which may limit a person's mobility, hearing, vision, speech, or mental function.

dress code A set of standards that companies develop to help provide their employees with guidance about what is appropriate to wear to work.

driver personality The personality type that wants to save time, values results, loves being in control, and does things his or her own way.

E

empathy The ability to understand another person's position without getting emotionally involved.

empowerment The act of giving a CSR the necessary power or authority to make administrative decisions based on corporate guidelines.

encoding process A step in the communication process that occurs when a message arrives from a sender; the senses pick up the message through signals and then relay it to the receiver's brain.

e-rep An online customer service representative.

expressive personality The personality type that values appreciation, enjoys social situations, likes to inspire others, and is extroverted.

external customers People outside of an organization that purchase and use a company's products and services.

F

Facebook A social networking website that allows users to add people as friends, send messages, and update their personal profiles.

feedback A step in the communication process that occurs when a message is transmitted back to the original sender.

filtering The tendency for a message to be watered down or halted completely at some point during transmission, which can result in deflecting or stopping the listening process.

first-call resolution (FCR) The process in customer service of resolving customer calls to service representatives on the first call or contact.

G

Generation X Born between 1965 and 1981, this generation is verbal, globally aware, street smart, process driven, and technically adept.

Generation Y Born between 1981 and 1990, this generation uses the Internet as their medium for communicating, entertaining, and learning.

Generation Z Born after 1990, this generation uses the Internet for the majority of their communication, possesses very low verbal communication skills, and spends much of their formative years in cyberspace.

H

homeshoring The practice of domestic companies hiring U.S. home-based call agents instead of in-house operators or offshore call center operators.

I

inbound telemarketing A marketing technique used by companies to take orders, generate leads, and provide customer service.

internal customers People within an organization who rely on colleagues to provide the support they need to serve their own internal and external customers.

Internet forum Also known as a message board. An online discussion site that contains a wide range of content, including news, gossip, and research.

K

knowledge base Computerized data compiled by customer service representatives and used to resolve problems with customers about service issues.

L

leading question A question that confirms information and helps speed up interactions with people who find it difficult to make a final decision.

lose-lose strategy A conflict resolution strategy that commonly occurs when one party attempts to win at the expense of the other.

M

Mature Generation Born prior to 1946, this generation has a strong work ethic and is fiscally conservative.

MeasuredUp A customer service resolution website where millions of connected, loyal, and involved customers share their experiences with each other and directly with companies.

mediation A process used to resolve differences between two parties conducted by an impartial third party for the purpose of bringing about a settlement or agreement.

messaging on-hold A system that plays a pre-recorded program for callers to listen to while they are on hold.

mixed message A single communication that contains two opposing meanings. Typically the verbal part of the message is positive, while the nonverbal component is negative and contradicts the verbal part.

moment of truth An episode in which a customer comes in contact with any aspect of the organization and thereby has an opportunity to form an impression.

mystery shopper A third-party person who anonymously and objectively evaluates a business for the purpose of analyzing customer service, product quality, store presentation, and other elements of the customer experience.

N

nearshoring A form of outsourcing in which business processes are relocated to locations that are low-wage, but close in geographical distance and/or time zone.

negative language Language that conveys a poor image to customers and may cause conflict and confrontation where none is necessary or desired.

negative stress A type of stress that comes from a person worrying about things he or she has no power to change.

negotiation An interpersonal process requiring a give and take between the participants.

O

open question A question asked in a way that requires a more complete answer than a simple "yes" or "no."

outbound telemarketing A marketing technique used by many organizations because of rising postage rates and decreasing long-distance phone charges in which the telemarketer cold calls prospects who are not expecting a call.

outsourcing The purchase of labor from a source outside of the company, rather than using the company's own staff; also referred to as subcontracting.

P

paraphrase The communication technique of repeating in a summarized form what has been said, using other words for clarification.

passive communication style An indirect communication style in which a person agrees externally with others in order to avoid expressing his or her true thoughts and opinions, although privately disagreeing.

personal digital assistant (PDA) An electronic handheld device that assists a person in organizing a busy schedule.

personal space The distance between people as they interact and communicate.

personality The pattern of collective character, behavioral, temperamental, emotional, and mental traits of a person.

ping-ponging The process of a customer being passed from one employee or department to another while he or she is trying to resolve a problem or concern.

positive language Language that projects a helpful, encouraging feeling rather than a destructive, negative one.

positive stress A type of stress that can be channeled into productive results that motivate and energize a person rather than making him or her anxious and frustrated.

post-episodical survey A satisfaction-type survey that gathers information from customers after they each complete one business transaction.

proactive problem solving The process of anticipating and resolving problems before they occur.

probing question A question that uses information already established to clarify points and elicit more details.

procrastination The act of putting off completing an activity until a later time.

R

reactive feedback A type of communication exchange that affirms the speaker's message.

relaxation A state of being that is self-initiated and provides relief from physical and psychological efforts.

responsive feedback A type of communication exchange that characterizes the listener's feelings.

role-playing A training method where learners use customer scenarios to act out situations encountered in the real world.

S

script A document used by customer service representatives when conversing with customers that states consistent responses to common customer problems.

selective listening The process of hearing only what you want to hear—filtering out what you think is not important or not of interest to you.

service animal Any animal that has been individually trained to provide assistance or perform tasks for the benefit of a person with a physical or mental disability.

service culture The aspects that make a business distinctive and make the people who work there proud to do so.

service infrastructure A framework for customer service strategy that includes concerns about hiring the best people, providing a quality management team for support, ensuring transparent communications throughout the organization, and consistently monitoring service policies and procedures.

service recovery A gesture of compensation, specific to the situation, that is offered to the customer who feels betrayed and not well served.

Smartphone A mobile phone that combines the functionalities of a PDA and call phone with Internet connectivity capability.

social CRM Social customer relationship management; companies unite contact interactions through social communication channels.

social data Information about an individual's relationship to other people, groups, events, things, and concepts.

social media Websites such as Facebook, Twitter, Yelp, and YouTube that allow customers to connect with each other and share their customer service experiences.

soft skills Also referred to as people skills. These include punctuality, positive attitude, and cooperation.

softening techniques Positive approaches that service professionals use when interacting with customers, for example, an open posture (no crossed arms) and kindhearted eye contact (no rolling of eyes).

standards A baseline description of service performance guidelines that tells workers what is expected of them, in terms of both the quality and quantity of their work.

stereotyping The tendency to categorize individuals or groups according to an oversimplified and standardized image or idea.

strategic plan A plan for an organization that includes objective, strategies, tactics, and performance indicators in order to create a strong service culture.

SWOT analysis A formal review of a business organization's strengths, weaknesses, opportunities, and threats, which ultimately contributes to a comprehensive strategic plan.

synergy In teamwork, the combined effect of individual efforts is greater than their individual efforts alone.

T

tiered service system A customer service approach in which the service level increases or decreases proportionally to the amount a customer is spending.

time management The conscious act of using time in the most effective way possible.

tone In written communication, a manner of expression that reflects the writer's attitude toward the reader and the subject of the message.

tweets Twitter messages sent to followers.

Twitter A social networking website that allows users to send messages up to 140 characters to a list of followers.

U

up selling The act of persuading the customer to buy a more expensive product compared to the one he or she asked for.

V

Voice over Internet Protocol (VoIP) A method for taking audio phone signals and turning them into digital data that can be transmitted over the Internet.

W

win-lose strategy A conflict resolution strategy that assumes one side will win by achieving its goals and the other side will lose.

win-win strategy A conflict resolution strategy that assumes a reasonable solution can be reached that will satisfy the needs of all parties.

Y

Yelp A website used to find and review local businesses that also allows consumers to find events, special offers, or talk with other users.

YouTube A video-sharing site that lets users store short videos for private or public viewing.

INDEX